THE PYRAMIDS OF GIZEH.

J Bowring
Cairo April 27 1838

APPENDIX TO OPERATIONS

CARRIED ON AT

THE PYRAMIDS OF GIZEH

IN 1837.

CONTAINING

A SURVEY BY J. S. PERRING, ESQ.
CIVIL ENGINEER,

OF

THE PYRAMIDS AT ABOU ROASH, AND TO THE SOUTHWARD, INCLUDING THOSE IN THE FAIYOUM.

By COLONEL HOWARD VYSE,
CORRESPONDING MEMBER OF THE ROYAL ACADEMY OF FINE ARTS OF FRANCE.

VOL. III.

LONDON:
JOHN WEALE, HIGH HOLBORN;
AND
G. W. NICKISSON, 215 REGENT STREET.

MDCCCXLII.

LONDON:
PRINTED BY MOYES AND BARCLAY, CASTLE STREET,
LEICESTER SQUARE.

CONTENTS

OF

THE THIRD VOLUME.

		PAGE
Remarks upon the Map		1
Pyramid of Abou Roash		8
— Zowyet el Arrian		10
— Reegah		10
— — Notes by Mr. Birch		12
Pyramids of Abouseir		12
— — Northern Pyramid		15
— — Middle Pyramid		17
— — Great Pyramid		19
— — Small Pyramid		21
— — Notes by Mr. Birch		22
Pyramids of Saccara		
— — The Map		37
— — No. 1 in the Map		39
— — No. 2 —		39
— — No. 3 —		41
— — No. 4 —		51
— — No. 5 —		51
— — No. 6 —		51
— — No. 7 —		52
— — No. 8 —		52
— — No. 9 —		52
— — Mustabet el Faraoon		53
— — Notes by Mr. Birch		53

CONTENTS.

	PAGE
Pyramids of Dashoor	56
— — Northern Brick Pyramid	57
— — Northern Stone Pyramid	63
— — Southern Stone Pyramid	65
— — Small Pyramid	70
— — Southern Brick Pyramid	70
— — Notes by Mr. Birch	72
Pyramids of Lisht	77
Pyramid of Meydoom	78
Pyramid of Illahoon	80
Pyramid of Howara	82
Pyramids of Biahhmoo	84
The Birket Kharoon	85
Pyramid of El Koofa	85
The Mummy Pits at Saccara	86
Discoveries at Tourah	90
— — Notes by Mr. Birch	93
Remarks on the Measures by which the Pyramids were built	104
The Sphinx	107
— Mr. Birch's Notes	114
— Notes on the Greek Inscriptions	118
Remarks on the Egyptian Army	120
Horses in Egypt and Syria	130

LIST OF PLATES

IN

THE THIRD VOLUME.

	PAGE
Portrait of Mr. Perring, (Frontispiece)	
Map	1
Ruined Pyramid and Causeway of Abou Roash from Kerdassy	7
Abou Roash	8
— Plans	9
Pyramid of Reegah	10
— — Hieroglyphics	12
Pyramids of Abouseir, Map	13
— — Northern Pyramid	14
— — Entrances to Northern and Middle Pyramids	15
— — Middle Pyramid	17
— — View of Roof, and Entrance to the Great Pyramid	18
— — Great Pyramid	20
— — Small Pyramid	21
Pyramids of Abouseir and General View of Saccara	22
Pyramids of Saccara, Map	37
— — No. 2	39
— — No. 3, (Great Pyramid) N.E. View	41
— — No. 3, Pl. A	42
— — No. 3, Pl. D	44
— — No. 3, Pl. C	46
— — No. 3, Pl. B	47

LIST OF PLATES.

		PAGE
Pyramids of Dashoor } Map and View		56
— Views of Northern Stone, and Southern Brick Pyramids		58
— Northern Brick Pyramid, Section		60
— — Hieroglyphics		63
— Northern Stone Pyramid, Section and Plan		64
— — Section of Passages		65
— Southern Stone Pyramid, View		65
— — Sections through W. and N. Entrance Passages, Pl. 1		66
— — Section of Northern Passage Entrance, Pl. 4		67
— — Western Entrance, Pl. 3		68
— — Portcullis and Hieroglyphics, Pl. 2		69
Pyramids of Lisht		77
View of Pyramid of Meydoon		79
Pyramid of Illahoon		81
Views of Ruins at Biahhmoo and Pyramid of Howara		83
Pyramids of Biahhmoo and Howara		85
View of the Tourah Quarries		90
— — Interior		91
Tourah Quarries, View from Interior		92
Plan of the Quarries at Tourah and Massara		93
Tourah and Massara Quarries, Tablets Nos. 1 and 8		94
Touarh Quarries, Tablet No. 2		95
— — No. 3		96
— — No. 4		97
Tourah and Massara Tablets, Nos. 5 and 7		98
Massara Quarries, Tablet No. 6		99
— — No. 9		100
— — No. 10		101
— — No. 11		102
Inscriptions from Massara and Tourah Quarries, Tablet 12		102
View of Sphinx during Excavations		107
Fragments of the Beard of Sphinx		109
Fragments found during Excavation of Sphinx, Plate A		109

LIST OF PLATES.

	PAGE
Ground Plan of Temple and Steps in Front of Sphinx	110
View of Temple between Fore Legs of Sphinx	110
Altar and Fragments found near Sphinx, Plate D	110
Building on Steps of Sphinx, Plate C	112
Inscription on a Building on Steps leading to Sphinx, T in Ground Plan	113
View of Steps leading to the Sphinx	113
Tablet between Fore Legs of Sphinx, Plate B	115
Smaller Tablet	117
Inscription on Paws of Sphinx, Plate E	118
Inscription found near Sphinx, Plate F	118
Tablet found during Excavations, Plate G	119
Inscriptions found near Sphinx, Plate H	119

PREFACE.

This volume is an Appendix to those which were published in 1841.

It contains the results of Mr. Perring's operations on the other Pyramids, after I had left Egypt; an account of the mummy-pits at Saccara; his remarks on the measures according to which the Pyramids were built; and some discoveries made by him at Tourah and at Massara, whilst he was employed in constructing a railroad from the quarries to the river.

It is unnecessary for me to advert to Mr. Perring's abilities and zeal in carrying on these inquiries, as they are fully exemplified by the numerous engravings in this book, and also by Part III. of the larger work.

Through the kindness of the Earl of Mountnorris, I have the satisfaction of publishing, together with Mr. Salt's plans, that gentleman's account of M. Caviglia's excavations at the Sphinx in 1816.

I beg leave to express my sincere acknowledgments to Samuel Birch, Esq., Assistant in the Antiquarian department in the British Museum, and Assistant-Secretary to the Archæological Institute at Rome, for his valuable Notes on the hieroglyphical inscriptions; and also to the Rev. Mr. Coleridge of Eton, for the kind assistance, which he has been pleased to afford, respecting the Greek inscriptions found near the Sphinx.

The remarks on the Egyptian army, and also on the horses of Egypt and of Syria, are inserted, because they are referred to in the former volumes.

As this volume completes the Work, I take the opportunity of returning my best thanks to Mr. Arundale, for the care and attention he has bestowed on the execution of the several plates.

Stoke, October 20, 1842.

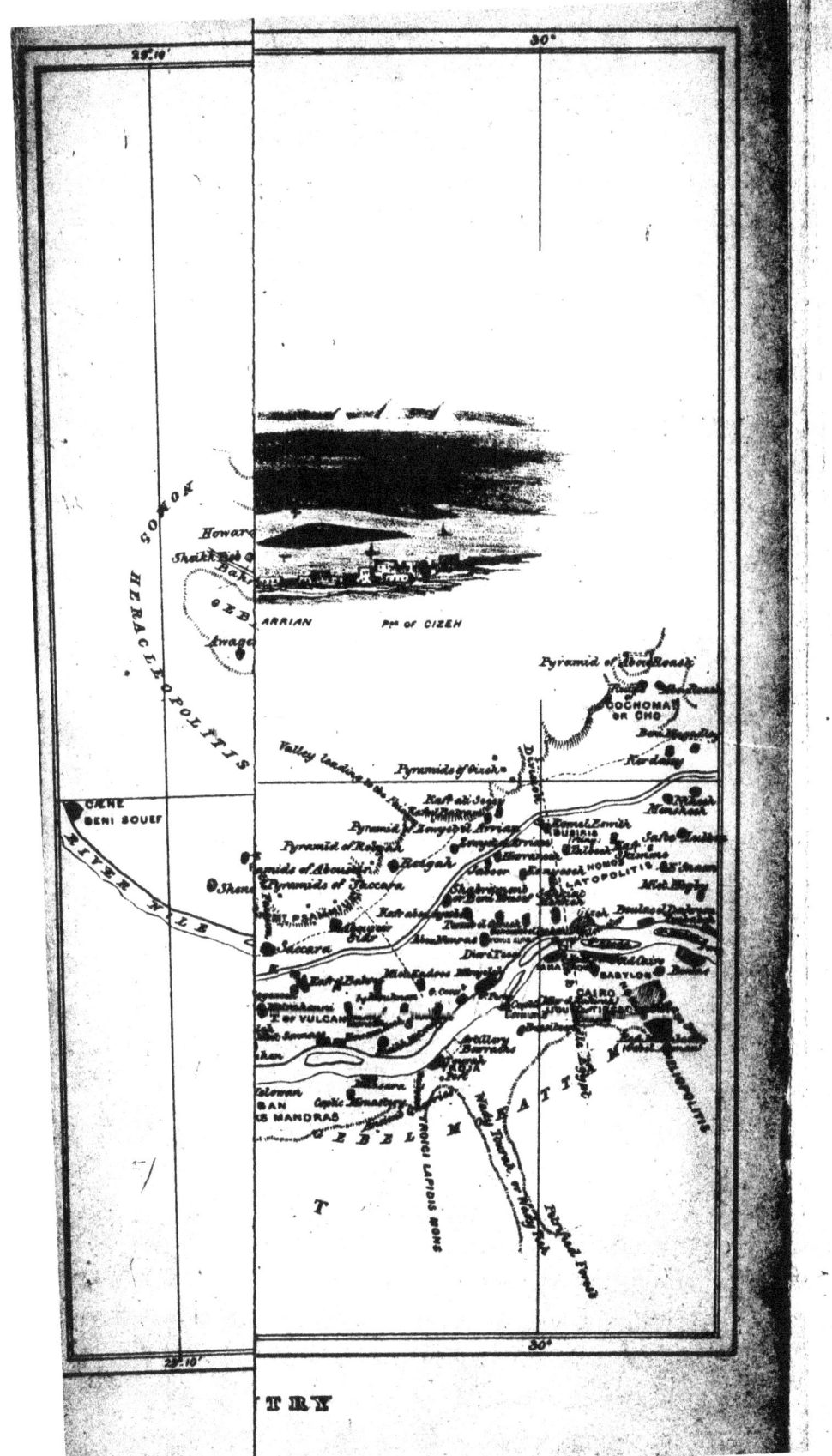

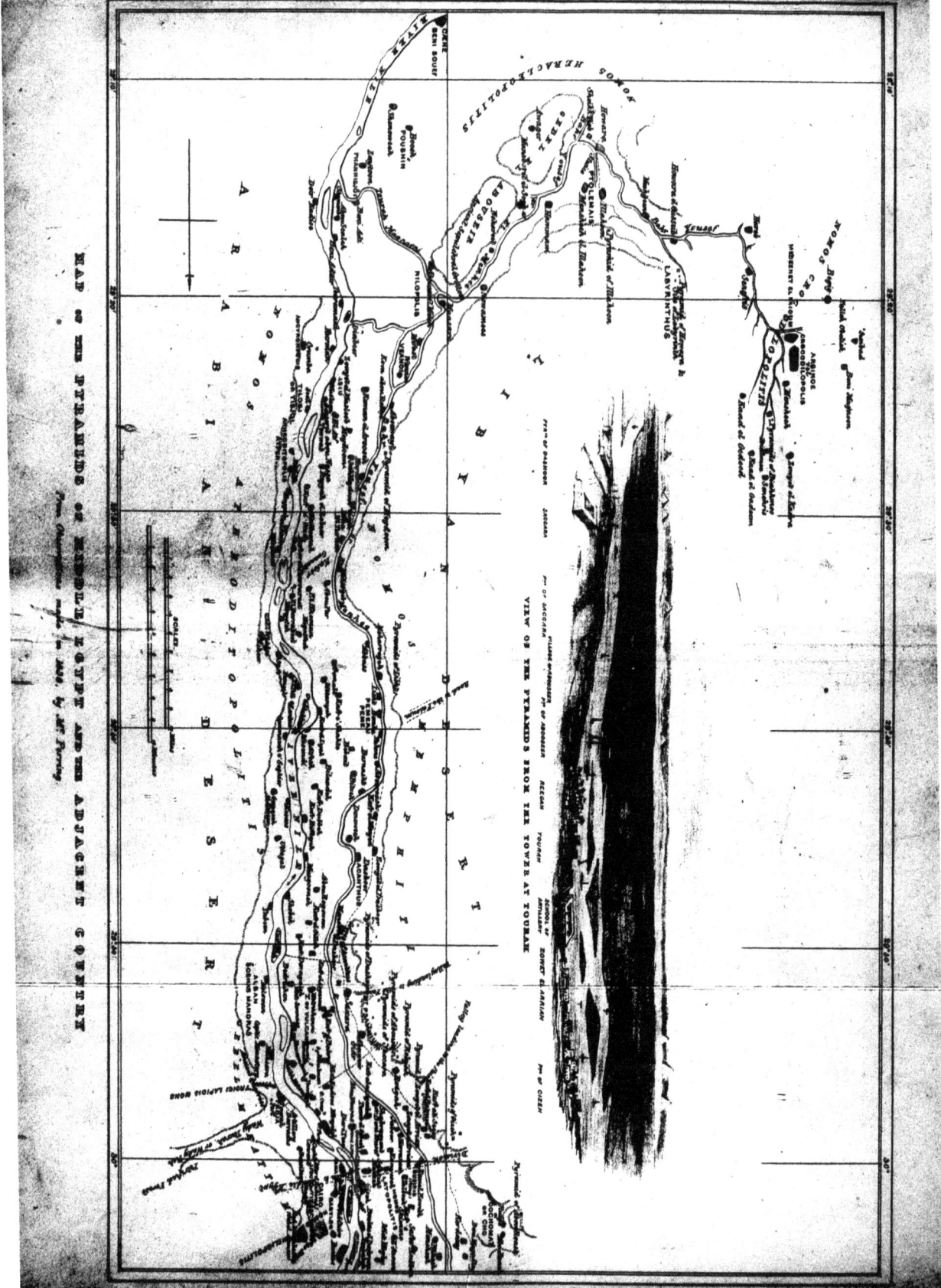

APPENDIX

TO

OPERATIONS CARRIED ON AT GIZEH,

&c. &c.

REMARKS UPON THE MAP.

EGYPT is naturally divided into the Delta, and the valley of the Nile, which extends from the Delta to Es Souan near the First Cataract, and which was subdivided by the antients into Middle Egypt, and the Thebaid. The former of these districts is now distinguished by the name of Bathree (*towards the sea*); and the latter is divided into Wustanee (*the Middle*), and Said (*the Upper*).

The thirty-six nomes, or provinces, are ascribed to Sesostris by Diodorus Siculus, who also says that they were equal in number to the apartments in the Labyrinth, which are supposed to have been twenty-seven; the nine others may, therefore, have included the different oases.

Middle Egypt, called by the Greeks Heptanomis, was, at a later period, included in the district, named by the Romans Arcadia in honour of the Emperor Arcadius; and, according to the "Notitia Imperii" (ascribed to the fourth century), Middle Egypt and part of the Delta formed the Provinciæ Augustannicæ.

The Pyramids of Middle and of Lower Egypt are thirty-nine in number. They are situated on the western side of the river, and chiefly on the desert hills, which form the western boundary of the valley of the Nile:—

    1 was in the Nome Latopolitis.
    33 - - - Memphitis.
    2 - - - Heracleopolitis.
    3 - - - Crocodilopolitis.

APPENDIX.

They extend from 29° 16′ 56″ to 30° 2′ 30″ north latitude, and occupy a space measuring, from north to south, fifty-three English miles. The map was laid down from a trigonometrical survey, carefully taken in 1839. It contains the sites of the Pyramids and the adjacent country, including part of the Delta, for, notwithstanding the supposed origin of its name, that province appears, according to Ptolemy, to have extended as far south as the Pyramids of Gizeh. Abou Fedeh also places the division between the upper and lower country at Fostat, or Old Cairo. Parts of five nomes, and the whole of another, are therefore inserted as follows:—

In the Delta, part of the nomes	Latopolitis. Heliopolitis.
The nome	Memphitis.
In Middle Egypt, part of the nomes	Aphroditopolitis. Heracleopolitis. Crocodilopolitis.

The situations of antient towns, as far as they can be ascertained, are also marked.

The account that Menes had diverted the river into its present course on the eastern side of the valley has been disputed by many commentators; but the antient channel has been shewn by Sir John Gardner Wilkinson, and may be traced in the low ground, between Kafr el Lyal and the Bahr Yousef, to the northward of Barnasht. Indeed, to the southward of this place, the Bahr Yousef evidently flows in an excavation; but to the northward of it, between the site of Memphis and the Libyan Desert, it apparently occupies the antient bed of the river, which, according to Herodotus, was used by vessels in their passage from Naucratis to Memphis.[1]

From the Bahr Yousef another canal of the same name supplies the Faioum with water. It is said to have been the work of one of the earliest kings, and is the source of the fertility of that district.

NOMOS LATOPOLITIS.

The site of LATOPOLIS has not been discovered. According to Ptolemy, it was near the river, and, by the "Itinerary of Antoninus," was twenty miles distant from Memphis; it may

---

[1] A branch from this canal probably passed under the Pyramids of Gizeh into the Bahr Bela Mar.

therefore be supposed to have been situated near the antient mounds called Kom Achmar. CERCASURA was probably at El Eksass. The ruins near the Pyramid of Abou Roash are supposed to mark the position of COCHONE, COCHOMA, CHO, or CHOE, because Cho signified a hill — and the elevation, upon which the pyramid was built, is higher than the surrounding country — and because the decayed state of the materials seems to correspond with the remote era of Venephres, the fourth king of the first dynasty, who, according to Manetho, erected a pyramid near that city.

NOMOS HELIOPOLITIS.

An obelisk and a few mounds are all that remain of HELIOPOLIS, famous for its grandeur, and also for the learning of its inhabitants. At this city Plato and Eudoxus studied, and Herodotus obtained materials for the history of Antient Egypt.

CAIRO occupies the site of an antient city, or probably, of two small towns called Liou and Tikes-chromi. The adjacent rocks have been excavated, and contain antient quarries, both of sandstone and of limestone; and Greek and Coptic inscriptions are found in some grottoes at a little distance to the south, which seem to have been the retreat of the early Christians.

The situation of the modern town of Cairo (Misr el Kahirah, built by Moez e Deen, 359 A.H.) was probably chosen on account of its strength.

BOULAC, the port of Cairo for vessels arriving from the northward, seems, from its name, to have had an Egyptian origin.

The Nilometer on the Island of Rhoda appears, from the length of the cubit employed, and from other circumstances, to be much older than the building, in which it is placed. The building, according to El Makim, was erected by the Kalif Soliman ebn Abd el Melik, A.H. 97, and was afterwards repaired under Almamon and Mutawakel. It is said that the French intended to build a fortified town on this island, and to have established a citadel on the island opposite to Boulac.

According to Strabo, BABYLON was an antient military post; and, according to Josephus, it was built by Cambyses, on the deserted site of Latopolis.[2] It was afterwards the station of a legion, and the present remains are evidently of Roman construction. Coptic authors state that it held out for seven months

---

[2] Many towns had this name.

against the Arabs, who built near it the first mosque, and Fostat the first Arab city, which were erected in Egypt. It is now called Old Cairo, and has a port, chiefly used by vessels coming down the river.

NOMOS APHRODITOPOLITIS.

This district commenced immediately above Old Cairo.

TAHA NOUB, which in Coptic signifies "*the place of gold,*" is now known by the Arabic name of Atar el Nebbi (*traces of the Prophet*). It is mentioned by the early Arab authors, and seems to be connected with Venus Aurea, now called Gezeeret el Dahab,— a place in the Memphite nome, on the opposite side of the river.

TROJA, now Tourah, supposed by Strabo to have been built by the Trojan captives carried off by Menelaus, is situated at the foot of a mountain, called by Pliny and by Ptolemy Troici Lapidis Mons, and mentioned by Herodotus to have supplied the stones for the erection of the Pyramids. It is composed of compact limestone, which has formed the casing of the exterior, and the linings of the passages and of the apartments in most of these buildings. The mountain is at present known by the name of Mokattam (*the hewn*), on account of the extensive quarries which were worked in it by the antient Egyptians, and which seem to have been abandoned since the time of the Ptolemies till 1838, when a railroad was made, by the direction of Mahomet Ali, from the quarries to the river.[a]

SCENAS MANDRAS was, by the "Itinerary," twelve miles from Babylon, and, according to the "Notitia," a military post. Under the Emperor Leo I. it was the see of a bishop. It seems to have been called in Coptic Alban, and is now Hellowan. The town was either rebuilt, or restored, by Abd el Azeez Ebn Merwan (a ruler of Egypt), who made it his residence, and adorned it with gardens. The adjacent land is very fertile.

APHRODITOPOLIS (by the Egyptians called Ipih, or Petfieh, and now Atfeh, is stated, in the "Notitia," to be a military post, and in the "Itinerary," to be thirty-two miles distant from Babylon); according to Strabo, and to other authors, it was

[a] This work was executed by Mr. Perring, who, in carrying the level to the river, discovered several antient tombs, which contained bodies wrapped in yellow woollen cloth, similar to that found in the Third Pyramid of Gizeh. See further account of these quarries.

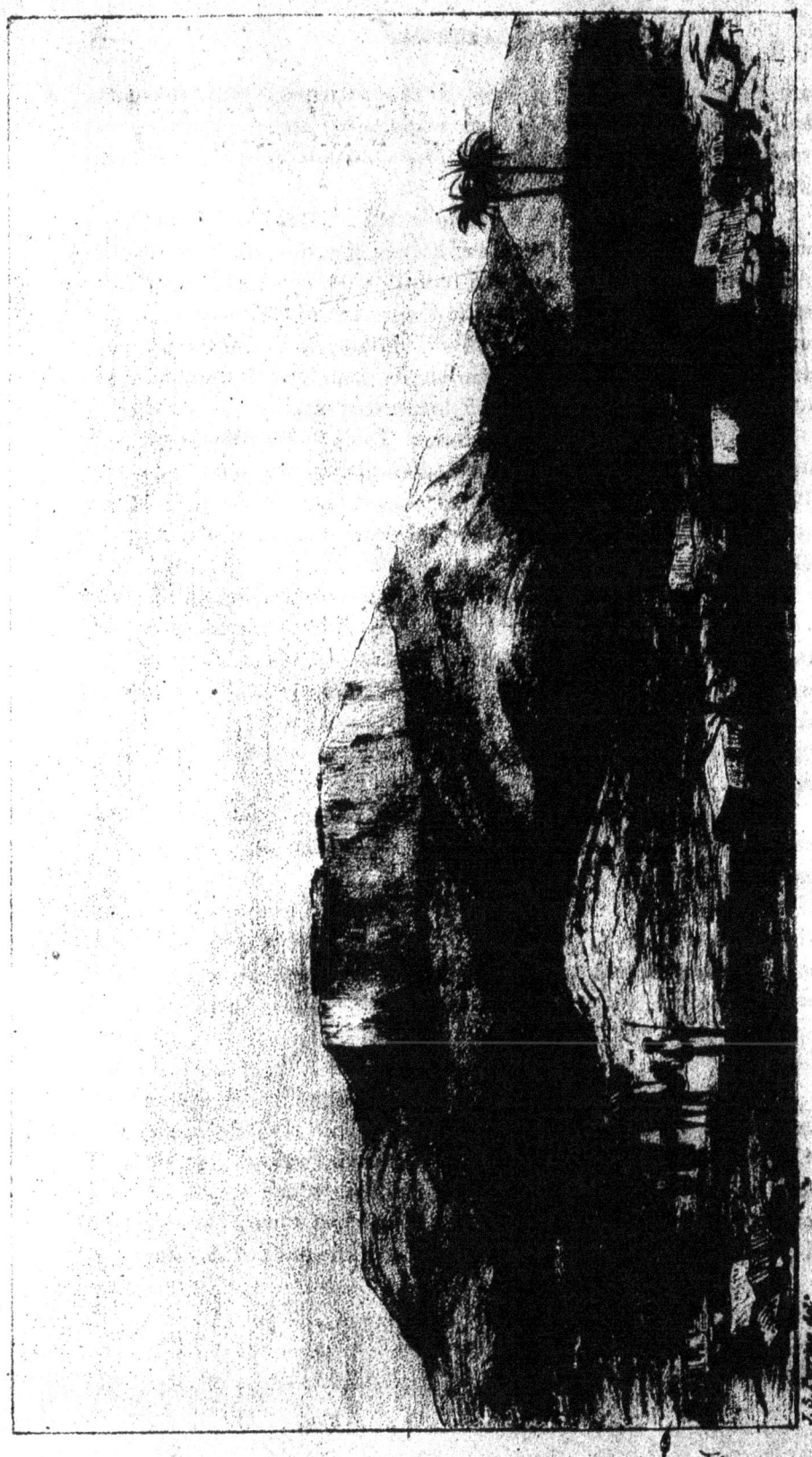

RUINED PYRAMID AND CAUSEWAY OF ABOU ROASH FROM HIRBASSY.

situated near the Arabicus Mons, and contained a temple, in which a sacred white bull was preserved.

Tilosj, or Tisjol, or Delass, said by Coptic authors to have been near Atfeh, and to have contained a convent, appears to have been at Soal, a large village near the river.

Ancyronpolis, so called by Stephanus of Byzantium, and Angyron by Ptolemy, was in this nome, and in the same latitude as Ptolemais. No traces of it are, however, to be found in that position; but the situation of Crumba has the appearance and the reputation of being an antient site.

Thimonepsi is described, in the " Notitia," to be a military post, and, in the " Itinerary," to be twenty-four Roman miles distant from Aphroditopolis. It was probably at Wady Bayad, opposite Beni Souef.

NOMOS MEMPHITIS.

Memphis, the capital of Lower Egypt, is supposed to have been built by Menes, the earliest king of the country. Diodorus describes it to have been nineteen miles in circumference; and his account is in some degree confirmed by the remains of buildings and of foundations. This great extent most probably occasioned the contradictory statements given by antient historians of its relative distance from the neighbouring places. Notwithstanding the antient grandeur of Memphis, Edrisi, who wrote in the twelfth century, says that it was then an insignificant place, and indeed it may be supposed to have supplied materials for the building of Cairo. Abou el Fedeh, however, 200 years afterwards, mentions extensive ruins, consisting of great blocks inscribed with figures; and at the village of Metrahenni a large tank may now be traced, near the foundations of a building, which appears to have been the temple of Ptah or Vulcan, mentioned by Herodotus, and by other antient historians; and a colossal statue near it was probably the image of Rameses, said to have been erected before the temple.[4] The city appears to have extended to the northward of the temple; but, as it was built upon low ground, the foundations have probably been covered by the annual deposit of the river.

Mons Psammius, near the above-mentioned city, was that part of the Libyan Mountains, upon which the Pyramids of Saccara[5]

[4] This statue was excavated by Signore Caviglia, and presented by the late Mr. Sloane, Vice-consul at Alexandria, to the British Museum.
[5] The name of the deity of Memphis was Pthah Sakari.

are built; and the Serapium was placed, according to Strabo, upon the plain near it; but no vestiges of it have been discovered.

VENUS AUREA. Diodorus speaks of a field called "Venus Aurea" in the neighbourhood of Meniphis; and an old site near the river, as has been already mentioned, is now called Gezeeret el Dahab (*the golden island or field*), which seems to be a translation of the antient name.

BOUSIRIS. This name was applied to various places in Egypt, where Osiris was worshipped in the form of an ox. The Busiris mentioned by Pliny has been generally supposed to have been at Abouseir, on account of the similarity of name; but, as the situation of that place appears to have been included within the city of Memphis, the name may be supposed to have marked the site of a temple dedicated to Osiris within the city; and if, as Pliny describes, Busiris was opposite the Great Pyramid of Gizeh, it may with more propriety be supposed to have been at an old site upon the adjacent plain, near the village of Kom el Eswith (*the black mound*).

ACANTHUS. The Egyptian name of this town is not known, but it is mentioned by Diodorus, Strabo, and Ptolemy; and Strabo assigns to it a temple of Osiris, and a sacred grove of Egyptian thorn (the acanthus of the Greeks). Groves of these trees are now to be met with between Saccara and Dashoor, and the town was most probably, therefore, situated on the edge of the desert near the hamlet of Zowyet el Dashoor.

PEME, or PEMBAU, is stated, in the "Itinerary," to have been twenty miles from Memphis. About this distance a place, called Bemah, has been constructed upon an antient site, and the Pyramids and a cemetery near them appear to establish the antiquity of the spot.

NOMOS HERACLEOPOLITIS.

According to Ptolemy, it was divided from the Nomos Memphitis by the river, which probably flowed near Kafoor el Gazaala, where a canal from the Bahr Yousef intersects the cultivated land.

ISIDIS OPPIDUM, ISSIU, or ISEUM, was, by the "Itinerary," forty miles from Memphis, probably at the site now occupied by the modern village of Zowyet el Masloob.

NILOPOLIS, where there was a temple dedicated to the Nile, under the personification of Osiris, and under the title of Bousiris, seems to have been at a place called Abouseir el Melik. Near it are the remains of an antient dyke constructed with masonry, and other works of considerable magnitude; and in the adjacent rocks are excavated tombs, but they do not appear to contain inscriptions.

PTOLEMAIS, called Ptolemaido in the "Theodosian Table," is described by Ptolemy to have been near the entrance to the Arsinoite Nome. It is now called Illahoon, and is at the entrance into the Faioum. The sluice for the admission of the waters into the canal called Bahr Yousef is evidently built on an antient foundation, and the shafts near the Pyramids seem to have formed the cemetery of the antient city.

VEANO. In the "Theodosian Table" we find that the distance from Veano to Ptolemaidon Arsinoitum was six miles. If six be supposed to be a mistake for eleven, the distance would coincide with that of some antient mounds, upon which is a village called Wennee.

POUSHIN, or BOUSHIN according to the Coptic, was at Boosh.

PHANNISJOIT appears to have been near Pouchin, and, according to Champollion, it was at the modern village of Zaytoon, the word Phannisjoît signifying in the Coptic, as Zaytoon in the Arabic, *a place of olives*.

IKEMEN, under the Emperor Diocletian, was a military post near the above-mentioned places.

CÆNE was at Benisouef. The only notice of it is in the "Itinerary of Antoninus," which states that it was about twenty miles from Isiu.

HERACLEOPOLIS MAGNA. The capital of this nome was, by the "Theodosian Table," six miles south of Ptolemais; and antient mounds and foundations near the village of Ahnas agree with this distance.

NOMOS CROCODILOPOLITIS.

This district was so called by the Greeks, but by the Egyptians Piom, because it was marshy and full of water. Under the Lagidæ the province, as well as the capital, was called Arsinoe. It is now known by the name of Faioum, which seems to be a corruption of its Egyptian name. The chief town, Medeenet el Faioum, is to the southward of the site of the antient Arsinoe.

PYRAMID OF ABOU ROASH.

This Pyramid is situated about five miles to the north-westward of those at Gizeh. The base (320 feet square) alone remains. The defective places have been made good with masonry, but the bulk of it is formed of the mountain (composed of a hard chalk), which has been reduced to a level around it. No part of the external casing is to be found; indeed the edifice was not probably ever completed, or even raised to a considerable height, for scarcely any materials, and very little rubbish, are to be seen, although the situation is difficult of access.

An inclined entrance-passage, and an apartment, lying east and west, have been constructed in an excavation, and have been lined with fine calcareous stone from the Tourah quarries.

The passage (about 160 feet in length) is in the centre of the northern front, and descends at an angle of 22° 35′. The dimensions of the apartment are about 40 feet by 15, and above it smaller chambers appear to have been constructed, similar to those over the King's Chamber in the Great Pyramid of Gizeh. Hieroglyphics have been inscribed with red ochre on some of the blocks at the western end, but they cannot be distinctly made out.

Upon the adjacent ground are heaps of broken granite, which may possibly be the chippings of the blocks, originally intended for an external casing, but afterwards broken up, and carried away for other purposes. The fragments crumble to pieces upon being handled, and are much decomposed and covered with moss, either from great antiquity, or from an exposure, not only to the corroding air of the desert, but also to the moist winds of the Delta.

Some other foundations are upon the same height, which has been already described to be composed of chalk, and which appears to have been worked in very early times (as at present) for the sake of the flints imbedded in it. The levelled space around the Pyramid is about 510 feet above the plain. The eastern and southern sides of the mountain are nearly perpendicular, and beneath it to the southward are antient remains. The northern side has been sloped away, and an inclined causeway has been constructed from the plain below (as is shewn in fig. 1). It is 4950 feet in length, 30 feet in breadth, and in

PYRAMID OF ABOU ROASH,
FROM THE S.W. ANGLE.

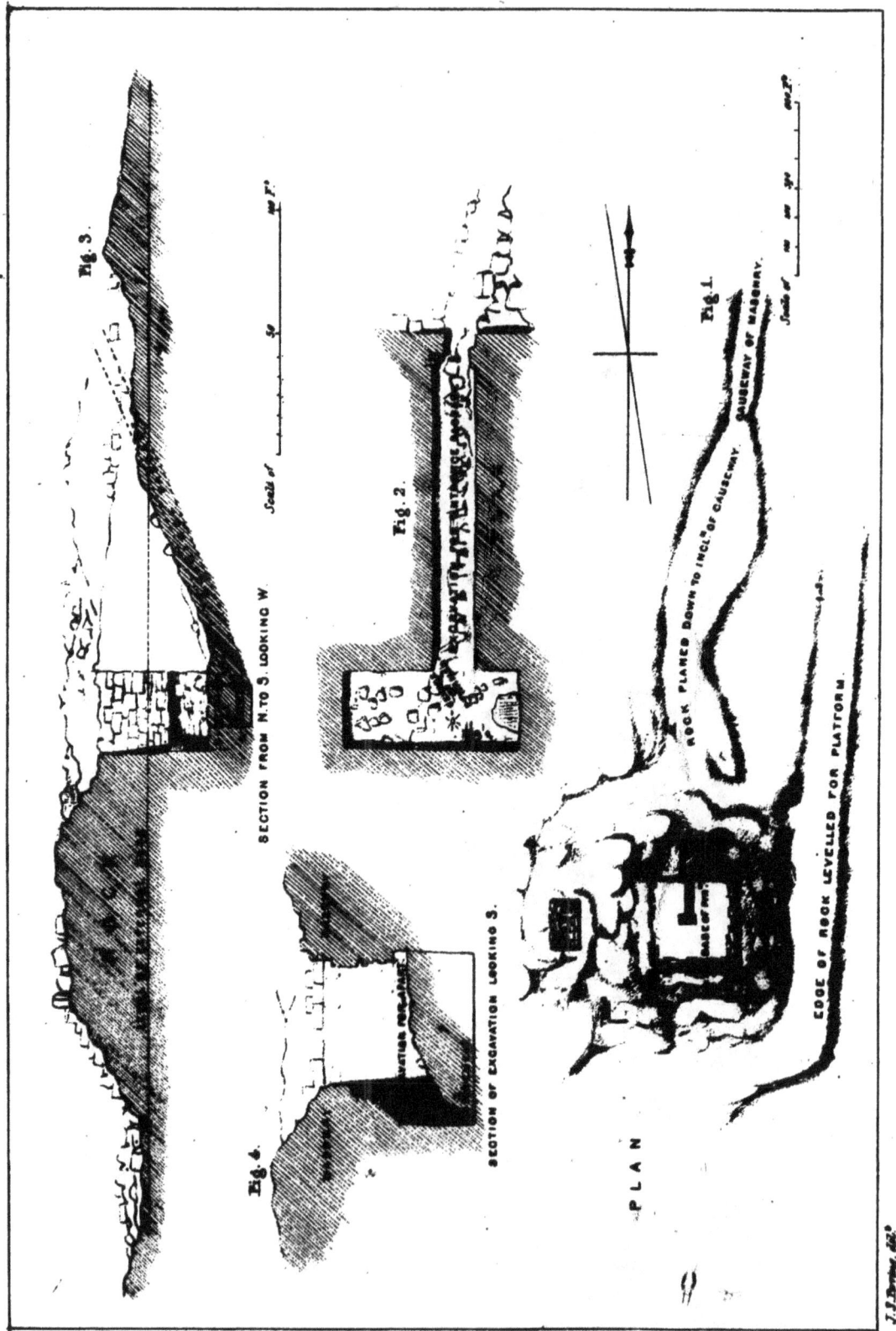

some places nearly 40 feet high. About half of it is constructed with masonry.

Fig. 1 is a plan of the Pyramid and of the hills upon which it is placed.

Fig. 2, Plan of excavation, wherein the inclined entrance-passage and the apartment have been formed.

Fig. 3, Section through the apartment, and along entrance-passage looking west.

Fig. 4, Section through apartment looking south.

A view of the Pyramid from Kerdassy, looking across the plain of sand, is also given; and also a view taken from near the south-western angle.

A valley to the northward extends to the Natron Lakes, and is the usual road of the western pilgrims from the Barbary coast. Mummy-pits and tombs were found in this valley, but they did not contain any inscriptions; the inhabitants of the neighbouring village, however, were said to have taken from them a variety of small articles, similar to those in the tombs at Gizeh, and mummy-cases inscribed with hieroglyphics. At the edge of the hills, on the northern side of the valley, are traces of an antient square building. It is called by the Arabs El Deir (*the convent*), a name, however, which is often indiscriminately applied by them to antient ruins.

Upon a projecting knoll, on the eastern side of the mountain, and near the village of Abou Roash, are also the remains of a building of considerable magnitude and solidity. It is composed of crude bricks, made of Nile earth, without any intermixture of straw. Small sepulchral grottoes at the bottom of inclined passages have been roughly hewn in the side of the mountain; they contain sarcophagi, which are without any ornament or inscription.

Upon a plain now covered with sand, between this place and the village of Kerdassy, the site of a considerable town may be traced. The name of it has perished, together with its edifices; but, from the apparent antiquity of the Pyramid in question, it was probably Cochoma, mentioned by Africanus as having existed under the fourth king of Manetho's first dynasty, Venephes (Enephes, or Venephres), son of Cencenes, "for that monarch is said to have erected a pyramid near the town of Cochone (Cochoma, or Choe)."[6]

[6] See Remarks upon the Map.

PYRAMID OF ZOWYET EL ARRIAN.

It is called by the Arabs El Medowareh (*the circular*), and is situated on an eminence near a sheik's tomb, about three quarters of a mile to the westward of the village, from which it takes its name.

It is mentioned in the "Description d'Egypte" (vol. v. p. 14), in connexion with two other buildings, the remains of which, after some trouble, were at length discovered; the one about half a mile, and the other about a mile, to the northward of the Pyramid in question; but they were so completely dilapidated, that their original construction could not be made out; indeed of the most perfect there were only to be seen a few stones, composing a parallelogram, twice as long as it was broad. The materials of the Pyramid of Zowyet el Arrian have been quarried from the adjoining hills, and consist of hard limestone, in which are many fossil shells. The blocks have not been squared, nor laid in regular courses, but form a sort of rubble work, in which clayey loam mixed with sand has been used instead of mortar.

Great part of the building has been removed for the use of the neighbouring villages; and it is only where the sand has been taken away in search of materials, particularly at the north-western angle, that the masonry is visible. The pyramidal form is entirely destroyed, and the general appearance of the ruin is that of a round hill.

No remains of a casing, or of the limestone from the Mokattam, were discovered.

> Present base, about 300 feet.
> Ditto height - - 61 feet above the rock.

The rock before the northern front had been scarped away, so as to form on the eastward an inclined approach from the plain beneath.

PYRAMID OF REEGAH.

It is situated on a hill, near the deserted village of Reegah, about three quarters of a mile north-west of the Pyramids of Abouseir; is called by the Arabs, Haram el Abou-Goorob, and

PYRAMID OF EILEGAH.

APPENDIX.

is composed of masonry superior to that of the Pyramids of Abouseir.

There appears to have been a temple before the eastern front, and a causeway communicating therefrom to another building on the plain. (See Plan, fig. 1.)

The Pyramid had been carried up in two inclines, like the Southern Pyramid of Dashoor. The casing of the lower part was of granite, and had an angle of 75° 20′; that of the upper part, composed of calcareous stone from the Mokattam, had an angle of about 52°.

The base was 123 feet 4 inches square.

Mr. Perring excavated in the centre of the northern front, and found amongst the rubbish fragments of stone which were rudely sculptured and coloured, and, in some instances, were marked with golden stars upon a dark-blue ground, as if they had belonged to the ceiling of an apartment; he also met with some coarse earthenware pots, and a mass of brickwork erected close to the Pyramid, upon the broken casing-stones; fragments of which, composed of granite, were found near the north-eastern angle. As Mr. Perring did not discover an entrance on the northern side, he extended his researches, but without effect, to the eastward, where brick-work had been also erected over the broken casing, and where more coarse earthenware, consisting of pots and of lamps of this shape were found, and likewise some round pieces of black basalt, from 3 to 7 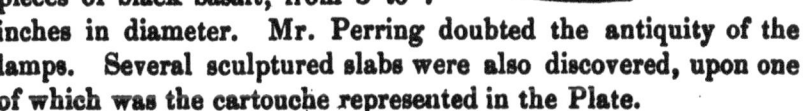 inches in diameter. Mr. Perring doubted the antiquity of the lamps. Several sculptured slabs were also discovered, upon one of which was the cartouche represented in the Plate.

The hieroglyphics were found upon blocks near the eastern front, and the stone marked fig. 7, and several others, upon which characters were rudely sculptured, had been apparently brought out from the interior of the building. Figs. 2 and 3 were well, but slightly engraved, upon four pieces of granite, which seem to have belonged to the temple already alluded to.

Fig. 3 had formed part of a doorway, for the hole A was evidently intended to receive the top of the heel-post of a door.

NOTE BY MR. BIRCH.

As two of these inscriptions are upon blocks, which according to Mr. Perring's account had been taken from another edifice before they were used in the construction of the Pyramid, they cannot be considered to be exclusively connected with the existing monument, and are therefore comparatively of less value. They are all likewise too imperfect to be completely understood. Figs. 2 and 3, at present separate, were no doubt originally connected together. Fig. 1 contains the name of the king Ousrenre; and on a line to the left the seated figure of the monarch may be traced. He is crowned with a teshr, or with the lower part of a pschent surmounted by two horns; and he holds a whip in his hand, in the same manner as the figure of the king Maire, or Piops, on a tablet at Chenoboskion, published by Sir J. G. Wilkinson. Before the monarch is the head of a person of rank, and also an imperfect inscription, in which can be distinguished a cord and an owl, phonetically expressing ⲥⲣⲣ, and part of the word ⲥⲉⲣⲣⲥⲓ, "*minister, officer, preferred.*" (Champ., "Gram. Egypt." p. 464.) Fig. 2 contains part of two vertical lines, which probably recount the address of a deity to the monarch, and the titles of the monarch, as, "*all stability,*" "*all power;*" and in the line to the right "*the king set up*" may be read.[7] Fig. 3 comprehends a long horizontal line of hieroglyphics, in which is "*of him the sun taking the heart. . . . .*" The inscription resembles those which have been discovered near the Pyramids at Gizeh. The lower part has contained one of the usual sacred representations, surmounted by the symbol of heaven, supported by a gom, or koucoupha sceptre.

PYRAMIDS OF ABOUSEIR.

They are three in number (besides the lower part of another, which has sometimes been called a temple, and the base of a fifth much smaller), and are situated to the south-eastward of the ruins of Zowyet el Arrian, and of Reegah, about seven miles S.S.E. of those at Gizeh, and about three miles N.N.E. of Saccara.

---

[7] Burton, "Excerpta Hier." Plate XXXVII. 20. Rosellini, "Monum. Tav." Cory (I. Preston), "Mythological Inq." 8vo. London, 1837. Title-page, D, Plate, where the deity says,—"*I set up the tosh (cap) on thy head like thy father Amoun-ra.*" Plate facing p. 184,—"*Who gives all life and power, all stability, all force, like the sun,*" are the titles of the Guardian of the South, the Hophioue of M. Champollion. Burton, "Excerpta Hier." Plate XXV. 5.

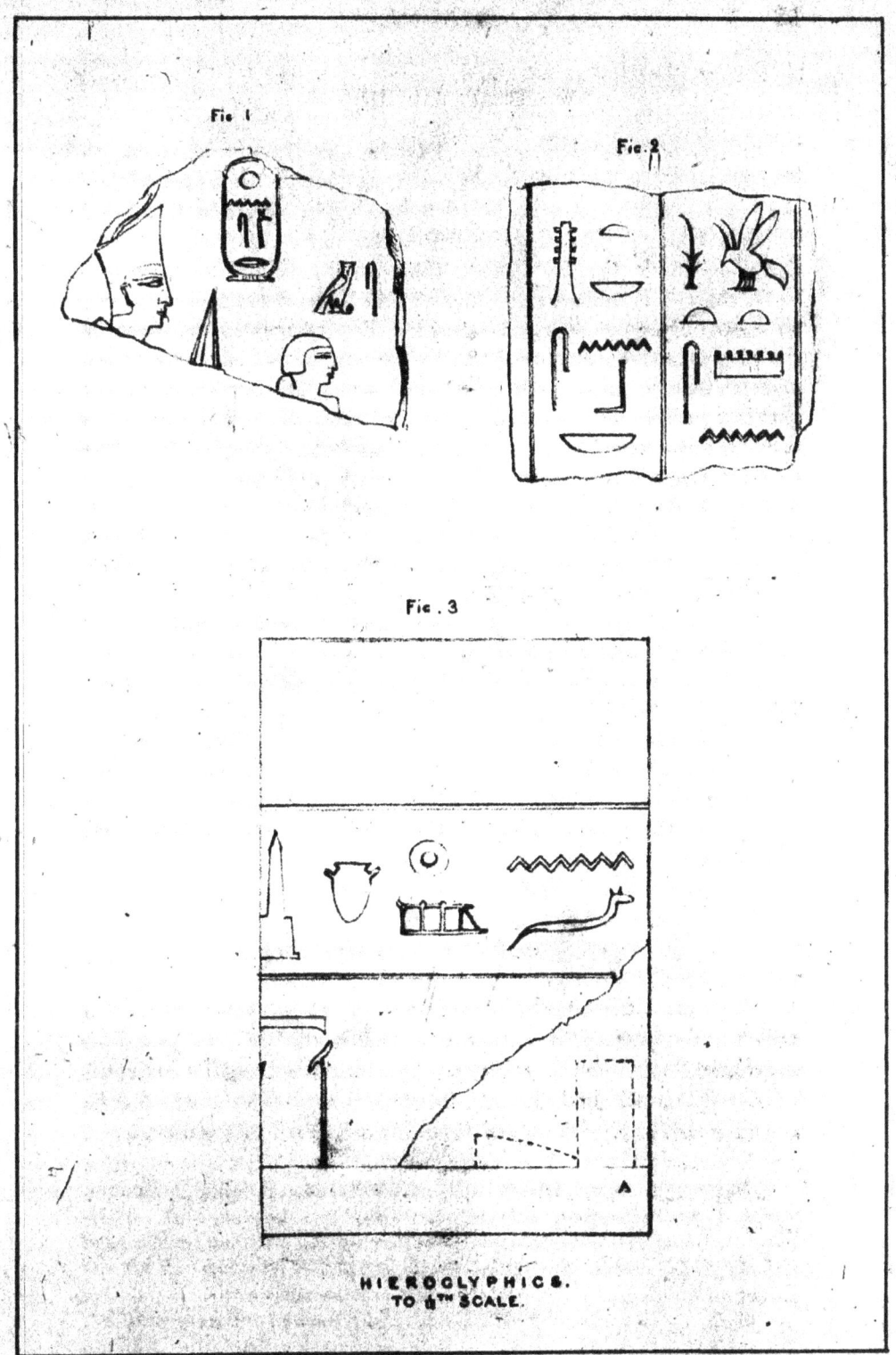

PYRAMID OF REEGAH.

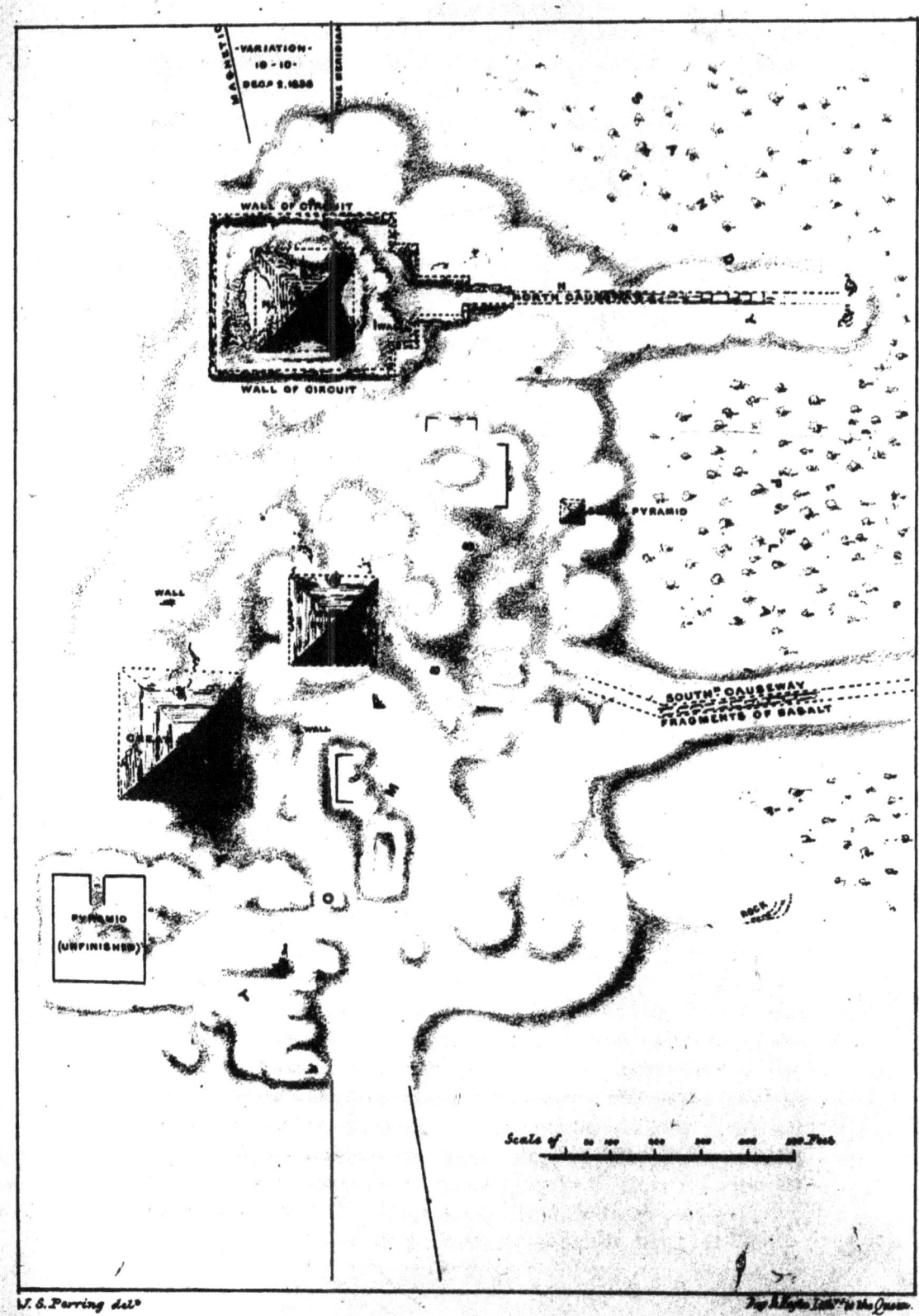

MAP OF THE PYRAMIDS OF ABOUSEIR.

They are on an elevation, which is about eighty feet higher than the adjacent plain, and is composed of argillaceous rock, unfit for extensive excavation; the few tombs which occur are therefore formed of masonry. A map of the Pyramids, and a general view of them, taken from the edge of the cultivated ground, are given.

Mr. Perring experienced a great deal of trouble in the examination of these Pyramids, and was unable to engage many labourers, on account of the people being employed in the Dhoorah harvest. He began with the Northern Pyramid, and removed the rubbish in the centre of the northern front, commencing at the peribolus and clearing away down to the platform. In doing so he first removed fragments of broken stones and sand, and found beneath them parts of the casing, which had consisted of granite and of the stone from the quarries at Tourah, one of which appeared to have been cut for the reception of a tablet like the tablets said by Herodotus to have contained inscriptions over the entrances of the Pyramids. The passage was full of stones and of rubbish, which continued to fall down from an opening in the ceiling; and while these were being removed, the side of the Pyramid gave way, and completely buried one of the labourers; who fortunately, however, did not sustain any material injury: for fear of a serious accident, Mr. Perring removed all the people except seven or eight of the best men, and these he had some difficulty in keeping to their work, as large masses of masonry, together with rubbish, from time to time fell in. On this occasion, as on many others, the courage and exertions of a Reis, named Abd el Ardi, were peculiarly conspicuous.

Mr. Perring succeeded in removing the hieroglyphics and the cartouche B from the retaining wall to the westward of the entrance, and was obliged to use gunpowder for that purpose. As the masonry, in which he was working, was composed of rubble work, and as the lining of the passage had been destroyed, some date-trees were procured from the village of Metrahenni, and he endeavoured to shore up the loose blocks, but, owing to the bad texture of the masonry, with little success. After ten days' labour he arrived at the apartment, which was completely ruined, and full of rubbish and of broken stones; his attempts to clear it were attended with great difficulty and risk, and the apartment was three several times filled up with stones, that fell through the broken parts of the roof. He continued his operations for above three weeks, notwithstanding that one man had his leg broken, and that several others were severely hurt. He found the long inscription A, and also part of D, inscribed with red ochre upon blocks of Tourah stone, near the entrance of the Pyramid.

The Northern Pyramid has been surrounded by a wall, and has also been connected with the plain on the eastern side by an inclined causeway, formed with rude blocks of limestone, quarried on the spot; and at the eastern extremity of the causeway there appears to have been a building.

Another inclined way seems to have formed an approach to the Middle Pyramid, although not in a direct course, owing, probably, to the profile of the ground. Upon the sides of a considerable part of it fragments of black basalt, at nearly equal distances, appear either to have belonged to an avenue of sphinxes, or to have formed part of a parapet wall, as may be seen in the Plate. These inclined roads were, no doubt, originally constructed for the conveyance of the stone, and of the other materials, used in the erection of the Pyramids; but they seem afterwards to have constituted the regular approaches. Herodotus mentions, that they were adorned with the figures of animals, which were probably either sculptured hieroglyphics, or an avenue of sphinxes.

The interior of the three Pyramids is upon the same plan. The entrance-passages, in the centre of the northern fronts, are at first inclined, and afterwards horizontal. The apartments in the centres of the Pyramids range from east to west, and are covered by inclined roofs, consisting of several courses of stone. The materials and the workmanship are also similar. The bulk of the building has been in the first instance carried up in degrees, and has been afterwards completed into a pyramidal form. The greatest part of the material consists of stone found upon the spot; but the exterior casing, the linings of the passages, and of the apartments, and the roof-blocks, are from the Tourah quarries, to which these Pyramids are exactly opposite.

The masonry is in general very rude, and consists of rough blocks of various sizes, put together like rubble work, with Nile earth instead of mortar. The exterior casing of all the Pyramids has been removed, and the masonry, when exposed to the weather, of course would be soon destroyed; but it is difficult to account for the disappearance of the materials, unless by supposing that they have been taken for other buildings;

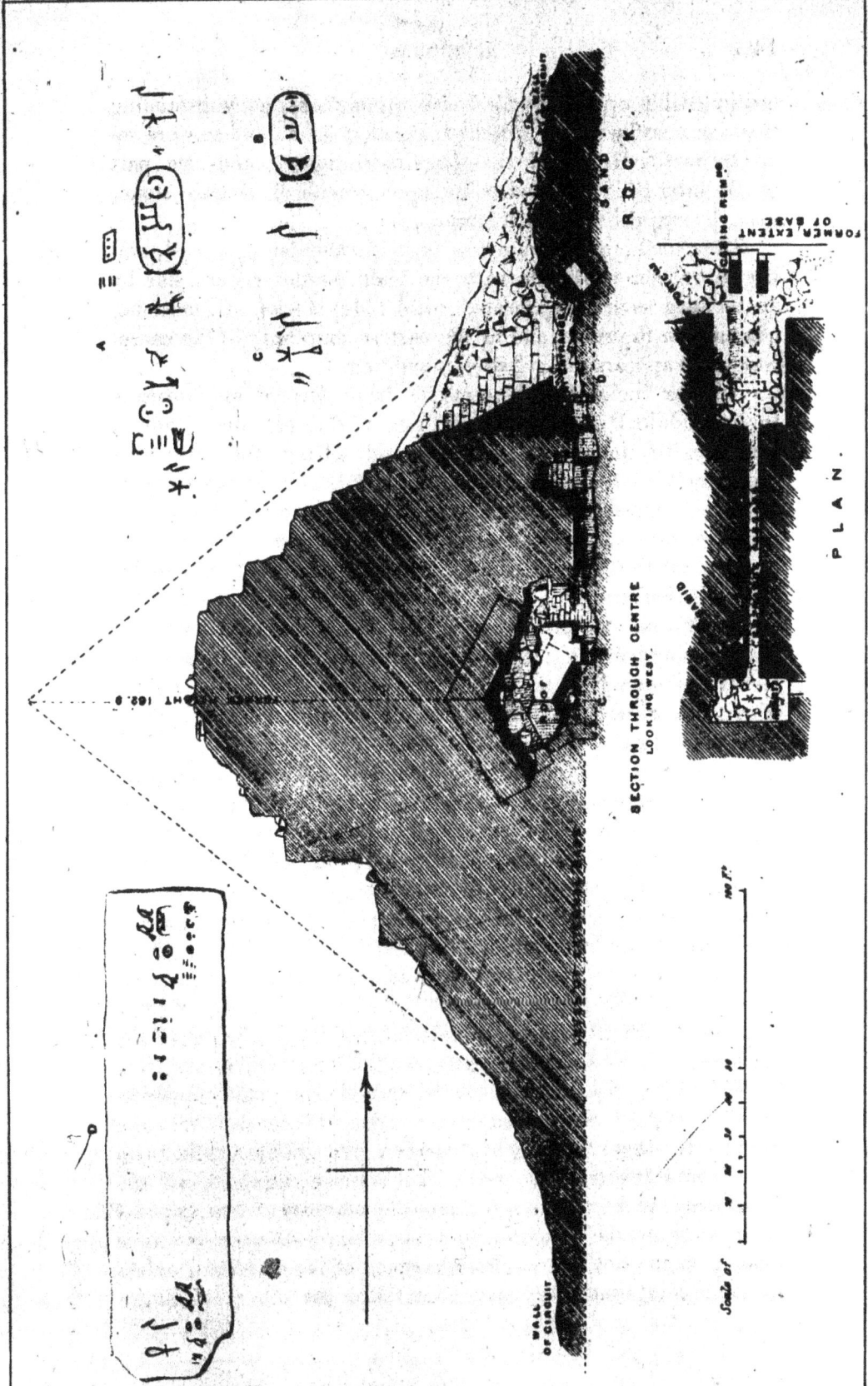

NORTHERN PYRAMID OF ABOUSEIR.

ENTRANCE TO THE MIDDLE PYRAMID.

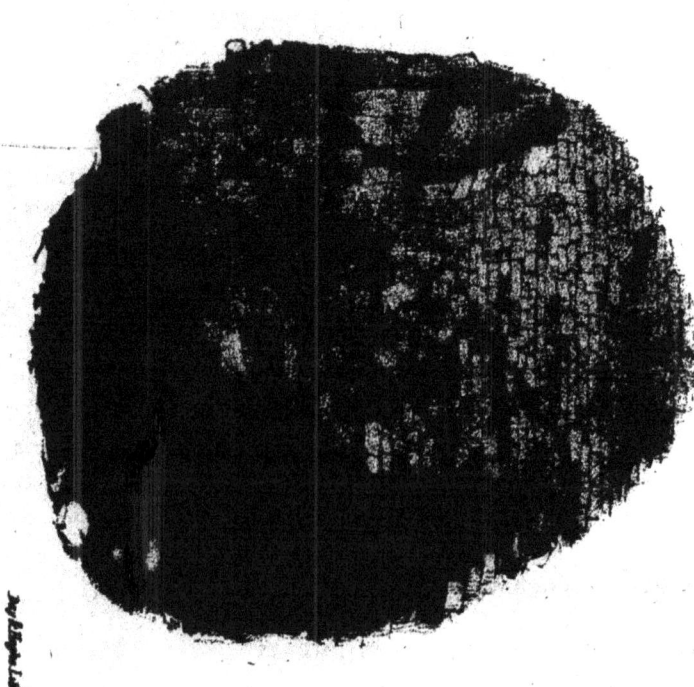

ENTRANCE TO THE NORTHERN PYRAMID.

PYRAMIDS OF ABOUSEIR.

APPENDIX. 15

and, as the Pyramids of Gizeh are more conveniently situated for that purpose, as regards Cairo, it may be inferred that these buildings were destroyed, at an earlier period, for the erection of a more antient town in their more immediate vicinity.

Near the south-western corner of the Great Pyramid are the foundations of another, in which an entrance on the northern side, and an excavation for a passage and apartments may be traced.

NORTHERN PYRAMID.

	Original.	Present.
Base	257 ft.	216 ft.
Perpendicular Height	162 ft. 9 in.	118 ft.
Angle of Casing		51° 42′ 35″

After the entrance-passage in the centre of the northern front was discovered, it was not practicable for a fortnight, owing to the broken stones and sand, and to the ruined state of the building. The passage descended at an angle of 27° 5′ for 14 feet, and then proceeded in a horizontal direction. At the distance of 27 feet from the incline, it has been closed by a portcullis, formed of a block of granite 1 foot 3 inches in thickness; and the same material has been employed in the passage, as far as the present entrance, 11 feet 6 inches beyond the portcullis. A view of the entrance in its present state is given.

	Feet.	Inches.	
Passage from Entrance to Portcullis	4	2½	high.
Ditto ditto	4	0	wide.
From present Entrance to Apartment	71	4	long.
Ditto ditto	4	2	wide.
Height at Entrance	5	10	
Height near Granite	6	4	
Height at Granite, B	4	5	
Height beyond Granite at Apartment	4	1½	
Apartment breadth North and South	11	8	
Height at Sides	9	4	
Height in Centre	12	6	

The apartment was in the centre of the Pyramid, and extended 9 feet 4 inches to the eastward of the entrance-passage, but its original dimensions are uncertain, and so indeed are the numbers and position of the apartments. Some however appear to have been placed under the eastern part of the edifice, and to have been entered by the low passage (C, in plan), but the place was full of rubbish, and towards the east had been completely ruined.

Most of the pavement had been destroyed, as well as a sarcophagus formed of black basalt, the fragments of which were well polished, but quite plain. Two small iron wedges, 4 or 5 ounces in weight, which might possibly have been used in destroying the building, were also found; they were about 3 inches in length, and 1¾ inch in breadth at the edge.

The granite in the sides and in the roof of the passage at B (in plan and section) was apparently intended to give strength to the masonry, where its solidity was weakened; and, as an additional security, there had been three tiers of roof-blocks, the footings of the upper rows of which had been carried beyond those of the lower, in order to distribute the pressure over as great a base as possible. These roof-blocks were of immense size, in some instances they were 35 feet long, 9 feet wide, and 12 feet thick; yet so completely had they been destroyed, that of the upper tiers only two perfect blocks, and fragments of two others remained.

The indefatigable exertions therefore of the people, who broke in and destroyed these Pyramids, cannot but excite surprise, and in some degree admiration, although they were probably occasioned by no better motive, than a desire to obtain the hidden treasures. The Earl of Mount Norris appears to be of the same opinion.[a]

The apartments and passages had been constructed with large blocks of Tourah stone, beautifully worked and well put together.

A recess in the casing above the entrance appeared to have been intended to receive an inscription, like that which we are informed by Diodorus was placed over the entrance of the Third Pyramid of Gizeh, and this circumstance may in some degree account for the inscriptions said by Herodotus and by other authors to have been seen upon the Pyramids.

DD, in plan and section, are retaining walls, about 24 feet asunder. They are composed of large blocks laid in more regular courses, and built with more care than the rest of the

---

[a] See Lord Valencia's "Travels," vol. III. page 433:—"I cannot but suspect that the conquerors of this country found treasures concealed in some of the stones of the antient edifices, and that the expectation of finding more led to the laborious destruction of these massive temples, which seem to have been constructed to bid defiance to time itself."

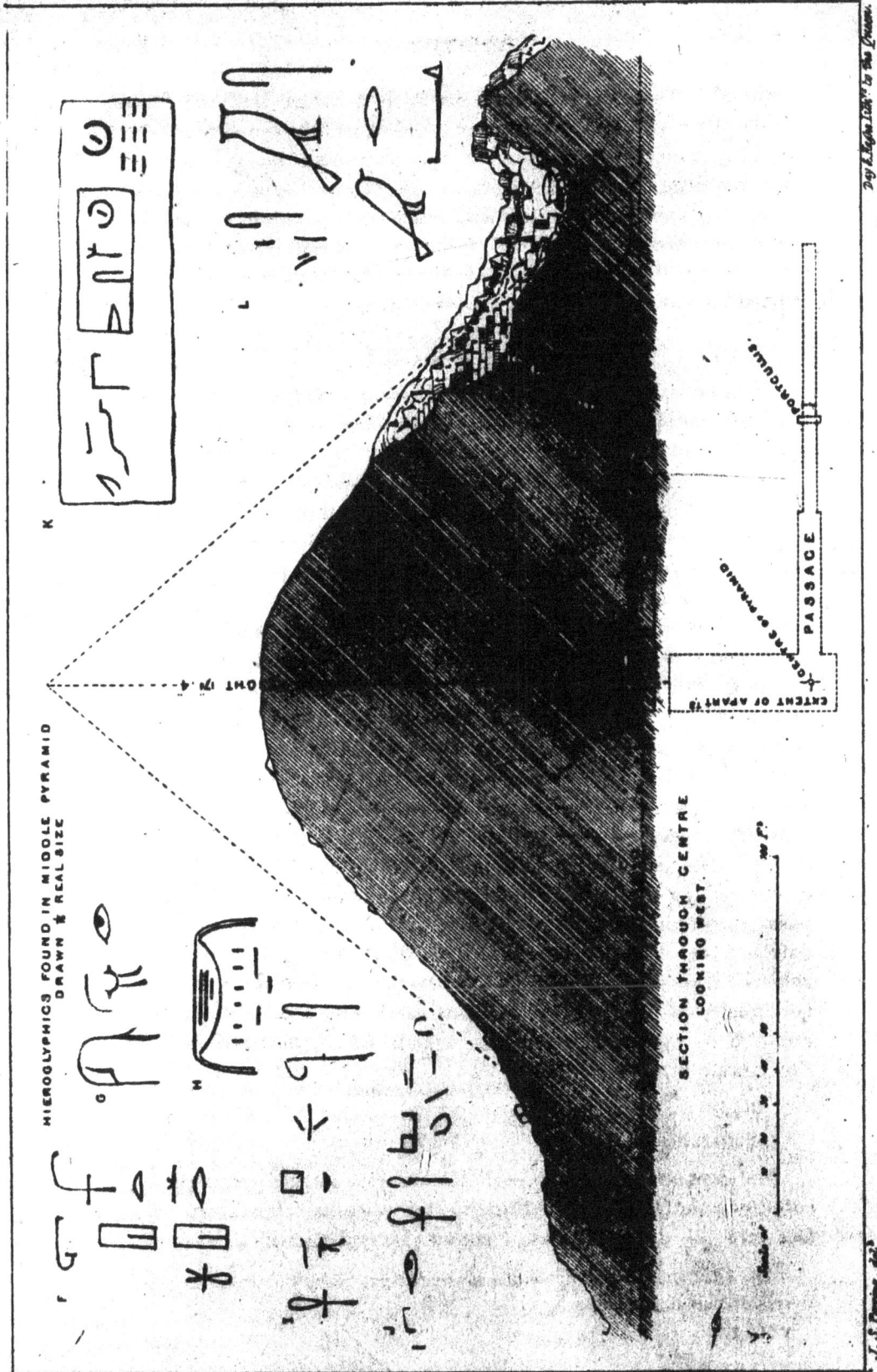

MIDDLE PYRAMID OF ABOUSEIR.

Pyramid. They were probably run up in order that the bulk of the Pyramid might be carried on before the passages were finished, which, on account of their superior masonry, must have required considerable time and attention. Upon these walls the hieroglyphics A, B, C, and D, were written in red ochre.

A pavement two feet in thickness, extended around the building to the peribolus; and where the rock was low, the pavement was placed upon a layer of sand.[9]

MIDDLE PYRAMID.

The appearance of this Pyramid is that of a square mound; and the masonry is only visible where the rubbish has been removed from the angles.

Mr. Perring employed all the people, whom he could spare from the Northern, upon the Middle Pyramid, and began to remove a great accumulation of rubbish near the base: after six days' labour the pit or hollow, A, was discovered; it was composed of small stones without mortar, and was apparently intended to prevent the entrance from being choked up by sand and rubbish; it was cleared out in eight days; a few pieces of granite were found in it, and fragments of stone inscribed with hieroglyphics. It then became necessary to clear away the front of the Pyramid, as the rubbish fell down upon the people employed in the pit. In ten days' time the entrance-passage, B, was discovered, and, as it was regularly filled up with masonry, it was evident that the Pyramid had been forced from above. After six days' additional labour a forced entrance was discovered by Abd el Ardi, which led down to a horizontal passage, running north and south from the bottom of the inclined entrance (see Plate). This forced entrance was choked up with rubbish; it was very narrow, and, in attempting to widen it, blocks continually fell in from the masonry above, which could only be removed by ropes and pulleys, so that it was eleven days before the passage was practicable.

	Supposed Original.	Present.
Base	274 ft. 0 in.	213 ft.
Perpendicular Height	171 ft. 4 in.	107 ft.

The present entrance (see Plate) is by a forced excavation, cut down perpendicularly through the masonry for about 40 feet into the regular passage near a portcullis, which, as well

---

[9] The lid of a wooden cup, containing red ochre, which was found at this Pyramid, had an iron fastening.

as the inclined entrance leading down to it, remained closed up with blocks of granite;[1] the passage is lined, and the portcullis is formed of the same material.

The horizontal passage from the portcullis to the apartment is 63 feet in length, 5 feet 10 inches in height, and 5 feet 1 inch in width. For the distance of 24 feet from the portcullis it had been broken up, and was much encumbered with rubbish.

The width of the apartment appeared to have been 14 feet, but it could not be correctly ascertained, as the place was filled up above the side walls with the fragments of the blocks, which had belonged to the roof.

The roof had been formed by three tiers of blocks, 48 feet 6 inches in length. Many of them had been destroyed, but upon the whole the interior was in a better state than that of the other two Pyramids; it was, however, completely ruined. The marks of wedges were every where visible; but it was difficult to imagine that any power, excepting that of gunpowder, could have effected so much destruction; it was not therefore cleared out. The condition, in which it was found, is represented in one of the plates; and in the section it may be observed that the roof-blocks had been laid with different degrees of inclination, in order that the vacancy between the tiers might relieve the ceiling of the apartment from the superincumbent weight. The skeleton of a starved tiger-cat was found in the apartment.

The position of the granite block in the casing of the passages beneath the roof (D in the section) is similar to that already described in the account of the Northern Pyramid, and was no doubt intended for the same purpose.

Figs. F, G, H, I, J, K, L, shew the principal hieroglyphics; but it is to be observed, that nearly every block belonging to the exterior contained larger or smaller inscriptions, written upon the light-coloured stones with red ochre, and upon the darker with white paint.

F was found upon two sides of a stone.

G the same.

J occurred several times, more or less distinctly.

All the characters were upon blocks found on the exterior of the building, excepting I, which was upon a roof-block, and was the only inscription observed at these Pyramids upon stone from Tourah; whereas the inscriptions found at Gizeh were invariably upon the blocks from the Arabian mountains.

[1] This is an additional proof that these buildings were merely tombs.

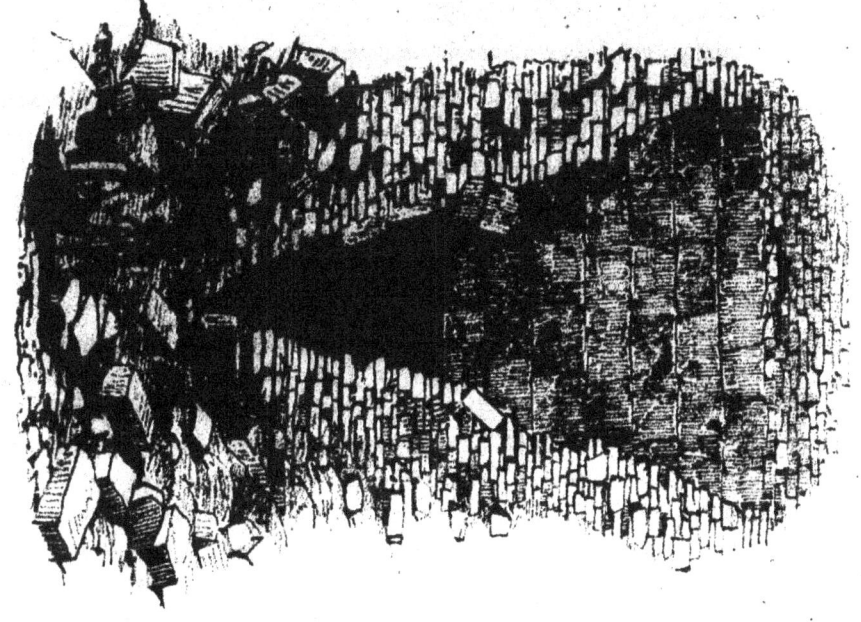

ENTRANCE TO THE GREAT PYRAMID OF ABOUSEIR.

VIEW OF THE ROOF, MIDDLE PYRAMID OF ABOUSEIR.

GREAT PYRAMID.

Mr. Perring then removed the stones and rubbish from the northern front of the Great Pyramid, and met with fragments of a casing composed of granite, which had been cut up for modern use, like the blocks belonging to the Third Pyramid of Gizeh; at the end of sixteen days he arrived at the masonry A, which had a casing in the form of steps, but he did not discover an entrance. He therefore proceeded to clear away the rubbish from the side of the Pyramid above it, when he found a space, where the masonry had fallen in; and in doing so he met with a pointed piece of sycamore wood, part of a head-rest, and a mallet about 11 inches long, 4¼ inches wide at the upper end, and much worn. It was similar to those represented by Sir J. G. Wilkinson, Vol. II. p. 181, and Vol. III. p. 335.

The building was in steps or degrees, covered over with flat stones (see a, b, c, in section, fig. 1), and the space between these and the pyramidal casing was filled up with a rubble work of smaller stones; so that it appears to have been the original intention to have left it in steps or degrees, like the present form of the Pyramid of Saccara.

The lower courses of the casing, and part of the entrance-passage, had been composed of granite. The masonry was somewhat better than that of the two other Pyramids, and the mortar, composed of Nile earth, had been mixed up with a small quantity of lime, or of pounded limestone.

	Supposed original.	Present.
Base	359 ft. 9 in.	325 ft.
Perpendicular Height	227 ft. 10 in.	164 ft.
From present Entrance to Apartment		104 ft.

The entrance-passage, in the centre of the northern front, had an inclination of 26° 3′. The horizontal continuation of it from D to D in section was constructed with large blocks of Tourah stone, in the singular manner (shewn in the cross-section, fig. 3), and a roof of inclined stones between two walls had relieved the passage from the superincumbent weight of the building.

The sides were however destroyed, and the roof had been broken up, with the exception of a few blocks, which had been left at intervals to support the superstructure. A long piece of wood had been worked into the masonry at E, in section, fig. 1, which though rather shaky, was completely sound.[a] Layers of split reeds were laid in many places upon the blocks of the roof of the passage. The reeds were like those used in the East for pens, and had been striped with red paint.

After ten or twelve feet of this passage had been cleared out, the people were alarmed by a loud noise, and had just made their escape, when a large mass of masonry above the entrance fell, and disclosed a wall composed of large blocks, C. It then became necessary to remove the rubbish, which amounted to several hundred tons. The lining of the passage was found completely broken up; but at length a small opening was discovered to the right of the excavation, by which Mr. Perring entered the apartment and found it in the same state as those in the other Pyramids.

This apartment had also been covered with a pointed roof of three courses of blocks. They were 45 feet in length, and had extended from east to west, but had been destroyed with a mischievous perseverance, which was truly wonderful.

A, B, C, D, E, contain hieroglyphics.

A, reversed, occurs in red upon a block in the passage.

B, C, D, are inscribed over the apartment in black, where most of the stones are marked thus in red.

E was found upon a loose block near the entrance.

The view of the entrance shews the casing of the story or degree, C in the section, fig. 1. It was marked with horizontal and with perpendicular lines, drawn in red ochre, and with a hieroglyphic at the rectangular intersections. A small figure of a female deity (Bubastes), composed of green glazed pottery, was found near this Pyramid.

---

[a] Part of it has been sent to the British Museum, and the following certificate was given to Mr. Perring:—

"*Cairo, April 27, 1839.*

"The piece of wood, taken by Mr. Perring from the Great Pyramid at Abouseir, must have been built in the masonry of the building at the time of its original erection—a considerable portion of the same still remaining inclosed amongst the stones, that have not been disturbed, and the mortar adhering to its surface, which could only have taken place when it was first laid on.

"Signed, CHARLES HAMILTON."

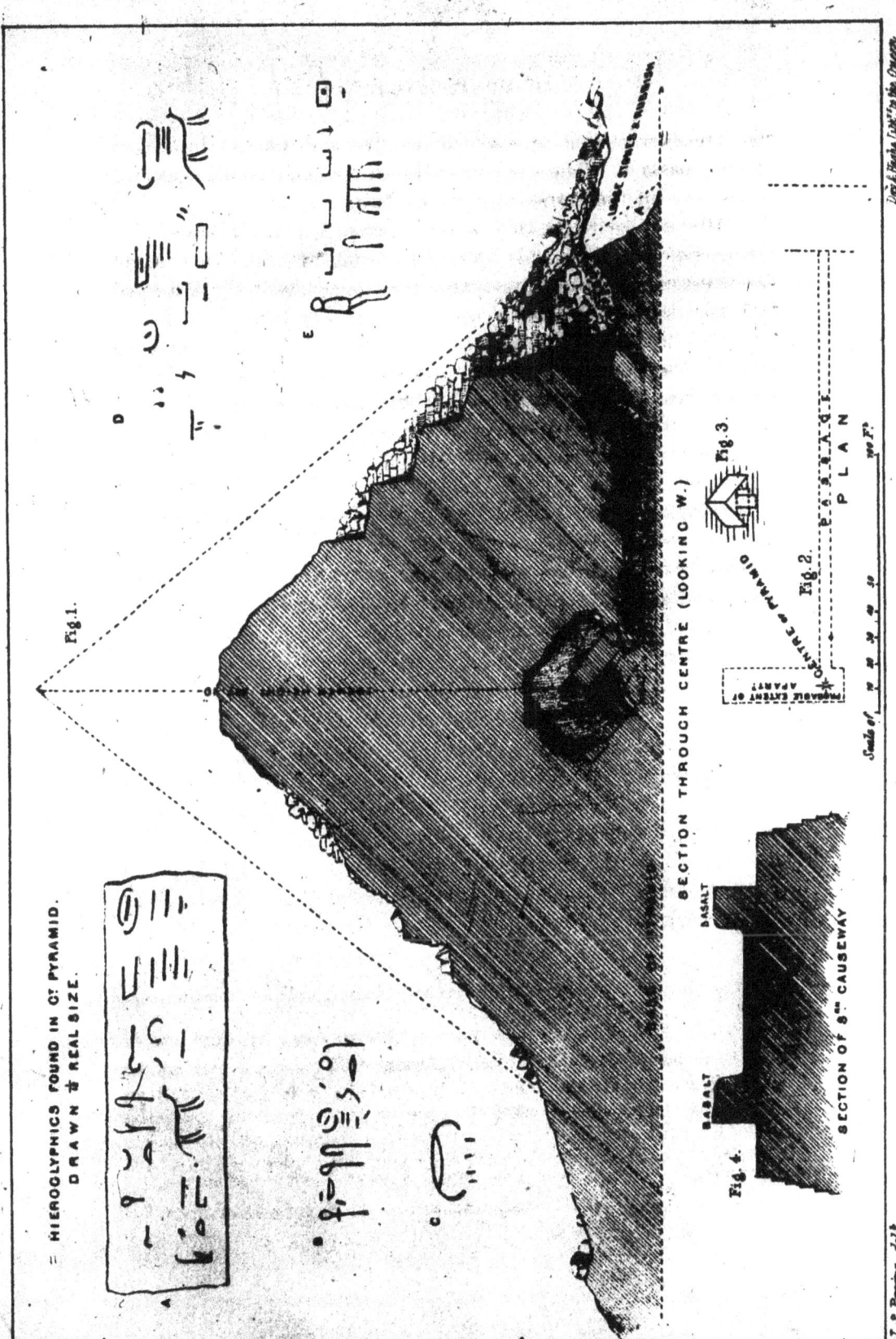

GREAT PYRAMID OF ABOUSEIR.

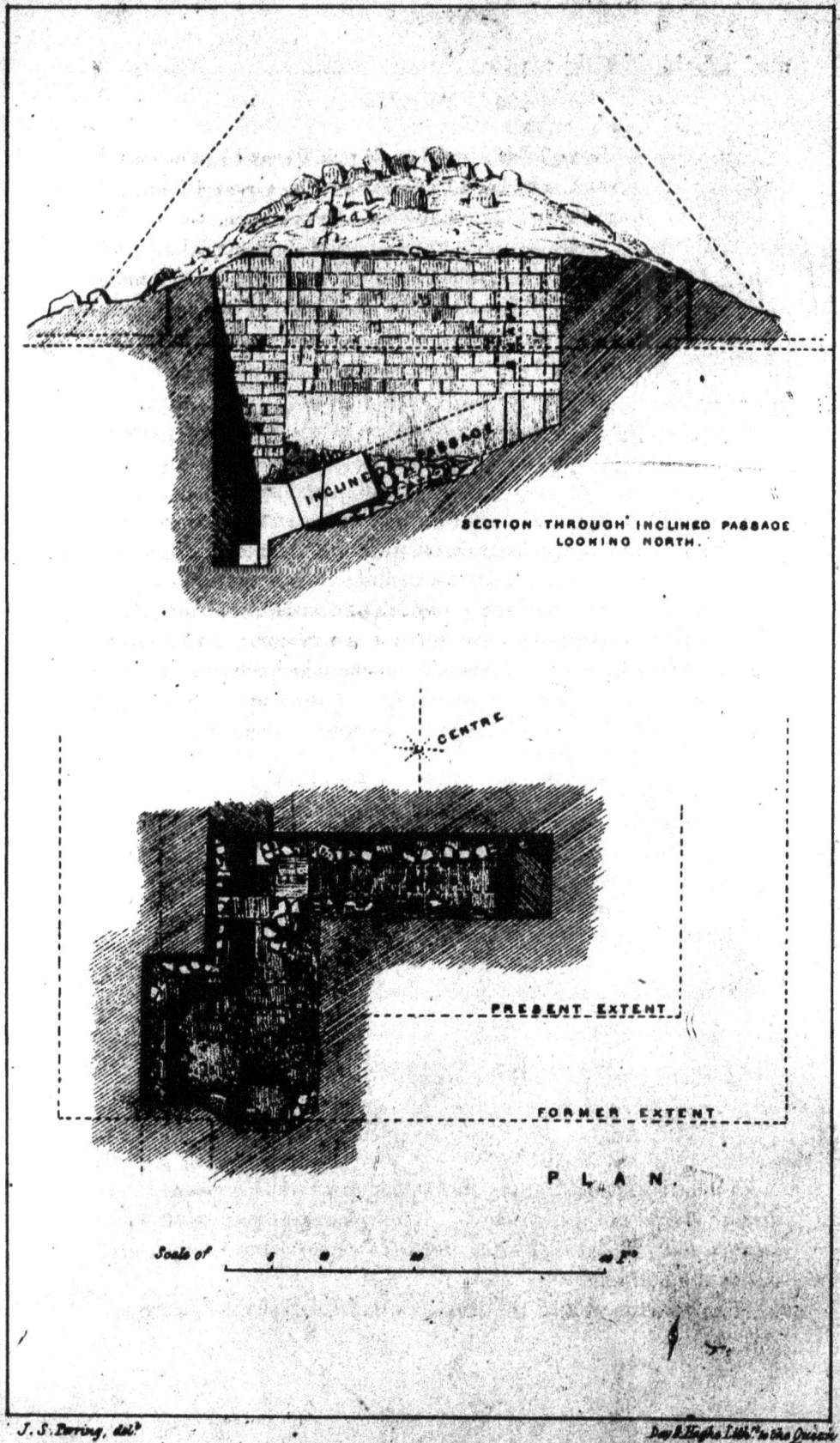

SMALL PYRAMID OF ABOUSEIR.

SMALL PYRAMID.

Mr. Perring turned his attention to this Pyramid, when the blasting of the blocks, which had fallen from the Great Pyramid, previous to their removal, or any other circumstance, set a few hands at liberty. In clearing the northern front several of the casing blocks were found, and it was evident that the Pyramid had formerly extended considerably beyond the present base. A range of mummy-pits had been excavated before the northern front, the entrances of which had been surrounded by walls of crude bricks three or four feet high. As Mr. Perring imagined that the entrance to the Pyramid might be found in these pits he examined them: one of them was unfinished; in another, which extended under the base of the Pyramid, plain sarcophagi, composed of calcareous stone, had been deposited in small recesses. But the pits did not communicate with the Pyramid. Mr. Perring, therefore cleared out a hollow in the masonry, which seemed to have been occasioned by the roof of the apartment having given way; and by these means he entered the interior. The roof of the apartment had been composed of blocks laid horizontally from east to west, and supported by side walls; they had all, however, excepting two, as well as those of the passages, been removed.

	Feet.	Inches.
Present Base	54	6
Former ditto	75	5
Apartment, length, East and West	12	2
.. breadth, North and South	10	6
.. height	8	7
Recess at South-eastern corner, breadth	5	1
.. depth	3	5½
Horizontal Passage from northern side, length	14	0
.. breadth	2	5
.. height	8	7
Inclined Passage, leading eastward, length	27	0
.. breadth	2	10
Angle	22°	10'

A shaft ascended from the upper part of the passage: its direction was not ascertained. It may have communicated with an inclined passage from the northern side, or have led directly out of the building.

The apartment and the passages had been formed in excavations, and had been lined, paved, and roofed, with blocks from the Mokattam.

Neither any hieroglyphics nor the remains of a sarcophagus were observed; but a piece of basalt of the following shape was found. Part of a glass bead, a small scarabæus, a common earthenware figure of a deity, and a small stone scarabæus, were found in the interior of this Pyramid.

NOTES BY MR. BIRCH.

ALTHOUGH these Pyramids are of less interest than those of Gizeh, the hieroglyphics upon them are of considerable importance, because they contain the dates, prenomens, and royal standards, of two monarchs. They are evidently quarry-marks; but, instead of having been inscribed, like those in the Pyramids of Gizeh, only upon stone brought from the Mokattam, they were found on the blocks quarried upon the spot. This is remarkable. In the former instance, they may have been intended to distinguish the materials, which had been prepared for a royal edifice; but in the present, their use is not obvious, and they can have only served to denote the founder of each particular Pyramid. It appears from them, however, as will be afterwards shewn, that the Northern Pyramid is the most antient, and the Southern, in which, however, no royal name was found, is the latest built.

In proceeding to examine the inscriptions, I shall therefore begin with those which were discovered at the

NORTHERN PYRAMID.

Figs. A, B, were found on the retaining walls. They contain the prenomen of the monarch, by whom, probably, the Pyramid was built. It has been already published by Sir J. G. Wilkinson,[3] by M. Rosellini,[4] and by Dr. Leemans;[5] although the last-mentioned author has confounded it with a prenomen, probably that of Shefre, or Chrefren. M. Lenormant corrected this mistake, and discovered the prenomen of Shore and of Nepercheres. The phonetic value of the middle character,

is uncertain; but it had probably the sound of ☉ or ḥ, from its resemblance to which is well understood. The

---

[3] Mat. Hieroglyph. Unpublished Kings, a.
[4] Mon. Stor. Teste, Tav. I.
[5] Monumens Egyptiens portants des Légendes Royaux, &c. 8vo, Leide, 1838, p. 20.

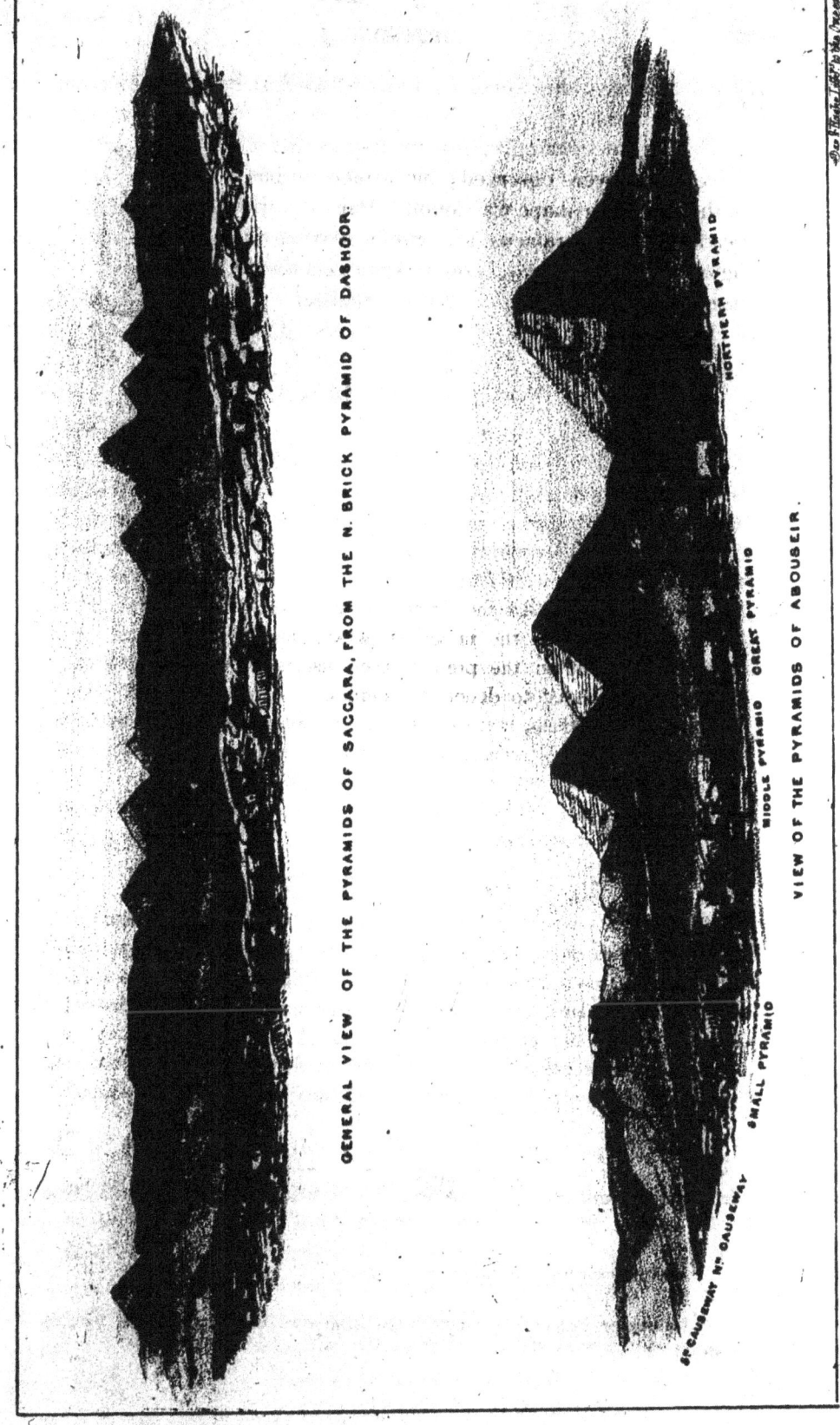

GENERAL VIEW OF THE PYRAMIDS OF SACCARA, FROM THE N. BRICK PYRAMID OF DASHOOR.

VIEW OF THE PYRAMIDS OF ABOUSEIR.

name, therefore, may be read Re-shou, or rather, Shou-re, by a transposition, which is proved by my remarks on the name Menkare⁶ to be often necessary. The symbols immediately above this name are clearly part of the designation of one of the last four months of the Egyptian year, *Pachon, Pauni, Epiphi,* or *Mesori;* but the inscription is imperfect, for it evidently began with a date, the greatest part of which is wanting. The following words may, however, be made out:—
" *In the year . . . . . month . . . . . . day . . . . . powerful and living Re-shou* (or *Shou-re*) . . . ." The rest of the inscription is not clear.⁷

Fig. C, merely contains the final titles represented by the gom and symbol of life, and which have been already said to signify "*powerful,*" "*living.*"

Fig. D, was taken from a large block in the retaining wall on the western side of the building, and had been originally concealed by the masonry. It begins with " *Horus of the two worlds, the hawk of gold;*" and then contains in two places the royal standard, composed of characters, in which " Ⲧⲙⲟⲩ or Ⲧϩⲟⲩ," *Tosh* or *Tokh*, can alone be satisfactorily read. Beneath the standard to the right is a date, " *the eighth day of Phamenoth;*" and above the one to the left is Ⲭⲟⲙⲙ-ⲟⲛⲉ, " *the mighty and living,*" or Ⲉⲕ-ⲟⲛϩ, " *restrainer of the living.*" It is to be remarked that these epithets likewise precede, and follow the titles found on the eastern side of the Pyramid. The name of the king *Shou-re*, and his standard appear, therefore, to be ascertained, and also fragments of two dates; but, whether they relate to the beginning, or to the completion of the Pyramid, cannot be positively determined.

The only other document, which relates to the reign of this king, is the sculpture on the rocks at Wady Magara, published in the Travels of M. Laborde,⁸ where the king Shou-re appears to hold in his left hand the hair of a captive, emblematic of some nation, which he has conquered, and to strike him with a mace held in his right. Behind the monarch is the peculiar sceptre, distinguished by a jackal and two deities, who

⁶ Inscriptions on the Mummy-board of the Coffin found in the Third Pyramid at Gizeh, fol. London, 1838, published by Mr. Fraser, Regent Street. Lenormant, " Eclaircissements sur le Cercueil du Roi Memphite Mycerinus, traduit de l'Anglais," 4to. Paris, 1839.

⁷ It consists of a man seated and a fowl, a suspended symbol, a moon, a solar disc, and a bar, meaning a month, a parallelogram and three horizontal bars, terminated by a lotus flower, and may signify, perhaps, one of the last three months of the year. There is also the koucoupha sceptre, the symbol of life. These are said to have occurred on one block, although they do not appear to be connected.

⁸ Voyage de l'Arabie Petrée, fol. Paris, 1830. Tableaux Hieroglyphiques, III.

carry wands and maces, and are crowned with the teshr, and ouobsh, or oueit. The representation is enclosed at the sides by two koucoupha sceptres, and is surmounted by the starry heaven. The inscription contains "*Horus, the lord of diadems, the king Shou-re, the giver of life for ever, the lord* (or *chief*) *of all countries, the establisher* (?) *of all countries.*" At the same place also are records of Maire (or Mœris), of Cheops, of the king Senophris, and of Ousrenre, another monarch of the same line. The plates in M. Laborde's works, however, have been so negligently transcribed, that some of the characters, those particularly in a group below the hawk, are quite unintelligible; but at all events it is clear that they do not describe the royal standard found at Abouseir.

MIDDLE PYRAMID.

Fig. F. These hieroglyphics apparently contain the title Souten Rash or Rokh, "*Royal tutor, orator,* or *guardian,*" followed by the symbols of "*abode*" or "*palace;*" and the title is repeated twice upon a block on the exterior, but the hieroglyphics are not clear. The initial signs are possibly the same as the title following those of Cheops.[9]

Fig. G, was found upon a block on the exterior. It cannot be completely deciphered, but it seems to signify *make to go.* (?)

Fig. H. The symbol *Noub,* "*gold,*" is on a large block from the quarries at Tourah, which had formed part of the roof of the Great Chamber, and it is the only inscription found on that kind of stone.

Fig. J, occurs several times, and appears to refer to *the abode of the living moderator* (*the monarch*).

Fig. K, is a quarry-mark on a casing-stone somewhat similar to that already cited. It is also imperfect. The dates of the year and of the month (which without doubt it originally contained) at present do not appear. The fragment is as follows: "...... *the ninth day of* (*the king*) *Re-ousr* (*Ousr-re*) ...... *ever* ......" It is extraordinary in this inscription that the cartouche of the king is rectangular, and that the characters are inscribed in the figure, which usually expresses "*abode, residence;*" but, as it is preceded by a date, it may be concluded that the name of the monarch is intended, and not "*abode*" or "*edifice.*"

Fig. L, is upon a block on the exterior. It contains, in unusually large characters, two phonetic groups — Ⲥⲁⲁⲥ-ⲱⲉⲡ, "*the great minister.*"

These characters are written in a careless linear style. The sense is not distinct, but as they express (like the inscription fig. G) "*made to go to*......" they were probably directions to the workmen for the position of the blocks.

[9] Operations carried on at Gizeh, Vol. I. p. 283, and Middle Pyramid.

It may here be remarked, that prenomens occasionally admit of slight variations in their forms, which in some instances are only complements of shortened or abbreviated expressions. Thus the prenomen of Thothmes the Third is written with three or four different symbols: with a disk, a sort of basket, and a beetle, or with an undulating line after the basket. The prenomen in the Middle Pyramid at Abouseir may therefore be the same as that at Wady Magara, which contains the undulating line after the disk, and either expresses, *Reenousr* " *the sun of vigilance,*" according to M. Rosellini, or *Ousr-enre,* " *the strength of the sun,*" according to my system. The same name was found at the Pyramid of Reegah; and it will therefore appear that the sculptures at Wady Magara, the inscriptions at Abouseir and at Reegah, and those in the plate headed the Pyramids, in Mr. Burton's " Excerpta Hier.." refer to the same monarch.

At Wady Magara the king is represented without any attendant deities, in a similar manner to the king Shore before described, The inscription at Wady Magara gives the usual Pharaonic titles and epithets —" *Horus the strength of the world, the giver of life for ever; the gracious god, the lord of the world, the king of the upper and lower regions, seated in all lands; the divine resplendent Hawk of gold, Ousrenre, the giver of life for ever; the gracious god Ousrenre, established in all lands.*"[1] Before the standard is a large vase of libations, inscribed with the name and titles of " *the king Ousrenre, giver of life, power, of dilated heart for ever.*"

The above-mentioned name likewise appears on a tomb near the Ninth Pyramid of Gizeh, and it is therefore connected with the successors of the line of Cheops.

These documents comprise all that is at present known about the reign of this early monarch, for a similar cartouche in the Tablet of Karnac cannot be ascribed to him, for reasons which will hereafter be given.

My opinion of the comparative antiquity of the Northern Pyramid of Abouseir is founded upon an inscription, No. 5 in Plate XXVII. of Mr. Burton's " Excepta Hier.," which was discovered near the Pyramids of Gizeh, and has been apparently copied from a tablet in the interior of a tomb. It represents a man named Otai, seated before a table or stand, with a peculiar reed-shaped top. The writing upon the area refers to an offering, which consists of a quantity of wine, bread, &c. Before the figure of Otai is the following inscription in three horizontal lines of large hieroglyphics:—" *An offering to Anoup (Anubis), resident in*

---

[1] The standard of Ousrenre is also published by M. Rosellini, " Mon. Stor." T. III. Tav. I. p. 46. It is analogous to that of Shore. It differs from M. Laborde, " Voyage de l'Arabie Petrée," fol. Paris, 1830, p. 71. M. Rosellini does not give M. Laborde's copy, but recites a Dr. Ricci's.

the divine abode, (may he give)[2] *a good and great embalmment in the Amenti and in the west, to the all true and devoted to his lord* ...... *an abode well provided for him* ...... *attached to the bards, delighting*[3] *his lord with his strains, excellent in* ...... *the great abode of the god Ra, of Athor the pure goddess,* ...... *Nofrekare the pure god,*[4] *Shou-re the pure god, Ousrenre the pure god, Otai.*" In No. 3 in the above-mentioned Plate, the same title follows the cartouche as in No. 5. This title has been already mentioned in the " Operations carried on at Gizeh," Vol. II. p. 9. In No. 5, Otai is represented to have been a bard under the kings Nofrekare, Shou-re, and Ousrenre: the precedence of these monarchs is therefore ascertained. Their names, however do not appear in the only copy of the Hieratic Canon of Turin,[5] to which I have had access, neither is their relative position with the dynasty of Cheops determined. It is, however, necessary to mention that in the restoration of Renofre, the two arms signifying Ka, are wanting, and that Nofre-ka-re, therefore, and Nepercheres, although highly probable, are not positively established; that the phonetic value of the central sign in the cartouche of Shou-re, and of the initial signs of Ousrenre, is not exactly determined, although the latter has been supposed to be " ou ;" besides that the list of Eratosthenes consists chiefly of names, and that the prenomen Ousrenre is apparently connected with prenomens totally distinct from that of Nepercheres, so that it may be supposed that different monarchs had the same prenomen. But the most probable solution of these difficulties seems to be afforded by the lists of Manetho, where, in the fifth Elephantine dynasty, immediately succeeding to that of Cheops, the first three names are Usercheres, Sephres, and Nepercheres,[6] which, if inverted, would greatly resemble the three in question; and their era, immediately after the Memphite dynasty, would coincide with the probable date of these buildings. It may be also remarked, that there is no evidence to shew that any of the Pyramids

---

[2] The parts between brackets are restored from contemporaneous monuments.

[3] The phonetic group expressing this has been translated by M. Champollion, to be " morose," Cⲱⲥϧⲉⲉ or Ϣⲱⲥⲉⲉ of the Coptic; but the correction is evident from the context.

[4] The term " ka " (offering) is wanting in the inscription; there can, however, be scarcely a doubt with regard to it. Wilkinson's " Manners and Customs of the Egyptians," Vol. III. p. 280, gives the cartouche in its full form.

[5] By M. Dulaurier, of Thoulouse. The liberality of the Sardinian government has allowed Dr. Lepsius a copy for his own use.

[6] Rosellini, " Mon. Stor." Tom. I. Pl. I. p. 28. According to this analogy, Usercheres would be Ousr-ka-re, not Ousrenre. That the name of Chnumis, or Chnouphis, the tutelary deity of *Elephantine*, appears in the cartouche of Cheops at the Great Pyramid, would induce a belief that the then reigning dynasty received its title from that island.

were constructed later than the eighteenth dynasty, but that they appear, on the contrary, to have been erected before the invasion of the Shepherd Kings. At the same time it must be confessed, that, from their situation, these tombs cannot, without some hesitation, be ascribed to an Elephantine dynasty, because the sepulchres belonging to the Memphite, the Theban, and the Saite dynasties, have been generally found near the respective capitals, whence the monarchs derived their names, and consequently, that the island of that name might be supposed to have contained the tombs of the Elephantine Kings. But the similarity of the names is at all events remarkable; and it is possible that the succeeding monarchs may have occasionally retained the name of the town, whence the founder of the dynasty derived his origin, without reference to their own actual residence, or capital city. By adopting a correction proposed by the ingenious criticism of the Chevalier Bunsen, and by striking out the name of Soris as an interpolation, Suphis I. (Cheops or Chemmis) will be the founder of the fourth Memphite dynasty; and he is expressly mentioned by Diodorus to have been an inhabitant of Memphis, and by Eratosthenes, to have extended his authority over Thebes, in Upper Egypt. Memphis was, most probably, at that epoch, the metropolis of Egypt, and continued to be so till the invasion of the Shepherd Kings; after which, on account of political circumstances, it was supplanted by Abydos and by Thebes, when the latter city, embellished by Remeses the Great (styled the King of Kings), surpassed probably the antient capital, and continued to be the seat of empire till the epoch of the Ptolemies, and was even then inferior only to Alexandria. On these grounds it may be presumed that the Elephantine Kings constructed their tombs of a similar shape and grandeur to those of their predecessors, and established them upon the rocky eminences, already consecrated for that purpose by former dynasties, in the neighbourhood of their actual residence.

The succession of these monarchs has indeed been stated in a different manner by M. Rosellini from memory, and also by Sir J. G. Wilkinson,[7] but, as in their lists the names are unconnected, and given upon inadequate authority, they cannot without further evidence be admitted. Sir J. G. Wilkinson, indeed, seems to have been aware of these difficulties, for in p. 507 of his work on Thebes, and General View of Egypt, he says,—" But I offer this table with great deference, and shall willingly yield to any opinion, that may be established on more positive and authentic grounds." It is indeed obvious that the regular succession of these antient monarchs cannot be established solely upon the authority of monuments, in different parts of which isolated names may have been

[7] Manners and Customs, Vol. III. p. 280. This ingenious and highly talented author, who has done so much for Egyptian archæology, says they are placed in chronological order. This succession would give Nouv-Shouf (Cheops), Shore (Sephres), Nofre-er-kare (Nepercheres).

occasionally inserted. This indeed I have already alluded to (see "Operations carried on at Gizeh," Vol. II. pp. 7 and 8), where it will appear that the most antient monarch is last mentioned. And in support of the assertion that the names of individuals were frequently composed of those of kings, I refer to a paper forwarded by me to the Society of Antiquaries,[s] in which the names of the children of an official character are composed, amongst other symbols, of the prenomen of the reigning monarch. This custom seems to have been universally prevalent, and the traces of it, if carefully investigated, may occasionally throw considerable light upon the individuals of the antient dynasties. I do not, however, positively insist, from the slight analogy of their names, that these monarchs belonged to the fifth Elephantine dynasty; but at the same time I must observe, that the tables hitherto published are not only at variance with the inscription in the tomb (called of Trades) at Gizeh, but likewise with those contained in Mr. Burton's "Excerpta Hier.," both of which are corroborated by the context, by certain connecting links between the several kings founded upon an analogy of the names and titles of various functionaries, and upon the tenor of several inscriptions relating to the monarchs in question at Wady Magara, and also near the Pyramids of Gizeh. I must likewise add, that the appearance of the same names at Wady Magara seems to shew, that these monarchs preceded the conquest of Egypt by the Shepherd Kings, because none of the persons belonging to the subsequent dynasties, who were driven by these invaders into Upper Egypt, are there recorded.

Another reference to a king Ousrenre, but which cannot possibly apply to the monarch mentioned at Abouseir, is contained in two inscriptions, which were published by Dr. Lepsius, and afterwards by M. Rosellini,[9] and were found upon a statue sent by the former gentleman to the Museum at Berlin. They contain a dedication by a Pharaoh, supposed to be Osortasen the First, to his father, Ousrenre, or Eian; and it is to be remarked, that the word "father," a general expression, is not followed by the pronoun "him," or "his," but by the seated image of a king, and that the name, as well as the prenomen, is preceded by a branch and by a bee, which have hitherto been supposed only to precede prenomens. It can be satisfactorily proved, however, that prenomens were made use of before the sixteenth dynasty, and the one in question is similar to that found at Abouseir, except in the substitution of an eye for a mouth in expressing the letter R, and in the insertion at the bottom of the cartouche of an undulating line (phonetically signifying N). By comparing the inscription on the statue with the Tablet at Karnac, in which a king named Re-en-ous,[1] Ousenre (probably an abbreviated form

---

[s] Archæologia, Vol. XXIX. p. 113, pl. XIV. fig. B, C.
[9] Rosellini, "Mon. Stor." Tom. III. Pl. I. p. 46.
[1] Burton, "Excerpta Hier." Pl. I.* Tablet of Karnac.

of Ousrenre), is placed before two kings, whose prenomens are almost similar in construction and in meaning to his own. It is to be concluded that the next king in succession, namely Osortasen the First, had been preceded upon the throne by two relations or brothers; although the succession of Karnac does not coincide with the list copied in Mr. Burton's " Excerpta Hier." from the tombs at Gizeh.

The Tablet at Karnac has not been satisfactorily explained. The Ousrenre recorded in it, although the same as that on the Berlin Statue, is evidently distinct from the Ousrenre of the Pyramids. The standard of the older king seems to have been more correctly given by M. Laborde, than by M. Rosellini. In both instances it commences, like that of Shou-re, with the word "Tosh," or "Tokh;" and the copy of M. Laborde[2] contains the epithet ⟨hieroglyphs⟩ ΟϓϹΡ-ΤΟΤΟ, "*regulating the upper and lower countries*," instead of the ⟨hieroglyphs⟩ of M. Rosellini.[3]

The dynasty of Cheops probably preceded that of the Osortasens by a much less space of time than the lists of Manetho hint. The analogy of this title with the names of the Osortasens is remarkable; but nothing has been satisfactorily made out before the time of Amasis: indeed, the arrangement of the seventeenth dynasty seems to be entirely conjectural. It is, in short, impossible to establish a distinct and satisfactory account of the succession and names of the early dynasties without more complete and connected information, than has yet been attained, and also without a more intimate knowledge of the language and method of communication, than has been at present acquired. For, although it may be reasonably expected that the hieroglyphical documents already procured —some of which are bilingual, and others Gnostic rituals, apparently containing the elements of more antient writings—may eventually afford the means of arriving at the most satisfactory results, yet, in the mean time, it is evident that perplexity and doubt are inevitably increased by premature and rash conclusions, unsupported by facts, and incapable of proof. To arrive at any certainty respecting these successive dynasties, it is necessary to compare the various inscriptions respecting them, and fully to comprehend their expressions and meaning. In this way alone can any positive knowledge of these curious and interesting particulars be obtained. All other statements, however ingeniously imagined, must be entirely hypothetical; and in adverting to the difficulties attending

[2] Laborde, "Voyage," &c. loc. cit.

[3] Rosellini, "Mon. Stor." Tom. III. loc. cit. It apparently means the "strength of the two worlds," or "having power over the two worlds," the ambiguity being in the word ΟϓϹΡ, which may be taken either as a verb or substantive.

this inquiry, it may also be observed, that the whole of the characters contained in a cartouche are not always to be considered as phonetic, but that, probably by a license incidental to a mixed mode of writing, they are partly syllabic, and partly phonetic; and likewise, that the characters are usually inserted in the cartouches, so as to please the eye rather than to follow the connexion of the pronunciation. The necessity for inversion in order to make out the prenomens of the more antient monarchs seems to be clearly proved by a reference to the lists of Manetho, by the texts themselves, and also by the explanation of the name of Menka-re, as well as of those of the monarchs found at the Pyramids of Abouseir. These instances must therefore be held in remembrance by those persons, who undertake the explanation of hieroglyphical inscriptions. In alphabetical languages a metathesis of the syllables of a word cannot take place; but in symbolical languages it is frequently used. Thus, in the Chinese, the radicals, or elementary characters, which answer to the class known in hieroglyphics by the name of determinatives, occasionally appear above, below, or at the side of the specific elements, without making any alteration in the character, because their ideographic meaning is not affected by position. In the same manner, in that language, the relative locations of the words are frequently overlooked. Thus, what expresses "*man-hand,*" or "*hand-man,*" equally means "*man's hand,*" or "*hand of man.*" The same principles apply to Egyptian hieroglyphics, and probably for the same reason — that the whole system is throughout *ideophonetic,* or of *ideal sound.* The cartouche, for example, of Re-nofre-ka, or Nofre-ka-re, contains three elements, every one of which is the image of an idea intended to be described. The circular disc indicates a sun, pronounced Ra in the Memphite, and Re in the Saidic dialect; the guitar, taken phonetically, stands for the letter N only when the idea "*good*" is to be expressed. The two uplifted hands, signifying Ka, or an offering, were exclusively used during the best epoch of Egyptian art, to express "*bearing,*" or "*offering;*" as Ka, "*to offer;*" Kot, "*to bear,*" or "*build,*" &c. Each symbol in the above name is, consequently, *emblematic* as well as phonetic, its relation to sound not being greater than to idea; and the whole group may be supposed to signify, either "*the good offering of the sun,*" "*good in offering to the sun,*" or "*the sun good in offering;*" and may, with great probability, be assumed to form Nofre-ka-re, which resembles the name of the monarch Nepercheres in the lists of Manetho.

M. Lenormant[4] has not only translated my account of the coffin of Mycerinus, as I have already remarked, but he has entered into consi-

---

[4] Lenormant (Ch.), "Eclaire. sur le Cercueil de Mycerinus," 4to. Paris, 1839, pp. 37-43, has been the first to publicly recognise Shore and Nofre-ka-re.

derable detail respecting the transposition of the symbols, which had been also adopted by two Egyptian scholars—M. Rosellini and Dr. Leemans, although by these gentlemen it has been limited to two names; by the one to Shou-re, and by the other to Merenre. M. Champollion does not seem to have entertained this opinion, excepting in the cartouche of the god Chnouphra; but the placing the dominant disc of the sun last is justified by a reference to the lists of Manetho, and by the inscriptions themselves. The analogy of the names obtained by this transposition has been amply and accurately detailed by M. Lenormant; it is therefore unnecessary to say more upon the subject, except by pressing it most strongly upon the attention of those who are engaged in the investigation of these antient characters.

The prenomens assumed by the Egyptian monarchs upon their accession, which were generally inscribed in ovals, preceded by the bee and branch, had most frequently a reference to the sun, generally in an active, but occasionally in a passive sense. The Tablet at Abydos consists almost entirely of prenomens; but that from Karnac comprehends likewise, several of the names of the monarchs, together with their prenomens, as may be seen in those of the Enentefs. The Hieratical Canon of Turin contains indiscriminately names and prenomens; and the Greek compilers, who no doubt derived their information from similar monuments, have also inserted in their lists both prenomens and names. In the same manner several of the kings of China are as frequently distinguished in the annals of that country by the "neen haou," or honorific name assumed during their lives, as by the "meaou haou," or appellation of honour after death. Such ambiguities will naturally take place where different titles are used; and the insertion, in antient inscriptions, of one name in preference to the other, most probably arose from temporary circumstances, which cannot now be ascertained.

It must, however, be confessed, that the propriety of this transposition of the disc must depend upon the construction of the sentence, and upon the meaning of the accompanying symbols, as may be seen by an analysis of the following royal names, particularly by that in a cartouche attributed to Amenemses by M. Rosellini,[5] the eight characters of which, if read as they are inscribed, will give—" *The sun established like, the sun approved of;*" but, as the three final symbols in the latter part are, by transposition, well known to mean "*approved of the sun,*" by a similar process the first five characters will likewise express "*established like the sun;*" and the transposition is in this case evidently necessary, for a king cannot be consistently styled "*the sun,*" and at the same time "*the approved of the sun.*"[6] The meaning, therefore, of the first part of the

---

[5] Rosellini, "Mon. Stor." Vol. II. No. 126.

[6] In "Ammian. Marcellin." lib. xvii. the Pharaoh is never called the sun, and the son of the sun, but Apollo, and the son of the sup. The parts

sentence, evidently requires that the symbol expressing the sun should be read last. The first part of a sentence can admit of inversion with as much propriety as the last; and it is well known that the Pharaohs were frequently termed " *Givers of life, like the sun, for ever ;*" " *Lords of the panegyries* (or festivals), *like their father Phtah.*"⁷ In this cartouche then at least, every symbol can be satisfactorily made out, and it is certain that the dominant disc of the sun must be put last.

In another cartouche, published by M. Rosellini, as belonging to Remeses the Eighth, the characters, as they are placed, read—" *The sun, the guardian of truth ;*" " *Amoun, the light of,*" or " *illuminated by.*" Here again there can be no doubt that the text must mean " *The sun, the guardian of truth, the light of Amoun.*" An important tablet in the British Museum gives the entire solution of this passage, " *The disc of the sun at Thebes Amon.*" The cartouche, containing a prenomen wherein the monarch is personified as " *The king of the upper and lower world, the sun,*" &c. must be considered to be his sacred name; and the second, in which he is styled " *The son of the sun,*" was probably his common appellation, in reference to his deification, as " *The gracious god, the good god, the living gracious god, the living Hor,*" &c.: epithets frequently inscribed upon the monuments of the Pharaohs. It may also be observed, that an examination of the hieroglyphics upon the coffin of Amyrtæus (?) in the British Museum, No. 10, will prove that the object of the sculpture was to declare that the deities would make the same adorations, and perform the same offices to the deceased monarch, which they did to the sun in its course. This mode of expression is, however, only found upon the monuments of actual monarchs.

The prenomen in the cartouche (No. 69 of M. Rosellini's " Monumenti Storici")⁸ also contains " *the disc the light of.*" The prenomen (No. 108) is preceded by the titles " *The son of the sun, living in truth,*" and contains " *the sun the light of, the sun approved of ;*" which of course means " *the light of the sun, the approved of the sun.*" Two other cartouches, which are inserted between those of Ousenr-re and Osortasen I. in the Tablet of Karnac, contain " *the sun render victorious of*" or " *by,*" and " *the sun render powerful of*" or " *by,*" which should no doubt be read " *the rendered victorious by the sun ;*" " *the rendered powerful by the sun.*" In No. 14 also of M. Rosellini, " *the sun,*

in cartouches appear to be ἡ "Ηλιος πρόληψιν καὶ "Αρης ἔλληνος Παρέσωσε, &c.; but this transcript is partly corrupt. The name of *Sesostris* has originated from some such adjunct. Sesoosis, a variation of it, approaches Shaa en shaou, similar to the Saa en saa of the Persian rulers. Mr. Osburne has suggested that Sept-en-re are the final symbols of his name.

⁷ Rosetta stone, Greek text. Monuments *passim.*

⁸ Dr. Leemans's " Monumens Egypt." 8vo. Leide, 1838, reads this name " Itenbashn, Apachnan (?)" The transposition gives Oubasheniten.

attached of," or "*beloved of*" or "*by*," signifies, in like manner, "*the attached* (or beloved) *of the sun*." These characters, considered phonetically, produce "*Snashtenre*," "*Merenre*," which are of the same construction with some names in the lists of Manetho.

In all these instances the proper position of the characters is indicated by the closing pronoun, and by the evident meaning of the sentences. In the name of Thothmes I. there is an adjunct[9] similar to those which frequently accompany royal names upon scarabæi, and small amulets. The characters Shaa, "*crowned*," or "*elevated*;" Re, "*the sun*;" She, "*like*," should be read Shaa she re, "*crowned like the sun*," according to the transposition adopted in Honshere,[1] one of the most familiar names in Egyptian archæology. The other names, Nepercheres and Shore, are not so completely determined, because in these words the characters admit of different readings. In the same manner Re-metaou-en may be Metaouenre,[2] like the Ousr-Ra, or Rauosis,[3] Princeps Robustorum of Eratosthenes. Re-mei-ophth (No. 56) may be Meiophthres, or Miophris; and in the various lists, "Re-mour-ka," Mourcheres; "Reka-mei," Moicheres. But these names cannot be depended upon, as they have been assumed upon no other authority than by a reference to Manetho. In many of the royal names the dominant disc of the sun seems to designate the celestial functions of semi-deified monarchs; yet in many others it may serve to represent, in the person of the king, some faculty, or power of that great luminary.

The transposition of syllables should be carefully applied to doubtful names, by which alone its value can be ascertained. Many other instances, besides those already mentioned, might be adduced; but an effectual examination of them would require a greater space than can be afforded in these observations, which are intended more especially to illustrate the quarry-marks of the Pyramids at Abouseir.

From a consideration of royal names I proceed to those of inferior persons, which have been found near the Great Pyramid at Abouseir, and which, it is to be remarked, in some instances have been written in black, and not in the usual red colour. Three of these inscriptions contain dates, which from analogy might be supposed to have been followed by royal names; but this has not been the case.

[9] Rosellini, "Mon. Stor." Tom. I. Part I. tav. V. 100 n. pp. 212, 213, and n. 2.

[1] Ibid. Tom. I. Part I. p. 271. Vide Dissertation, by Dr. Lepsius, on the same statue, in the Proc. of the Arch. Inst. of Rome.

[2] Rauosis may be an inversion of Ousra, from reading the cartouche directly. Leemans's reading is incorrect, and Segato's scarcely worth criticising.—"Mon. Egypt. port. des Légendes Royales," p. 20. Cf. Lenormant, "Eclairciss. de l'Inscr. sur le Cerc. du Roi Memphite Mycerinus."

[3] Where a cartouche is composed of the disc of the sun and an adjective only, it may be read directly.

In the formula of dates the royal titles, or those inserted in the standard, generally follow the cypher, as "*the living Horus*," &c. The first of the symbols is an *S*, the second possibly a reed, but the third and fourth are *differently represented;* as in one instance the third is apparently the upper part of a sieve, and the fourth a mouth, signifying S H and R; while in the other they are decidedly an N and K: the last, in both cases, is the symbol of life.

A similar group from the Middle Pyramid contains three symbols, then an indistinct character, afterwards a block (phonetically, P), a basket, a diadem, a belt upon two human legs, and the symbol of life. These characters I cannot satisfactorily explain; but I conceive it just possible that they may describe the title of some great official personage, similar to those conferred upon high functionaries under the dynasty of the Osortasens, and to those which I have already noticed in my observations upon the quarry-marks found in the Great Pyramid of Gizeh. And this supposition is rendered more probable by the appearance of a group beginning with a jackal, which apparently describes a name. I only know, however, one name, Eimothph, beginning with a jackal, and that, although of frequent occurrence at the time of the Ptolemies, does not occur at an earlier period. The name, however, cannot be made out in the present instance.

THE GREAT PYRAMID.

Fig. A, contains in the first part of the upper line a date in the month of Mesore, but the day cannot be distinguished.

According to the usual mode in which dates are inserted, these symbols delineate either the standard, or the titles of the king, and phonetically signify Cαp; but they are too imperfect to be exactly explained, although it may be conjectured, that the lower line contains the name of a woman, or of a female deity, which seems to be represented in B. The jackal has various significations; sometimes that of a guardian (generally sacerdotal), at others of a son, and frequently, when combined with other characters, of the name of the god Eimothph, or Imouth; and in sepulchral monuments during the Ptolemaic era, and in a few more antient a jackal precedes in the name of the above-mentioned deity.

B. This inscription contains a date, in which the year, the month, and the day, are expressed; but it is imperfect, and the fourth day can only be distinguished. The other characters resemble those in A, C, D.

C. These characters are like those in B. They are inserted in black, and with bars which are vertical, and therefore unlike those in A and D, which are horizontal. A fourth month is recorded, but, as the season is not mentioned, it cannot be ascertained whether it signifies Choiak, Pharmuthi, or Mesore.

D. The upper line contains a portion of a date, viz. "the eighth of Epiphi," the third month of the last Egyptian season. The lower line somewhat resembles A. The determinative image of a man seated upon a chair seems to indicate that these two lines express a name. The characters are not perfectly defined, but the upper line contains an inscription similar to the cartouche of a king, and ends with three pairs of uplifted hands, preceded, either by a branch (see Champol. " Gram. Egypt." p. 43, n. 165), or else by the symbol (*ibid.* p. 40, n. 94); and immediately before it is a horizontal line and a parallelogram. The lower line contains the expression " Penti," and the symbol, a T, initial of Tot, inserted in Champol. " Gram. Egypt." p. 43, n. 158. It is also to be remarked, that a name, resembling in its composition the one in the upper line, occurs in an inscription upon a tomb found at Gizeh. See Nos. 61 and 64, Egyptian Saloon, in the British Museum.

The following is the substance of a letter from Mr. Harris of Alexandria to Mr. Perring,[4] dated April 18, 1839:—

I promised to send to you the observations that had occurred to me upon examining the quarry-marks which you found upon the stones of the Pyramids of Abouseir. The interest which they excite, arises from the supposition, that these writings, being directions to guide those, who embarked the stone at the quarries, who conveyed it to its destination, and who built with it when there, will contain a more matter-of-fact meaning than the more recondite inscriptions that adorned the fabric after it was " completed."

Some of the characters evidently indicate the building, for which the stones were destined, and others the position, in which they were to be placed; this last direction could not be necessary in regard to all the stones of a building, but would be requisite for all, or most of those composing the linings of the chambers, passages, &c. the angles, and other particular positions.

NORTHERN PYRAMID.

A. Here we have the name of the king, for whom the Pyramid was probably erected as a tomb.

The position, in which the stone was to be placed, seems to be indicated by the marks ≡ ⬜ ☉ ≣ the meaning of which it would

---

[4] Mr. Perring states that Mr. Harris has lately discovered at Alexandria, a statue of Jupiter Serapis, which has been broken exactly in the manner described by Mr. Gibbon, in his account of the destruction of the Temple, A. D. 389. See Vol. III. p. 86, chap. 28.

not be difficult to find out by observing the stones in their respective places, and by comparing the situation of others, that are written upon.

B has the name only.

C. The name may possibly have been effaced or cut off, if the stone required any fitting on the spot.

D. Here we have the name of the king again, but in another form, whereby we learn the value of the unknown character ⟨glyph⟩; for ⟨glyph⟩ is the splendid *Ra*, or ☉ *Ra*. ⟨glyph⟩ T ⟨glyph⟩, or ☉ ⟨glyph⟩ equivalent to ⟨glyph⟩, *tsh* or *thsh*. ⟨glyph⟩ ꚍꚍꚍ or ꚍ . . . . . ⟨glyph⟩ making *Rathsho*.

This group looks amazingly as if two brothers or two sisters were spoken of. There are two hawks, as if it meant two kings; and what follows appears like ⟨glyph⟩ : — ⟨glyph⟩ and ⟨glyph⟩ signify "*Brother-loving*;" and by the same rule ⟨glyph⟩ would be "*Sister-loving*."

The fifth king of the fourth dynasty *Rhatoises*, and *Rau-osis*, and the eleventh king of the eighteenth dynasty, is called *Rathos*, *Athoris*, or *Rathosis*, all of which names bear a great resemblance to the one we have deciphered; but I am of opinion, that it is premature to begin to class these names before a sufficient number of them is collected from the tombs, and their relation to each other noticed. To pursue the inquiry, the sand ought to be cleared out of all the tombs about the Pyramids of Gizeh.

What follows the name, I do not pretend to understand, but the characters in the lower line indicate the position, as in A.

MIDDLE PYRAMID.

F, G, I, and K, I must pass over.

In J ⟨glyph⟩ signifies "*to make live.*"

⟨glyph⟩ is a verb of action, "*to do*," or "*to execute*."[5]

⟨glyph⟩ signifies "*a dwelling*."

The whole may mean "*an eternal habitation*," or "*a Tomb*."

L. ⟨glyph⟩ may have the same signification as the above.

[5] Champollion.

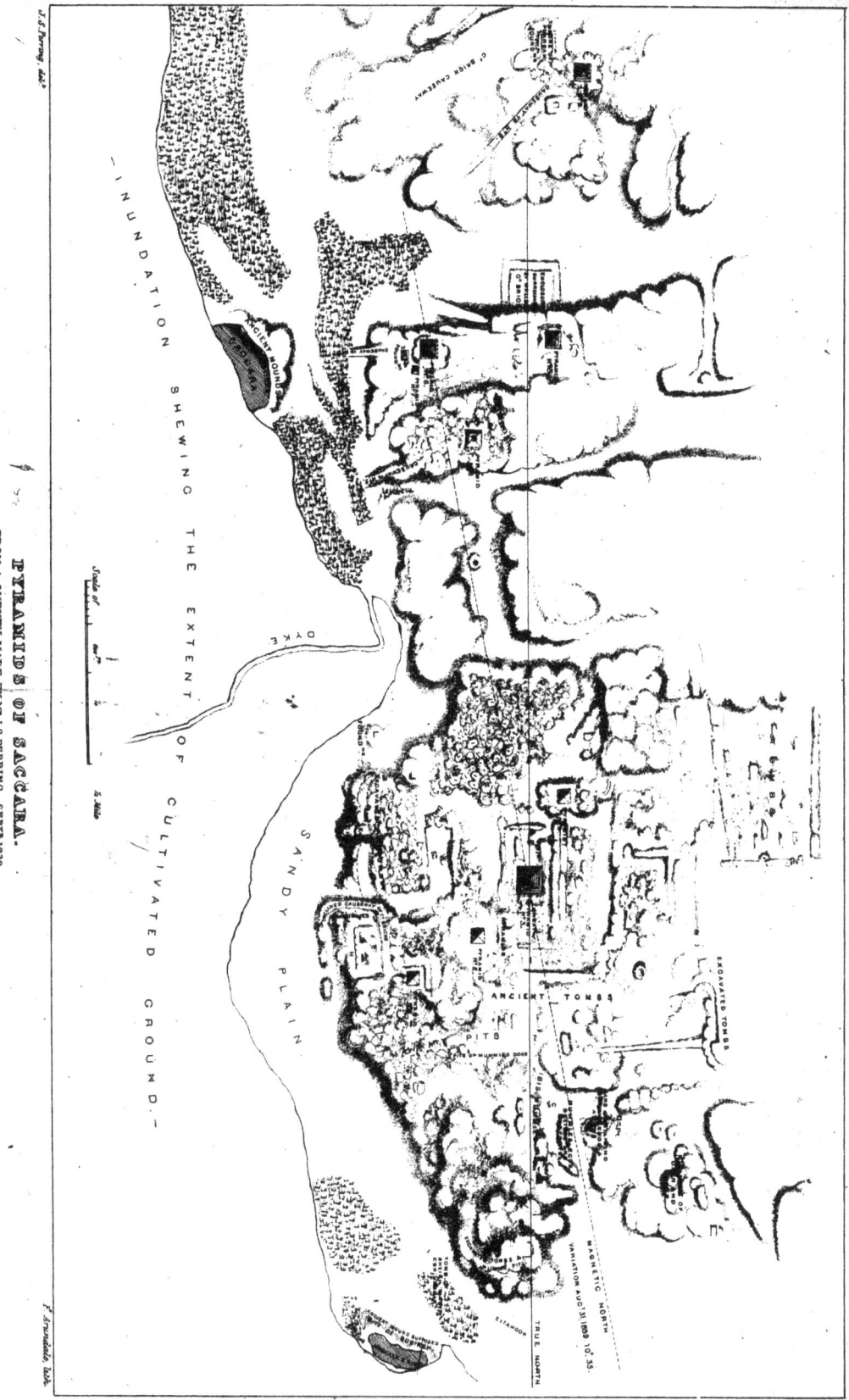

H. The character here given ▨ is a symbol of gold, and being on the roof-block of the apartment, it seems to indicate that the stone was intended for the ▨ which, according to Champollion, expresses "an *habitation, the sepulchral chamber of a tomb.*"

GREAT PYRAMID.

D resembles the foregoing, and so does the initial character of B. It appears that these characters were found in the sepulchral chamber, and that A was in the passage leading to the apartment, which, with the addition of ▨ implying "*to move,*" "*to enter,*" or "*to go out,*" has also the same initial character.

E seems to be a name. ▨ is for ▨ "*the tomb,*" ▨ "*of the king,*" named, for example, "*Koncharis.*"

PYRAMID OF REEGAH.

Taking the value of the characters, as expressed in Coptic letters, they shew ⲥⲟⲩⲧⲛ̄ ⲥⲁⲉⲛ ϯⲩ (ϯⲓⲟⲧ, ⲧⲁⲭⲣⲏⲟⲩⲧ) ⲥⲛⲃ; or if the perpendicular line in ▨ be inclined thus ▨ marking ▨, it may be ⲥⲟⲩⲧⲛⲥⲁⲉⲛ ϯⲩⲥⲛϯ, which appears to be of the king, monument of the king to lay the solid foundation. ⲥⲁⲉⲛ signifies "*to place,*" "*to dispose,*" "*to prepare;*" ⲥⲛϯ, "*foundations;*" and ⲥⲁⲉⲛ ⲥⲛⲉ means "*to found,*" "*to lay a foundation;*" ⲥⲛⲃ, ⲡⲥⲛⲃ, is translated by M. Champollion "*la force;*" but it is not in the dictionary.

▨ appears to be the sign of the plural number, &c. &c. &c.[6]

PYRAMIDS OF SACCARA.

THE MAP.

Mr. Perring considers that the range of mountains from Dashoor to Abouroash contained four cemeteries; the most Northern belonging to Latopolis, that near Gizeh to Heliopolis, the one at Saccara to Memphis, and that at Dashoor to Acanthus. In

---

[6] It will be evident to the hieroglyphical scholar, that these conjectures by no means coincide with Mr. Birch's explanations.

order, therefore, to comprehend the whole of the cemetery of antient Memphis, this Map extends as far northward as the village of Abouseir.

The Pyramids of Saccara are eleven in number,[7] exclusive of the large building, called "The Throne of Pharaoh." They are built with stone, and were approached by inclined roads or causeways from the plain below. They are all much decayed, excepting the large one built in degrees, which, together with another towards the north-east (No. 2 in the Map), are the only two at present open.

A space around the large Pyramid (about 8200 feet in length), abounds with mummy-pits, and also with tombs, although of the latter but few remain, as they have been subject to continual devastation for the sake of materials for building. The most interesting at present are those marked G and K on the Map.

In G are the cartouches of several kings of the early dynasties. K is an excavation and contains the name of Psammetichus II.; and, although the roof is not a regular arch, yet the way, in which it is built, evidently shews that the principles of an arch were known when it was formed. The space (F in the Map) to the northward of the Great Pyramid is supposed to have been used for the interment of criminals, because the bodies were placed, without coffins, in small recesses lined with crude bricks, and had been mutilated by the loss of the hands, or of the feet, which had been separated at the joints.

The Serapeum is said by Strabo to have been built on a sandy spot, and traces of it have been looked for (but without success) amongst the mounds and antient substructions near this place.

A sketch of the Pyramids of Saccara, as seen from the northern brick Pyramid of Dashoor, is given in Plate IX. Fig. 5; and Bruce probably alluded to this view, when he observed, that "the traveller is lost in the immense expanse of desert, which he sees full of Pyramids before him; is struck with terror at the unusual scene of vastness, and shrinks from attempting any discovery amidst the moving sands of Saccara." Bruce's "Travels," Vol. I. p. 66.

---

[7] Nine of them are numbered from north to south in the Map.

PYRAMID No. 1 IN THE MAP.

This pyramid seems to have been of a later date than the two following, because the road for the conveyance of materials to it has been constructed with crude bricks from a causeway, which had been previously formed in the rock to Nos. 2 and 3. The bricks are large, and are made of alluvial soil, with but little straw, excepting on the outside; and almost all of them are marked, apparently by the fingers having been brought close together, and thrust in thus

The pyramid is much decayed, and presents the appearance of a mass of rubbish. The masonry is only visible at one place on the southern side. It appears to have been built in steps or degrees.

Attempts had been made, both on the northern and on the southern sides, to open it, but without success; and an excavation, about 8 feet deep, had been begun at the top.

Present Base, about	210 feet.
Ditto Height	59 feet.
Platform at top, about	50 feet.

PYRAMID No. 2 IN THE MAP.

Mr. Perring proceeded to Saccara during the inundation on the 24th July, 1839; and, notwithstanding the great heat of the climate, the thermometer in his tent being 114° at 2 P.M., and 112° at 5 A.M., he began his operations upon this pyramid. It is called by the Arabs, "Haram el Mekurbash," the Broken or Serrated Pyramid, and was opened by a Signor Maruchi, in 1831 or 1832; but was again closed up by the falling in of the masonry.

It is built with large, unsquared stones, rudely put together. There are no remains of a casing, and the whole is much decayed.

The regular inclined passage in the centre of the northern front remains closed up with masonry; and at the opening, C, Figs. 1 and 2, it was found to be lined, and also to be stopped up with blocks of granite. To avoid these obstructions, therefore, when the Pyramid was broken open, the present entrance was probably forced into the lower end of the inclined passage, which thence proceeds in a horizontal direction, and has been closed near the middle by a portcullis, consisting of a slab of granite, about half of which remains. Above this portcullis, a perpendicular excavation is apparently connected with the horizontal passage, D, Fig. 1, which had been forced from the entrance.

A little beyond the portcullis on the eastern side, a passage communicates with two side-rooms excavated in the rock, and originally lined with fine masonry, the fragments of which at present nearly fill them.

The two principal apartments have pointed roofs, and are lined with calcareous stone from the quarries of the Mokattam. The blocks which form the sides are not laid on horizontal beds, but slope away with an incline, like the beds of those in the Queen's Chamber in the Great Pyramid of Gizeh.[8]

Nearly the whole of the pavement has been removed, and the stones are scattered about the floor, and in the passages.

In the inner of the two principal apartments the remains of a small sarcophagus, made of plain basalt, and without any ornament, were found. The sarcophagus had been removed from its original position.

In the northern and southern walls (at BB, Fig. 2) are cavities, apparently intended to receive the ends of beams, used for lowering the sarcophagus into its place.

The whole of the passages and apartments are excavated in the rock, and are below the base of the Pyramid.

	Original.	Present.
Base[9]	231 ft. 3 in.	210 ft. 0 in.
Height	146 ft. 6 in.	108 ft. 0 in.
Length of Inclined Entrance-passage, closed up with masonry, about		78 ft. 9 in.
Angle of ditto	26° 35'	

	Feet.	Inches.
Horizontal Passage, length to Portcullis	31	3
Thickness of Portcullis	2	3
Portcullis to Apartments	26	9
Total length	60	3

	Feet.	Inches.
Width of Passage	4	2
Height to Granite Heading, A	6	1

---

[8] "Pyramids of Gizeh," Plate VIII. No. 1.

[9] The base appeared to be longer from north to south than from east to west; but it is supposed that it was a square, and that the apparent irregularity was owing to the rubbish, and to the ruined state of the building. The rock, and the different sorts of masonry, are distinguished in the plans.

GREAT PYRAMID OF SACCARA, N.º 3. N.E. View.

		Feet.	Inches.
Height beyond ditto		4	2
Outer Principal Apartment, length, East and West		13	7
.. breadth, North and South		10	3
.. height at Sides		10	5
.. height in Centre		14	2
Passage between Apartments, length		5	6
.. width		3	11
.. height		3	11
Inner Apartment, length, East and West		25	7½
.. breadth, North and South		10	3
The height is the same as that of the Outer Apartments.			
Passage leading from the principal Entrance-passage to the Side-rooms, length		13	0
.. width		2	8
.. height		4	2
First Room, running East and West, length		18	0
.. .. width		8	0
Second Room, running North and South, length		34	0
.. .. width		7	3

THE GREAT PYRAMID, No. 3 IN THE MAP.

Mr. Perring then examined the pyramid called by the Arabs, "Haram el Modarrggeh," the Pyramid of Degrees. It is situated on an elevation of about 91 feet above the plain, whence, by scarping the rock into a regular incline to the base of this Pyramid, and also to that of the one marked No. 2 in the Map, roads have been made for the conveyance of the stone used in the buildings, which was principally taken from the eastern face of the mountain, where tombs were afterwards formed in the quarryings, and likewise for that of the finer blocks, which were brought across the river from the Mokattam. It was opened by the Baron von Minutoli in 1821, and is the only Pyramid in Egypt, the sides of which do not exactly face the cardinal points, the northern front being 4° 35' east of the true north. It also differs from the rest in many other particulars, namely, in the form and mode of building, in the number and complexity of the passages, in having four entrances (one of them in the southern front), and also a variety of small excavated chambers, upon the walls of two of which hieroglyphics and peculiar ornaments are to be seen; in containing a large apartment covered in with timber, and furnished with a hidden chamber, and not apparently intended for sepulchral purposes, and likewise a great quantity of fragments of marble, and of alabaster vases, and of sarcophagi, which give to the building the character of an extensive catacomb, rather than that of the tomb of a single individual.

It is evident that the exterior of the edifice originally consisted of six degrees or stories, each of which had the shape of a truncated Pyramid, and was successively smaller than that below it; but, by the effects of time and of violence, the whole of the eastern, and nearly the whole of the northern and of the southern sides of the lowest tier have been removed. Two attempts have also been made to force an entrance on the southern side, and the French are said to have employed artillery for that purpose.

The bulk of the masonry (see fig. 1, Plate A) consists of loose rubble-work, and is inclosed by the walls, CC, which are about 9 feet in thickness, and are composed of rudely squared stones set to the angle of the face; and the breadth of the building from north to south has apparently been increased by an additional wall on each of those sides. The walls of the lowest tier are 10 feet thick. The stones have been quarried on the spot, and a great deal of mortar has been used; in some places on the southern side the masonry is of a better quality. The mortar is of various kinds, but it is principally composed of the gravel of the desert and of lime, or of Nile earth and of small pieces of calcareous stone.

	Feet.	Inches.
Original Base,[1] North and South	351	2
.. East and West	393	11

It seems to have covered an area of 15,372 square yards; but the present base is irregular, in consequence of the partial removal of the lowest tier.

	Original.	Present.
Platform at top, North and South	42 ft. 10 in.	24 ft.
.. East and West	85 ft. 8 in.	55 ft.

The degrees or stories vary in height, and gradually diminish towards the top.

---

[1] The base of this pyramid from north to south appears to have been originally 331 feet 2 inches, and to have been afterwards increased by the additions of a wall, 10 feet thick at each end, to 351 feet 2 inches.

		Feet.	Inches.
1st	- - - - - -	37	8
2d	- - - - - -	35	11
3d	- - - - - -	34	3
4th	- - - - - -	32	7
5th	- - - - - -	30	10
6th	- - - - - -	29	2
		200	5
Present height above Base	-	196	6
.. above Sand	-	190	0 (in places less).

The face of each story or degree has an angle of 73° 30′ with the horizon.

The entrance, which is in a pit, at the distance of 52 feet from the building, and 11 feet to the westward of the centre of the northern front (see *a*, Figs. 1 and 2, Plate A), is generally closed up by the sands of the desert, and often, indeed, by the Arabs, in order to gain money from strangers who wish to visit it.

The pit opens into a passage, which is nearly horizontal for about 120 feet, and afterwards descends, in the circuitous and irregular manner shewn in the drawings, to the lower part of the large apartment. It is an excavation, and appears to have been intended for a secret communication with the large apartment, and also with the small chambers and lower passages.

Near the entrance of the passage is a hole for the pivot of a door.

The centre of the principal entrance is 36 feet to the eastward of the centre of the northern front. The passage is stopped up with masonry; it has been irregularly cut out, but the general inclination is 23° 20′; it is 3 feet 5 inches wide in the centre, and has a ramp on each side. It is 176 feet 5 inches long, and it enters the apartment 7 feet 6 inches above the floor. The excavation made for it was originally more than 10 feet in width, and for 76 feet it was an open cutting, beyond which it has been tunnelled in the rock. The roof of it is therefore horizontal, and is 20 feet 9 inches below the base of the superstructure. The reason for the great size of the excavation appears to have been to facilitate the removal of the stone, and of the chippings, &c. from the large apartment, after it had been covered in by the erection of the Pyramid.

The passage was formed with masonry in the bottom of the excavation, and the vacant part was filled up with rubble-work, which has been partially removed. The passage is still closed up with large blocks.

Another passage, 179 feet 6 inches in length, about 4 feet 2 inches in height and in breadth, irregularly excavated in the rock, commences 5 feet without the building, and 5 feet to the eastward of the centre of the northern front (see Plate A, Figs. 1 and 2). A track had been worn down the middle of it, and a few stones had been piled up on the western side. It communicates in a horizontal, but not quite straight direction, with a recess in the upper part of the western side of the large apartment, where a groove had been cut across the floor, apparently for the insertion of a beam, whence a rope had probably been suspended. This passage was discovered by Mr. Perring, in August 1839, whilst he was in search of a chamber under the western part of the Pyramid, as those, which he had entered, were under the eastern part of the building.

A fourth entrance, proceeding from a pit (*d*) 14 feet square, and about 7 feet to the eastward of the centre of the southern front, had been previously found, and was supposed by Mr. Perring to be the only passage then discovered from the southern side of a Pyramid.

This entrance communicates by a horizontal gallery, 166 feet 3 inches long, 6 feet 4 inches high, and 10 feet wide, with a recess at the south-western corner of the large apartment. The recess was 70 feet above the floor, the texture of the rock could not be depended upon, and poles, above 6 feet in length, could not be introduced: the examination of the recess was, therefore, attended with some difficulty. The gallery is an excavation, but, as the rock above it has not been left of sufficient thickness to sustain the weight of the superincumbent masonry, the ceiling is supported by a row of twenty-two short columns, formed with blocks of compact limestone. They are roughly worked excepting the one *x*, Plate A, which has been inscribed with four rows of hieroglyphics (see Plate D, Fig. 5). The characters are badly engraven, and the stone seems to have belonged to some other building, as part of the inscription has been cut away, in order to fit the block for its present position. These columns have been brought to their bearings by wedges of wood, inserted both above and below them; and most of them are cracked by the superincumbent weight. The southern end of the gallery was stopped up with sand, but for the length of 160 feet from the interior it was open, and did not seem to have been previously visited, as nearly thirty mummies were found in it, apparently undisturbed.

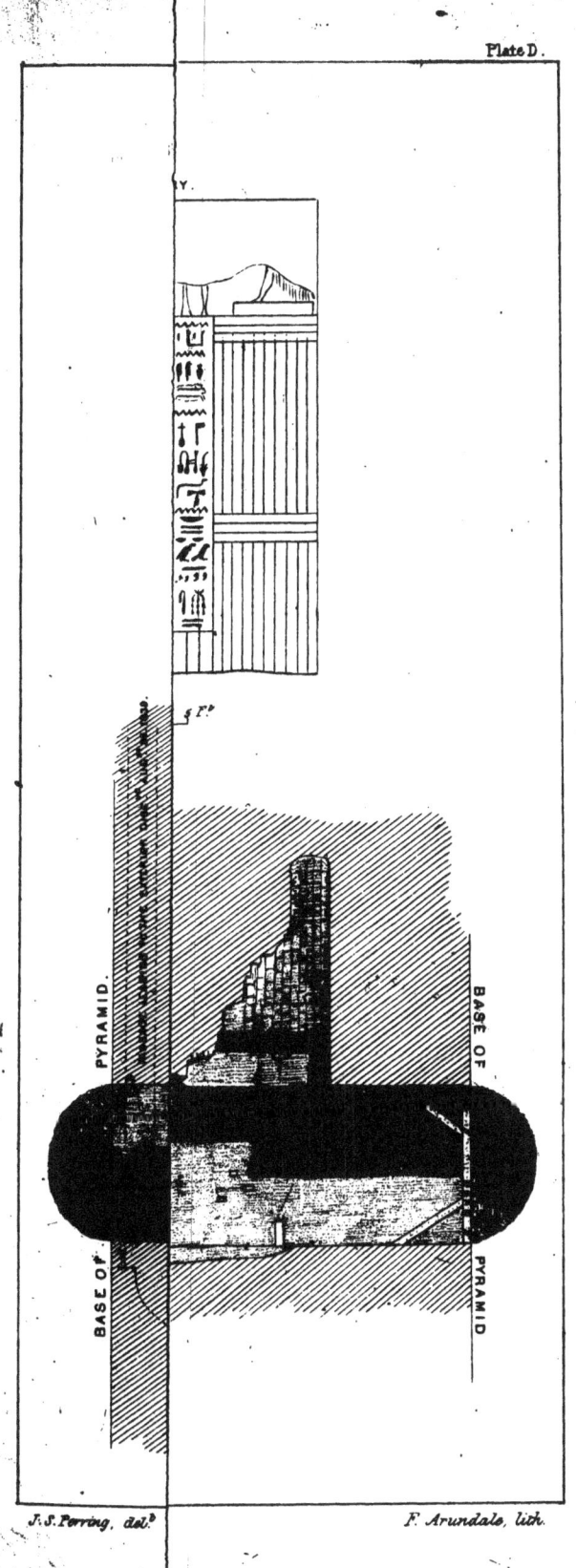

Plate D.

J. S. Perring, delt.   F. Arundale, lith.

Plate D.

FIG 6. STOPPER OF SANCTUARY.

FIG. 2. SECTION LOOKING NORTH.

Scale of 10 20 30 40 Ft.

FIG 5. SURFACE OF COLUMN IN GALLERY.

Scale of 1 2 3 4 5 Ft.

FIG. 3. SECTION LOOKING WEST.

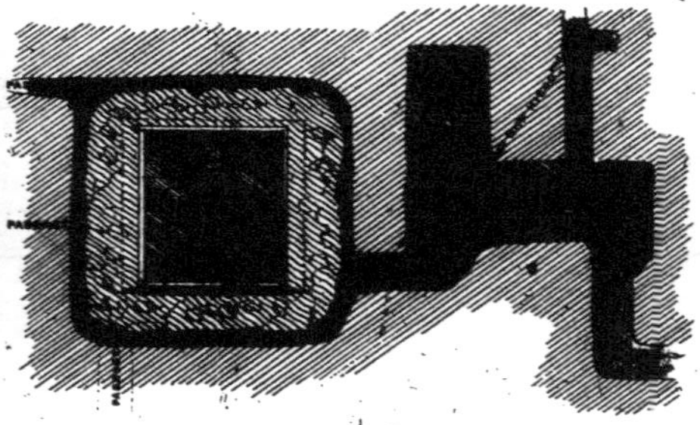

FIG. 1. PLAN THROUGH A.B. IN SECTIONS.

FIG 4. SECTION LOOKING EAST.

J. S. Perring, del.

F. Arundale, lith.

PYRAMID OF SACCARA, No. 3.

SECTIONS OF APARTMENTS, &c.

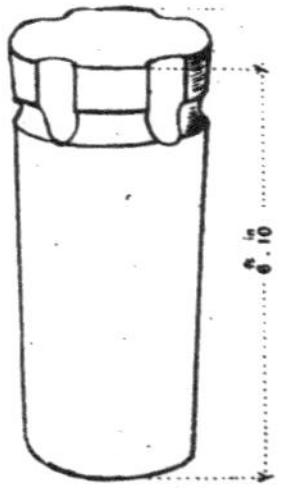

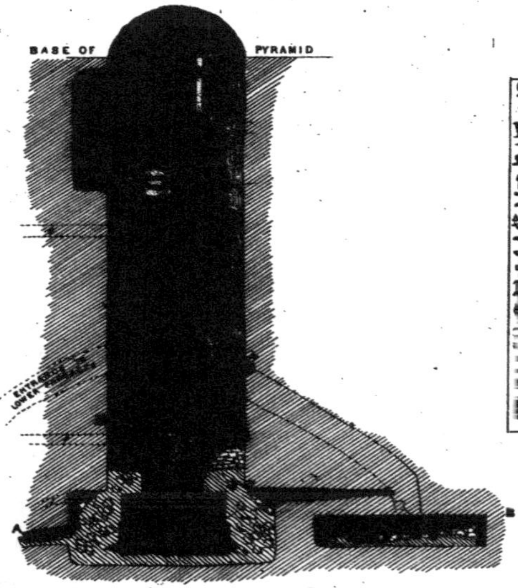

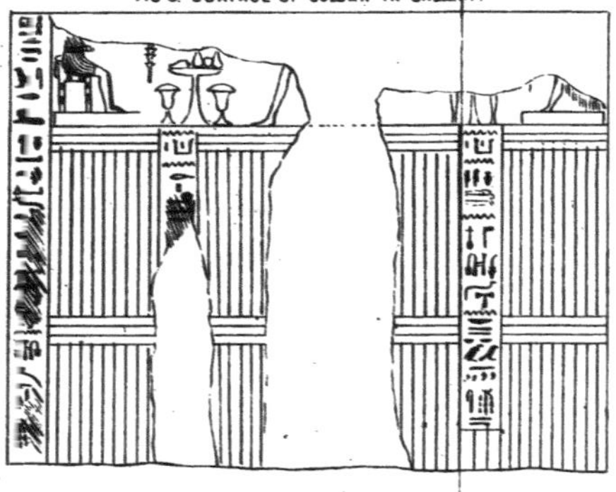

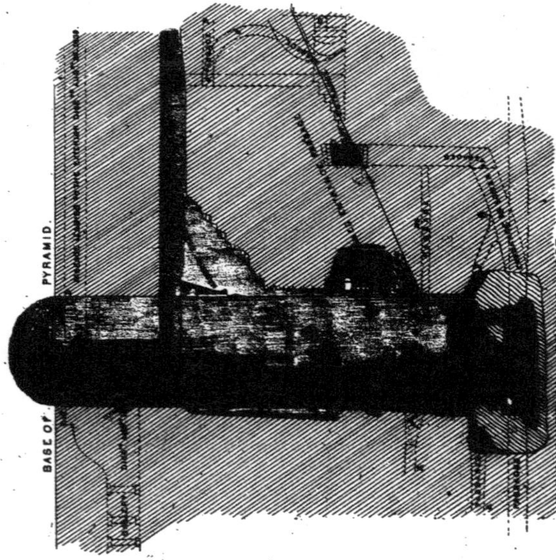

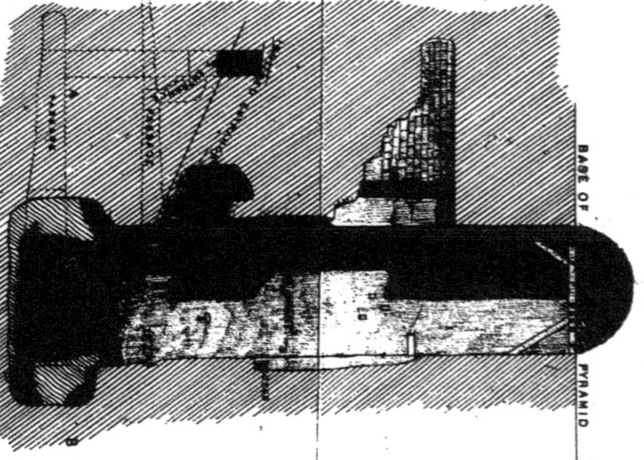

They had neither coffins nor sarcophagi, nor, with the exception of three or four, any painted decorations. They crumbled to pieces upon being touched, and could not be removed. Mr. Perring therefore proceeded to examine them. He found them inclosed in wrappers, with pitch and bitumen, but he did not meet with any of the objects usually deposited with mummies, excepting some of the common stone idols upon the body of a female; he therefore concluded that they were the bodies of persons employed in the building. A few pieces of decayed wood, apparently belonging to date-trees, were also found.

The large apartment is likewise an excavation; the western side of it is 25 feet 6 inches to the eastward of the centre of the Pyramid from north to south, but it is immediately under it from east to west. It measures 24 feet by 23, and is 77 feet high from the floor to the original ceiling, which he examined by the help of torches made of greased rags, and ascertained it to have been formed with planks, supported by a platform of timber, consisting of cross-bearers and of two principal beams. One beam remained in its place, but was broken in the middle; the other, together with the platform, and about 9 feet of the masonry, had fallen down, and the room was therefore covered in by the rubble-work, which composed the interior of the Pyramid, and which was retained in its place merely by the adhesion of the mortar, and of the materials. The apartment was filled with rubbish to the height of 25 feet, and the sides of it were blackened by the smoke of torches. They are roughly hewn, and have probably been cased with masonry.

The Arabs informed Mr. Perring that, when Baron von Minutoli first opened the Pyramid, a broken sarcophagus was found in the large apartment.

In the floor (which consists of blocks of granite) a remarkable chamber, 10 feet long, 5 feet 4½ inches wide, and 5 feet 4½ inches high, had been formed, the entrance to which had been closed by a conical block of granite, shaped like the stopper of a bottle; it was above four tons in weight, and was grooved round the top, as shewn in the perspective representation, see Plate D, Fig. 6. A few hieroglyphics were slightly engraven near the south-western corner of the chamber, but had been partially concealed by a joint.

The Baron von Minutoli[2] says, that this chamber is "a small

---

[2] See "Recollections," p. 83.

sanctuary, formed of several blocks of stone placed one upon another, into which a man could easily enter, and from which the voice of an oracle was probably made to issue." Mr. Perring does not, however, coincide with the Baron's opinion, but is inclined to believe, that the place was intended for a treasury, because there did not appear any secret entrance, by which a man could easily have got into it, and because the ponderous block, by which it was closed, did not seem fitted for mysterious purposes, as a number of men, and machinery also, would be required to raise it; because, likewise, no acoustic effect was perceived, which would peculiarly qualify the place for an oracle; and because it was well adapted for a secure and secret treasury. At all events, it did not appear to have been used as a tomb; for, had a body been placed within it, some remains would probably have been found, as it could not have been conveyed away through the present forced entrance, unless it had been broken into small pieces.

The granite blocks, belonging to the floor of the large apartment, are from 3 feet 6 inches to 4 feet 6 inches in thickness; and a reference to the sections (see Plates A and D) will shew that they are supported by short pillars of loose stones, placed together without mortar, and wedged up with wood to an uniform height.

In many places broken pieces of wood, crooked branches, &c. have been inserted between the pillars to tie them together. It has been already remarked, that the employment of wood is peculiar to this Pyramid.

Mr. Perring observed upon many of the stones characters, which had been indistinctly written in red ochre.

From the south-eastern angle of the large apartment, a passage below the level of the floor communicates with the smaller rooms. The doorway in one of them is bordered with hieroglyphics in relief, and that in another has a similar inscription traced in black. The characters had been much defaced since Mr. Burton copied them: they contain the title, but not the name, of a very early king. See Plate C. The headings of these doorways are covered with small stars, sculptured in relief.

The first apartment (see Plate B, Fig. 3) is 20 feet 6 inches in length, north and south, 5 feet 1½ inch in width, and 6 feet 5 inches in height; the other is 18 feet 8 inches in length, east and west, and of the same width, and height as the former. From the south-eastern angle a small doorway opens into an excavation,

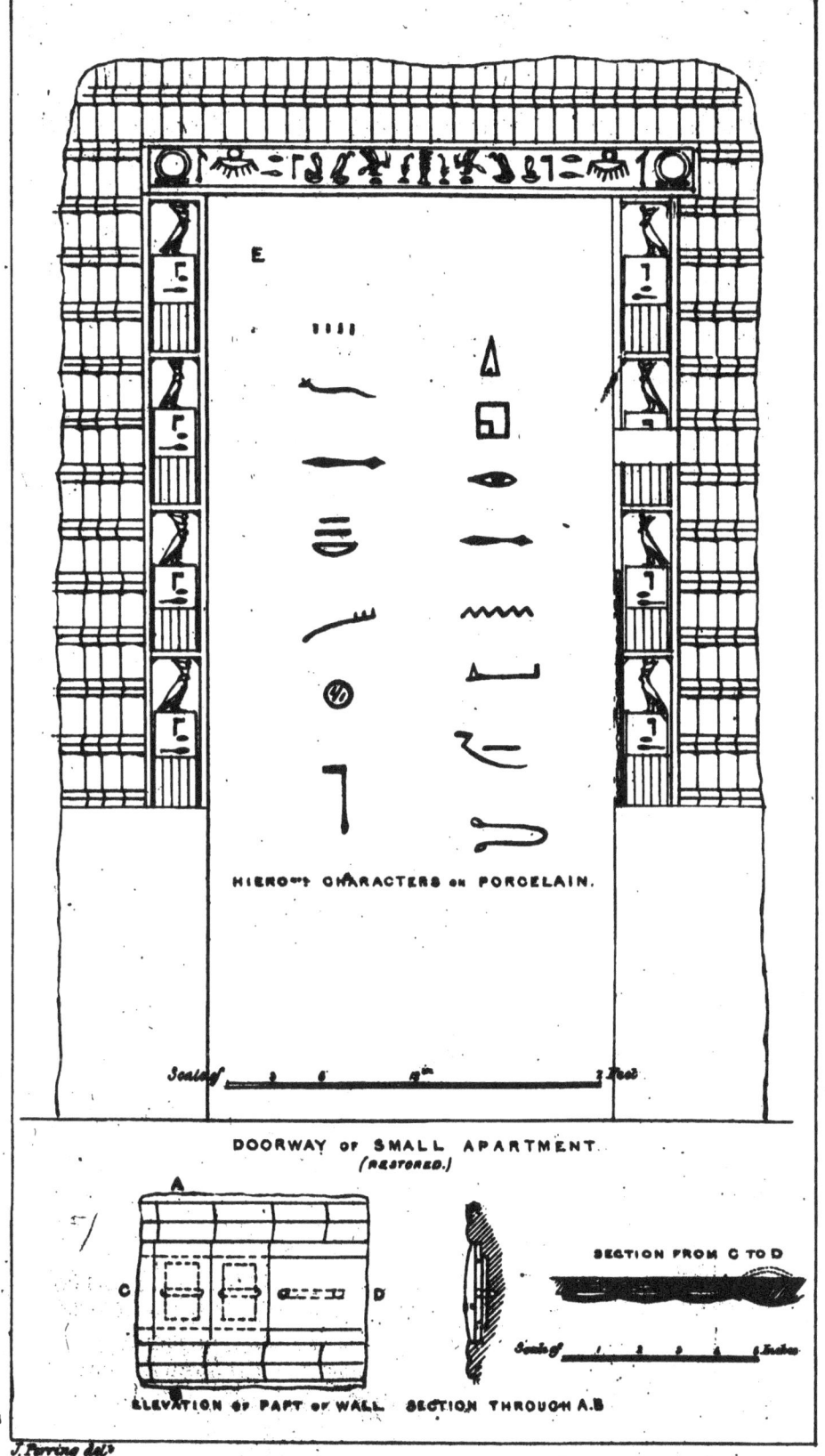

PYRAMIDS OF SAQQARA, N° 3.
PLANS OF PASSAGES AND APARTMENTS.

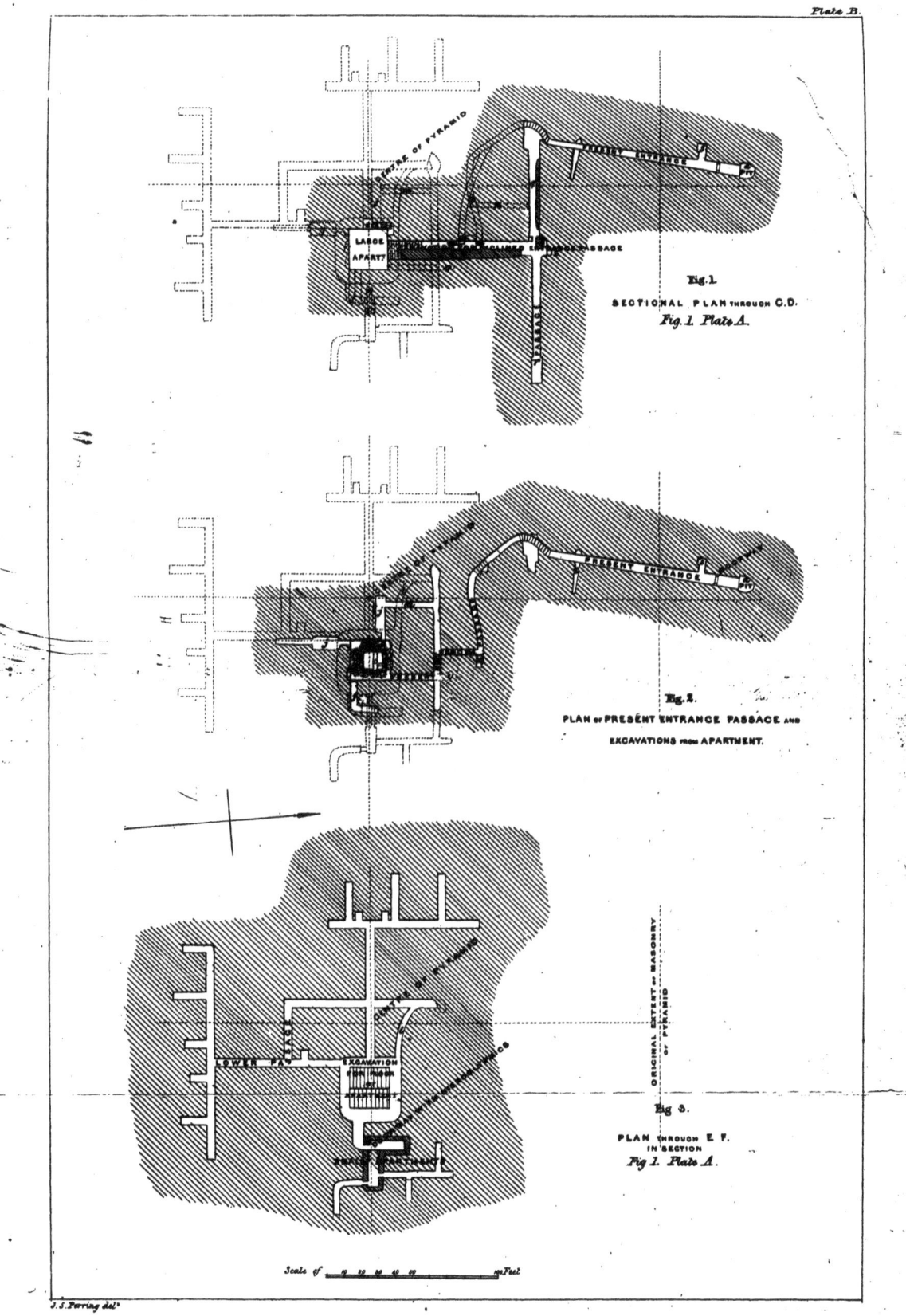

in which another room of the same kind may formerly have been constructed.

The sides of these apartments had been lined with calcareous stone, and ornamented with rows of convex pieces of bluish-green porcelain, inscribed on the back with a hieroglyphic, the impression of which remained on the cement. See Plate C. The porcelain had been removed, but from the fragments found in the upper passage, Mr. Perring was enabled to ascertain the form of the several pieces. The rock, made good and level with plaster, formed the floors, and the ceilings.

From the northern side of the second apartment an excavated passage inclines to the westward, and communicates with the present entrance-passage.[3] Mr. Perring is of opinion that the communication, leading from the entrance-passage below the level of the great apartment, was not only intended to facilitate the construction, and to open into the lower excavation, but that it has also served for a catacomb, because the recesses in the sides of it (which are as large as the nature of the rock will allow) are sufficient to contain sarcophagi; and because the sanctity attached to the Pyramids may have authorised the interment within them, of the people employed in their construction, and likewise that of the attendants of the deceased king.

The lower passages (about 5 feet in width) were nearly filled with broken vases composed of marble and of alabaster, with fragments of sarcophagi, and with broken stones, upon which stars, a common ornament of Egyptian ceilings, were observed. These passages were very intricate, in some instances leading to the excavations for the floor of the large apartment; in others, to small recesses, which might also have been supposed to have been intended for the bodies of the workmen employed in the building, had they not contained the fragments of valuable sarcophagi.

A small passage near the doorway appeared to communicate with the recess at the upper part of the western end of the apartment; but upon examination it was ascertained to end in the rock. The lowest passage to the westward, which Mr. Perring had imagined to be connected with one on the right-hand side of the entrance, was also found to be similarly constructed.

---

[3] Sir J. G. Wilkinson conjectures that these apartments and passages are of a later date than the rest of the Pyramid. See "General View of Egypt and Thebes," p. 337.

48   APPENDIX.

Mr. Perring endeavoured to ascertain whether any apartment existed to the westward of the large one, which has been described to be to the eastward of the centre of the Pyramid, although directly in it in the other direction.

He also cut a communication along the face of the excavation from the top of the main entrance, to find whether any passage existed from the recess in the western side of the apartment; and in six days he had contrived to penetrate to the apartment, and to form a ledge along the northern and western sides to the recess, which has been described to communicate with a passage 179 feet 6 inches in length, towards the northern end.

Plate A, Fig. 1, is a vertical section of the Pyramid through the centre of the principal apartment, along the line G, H, in Fig. 2, which is 37 feet eastward of the centre of the Pyramid.

Plate A, Fig. 2, is a sectional plan through A, B, in Fig. 1, at the level of the gallery discovered August 15th, 1839. The passage leading to the northward from the recess at the upper part of the western side of the large apartment (drawn in small dotted lines) is above the plane of the supposed section.

Plate B, Fig. 1, is a sectional plan through C, D, in Fig. 1, Plate A, on a level with the roof of the excavation for the principal entrance-passage.

Plate B, Fig. 2, is a plan, following the passage, by which the Pyramid is usually entered, and shewing the side excavations, which are 5 feet 6 inches above the floor of the large apartment, and which constitute small chambers.

Plate B, Fig. 3, is a sectional plan, E, F, in Fig. 1, Plate A, through the lower passages and small apartments.[*]

Plate D, Fig. 1, is a sectional plan, shewing the chamber in the floor, and the small apartments.

Fig. 2. A vertical section, looking northward, through the large apartment, the chamber in the floor, and the small apartments.

Fig. 3. A vertical section, looking westward, through the large apartment, the chamber in the floor, and the inclined entrance.

Fig. 4. Ditto, ditto, looking eastward.

Fig. 6. A representation of the granite stopper, which closed the opening of the chamber in the floor.

Plate C. The doorway of the small apartment, with the

---

[*] The chamber, in the Plate D, is called "a sanctuary."

hieroglyphics in bas-relief (with the broken parts restored), and with the convex pieces of porcelain inserted upon the walls.

Plate C. Details of the pieces of porcelain, and of the manner in which they were fastened to the walls. A is the masonry; B, the piece of porcelain attached to the masonry by stucco, which was chiefly composed of plaster of Paris. At the back of each piece of porcelain was a projection pierced through with a hole, into which the moist stucco upon the wall entered; and in some instances, to increase the adhesion, the wall was also perforated in the same manner.

Plate C contains the hieroglyphical characters on the porcelain which were impressed upon the plaster. The marks, such as E, which denote various numbers, from 1 to 8, frequently occurred.

Plate D, Fig. 5. The surface of the column x, in the gallery, and the inscriptions upon it.

> The following Letters of Reference are common to Plates A, B, and D.

a The usual entrance by the pit opened by Baron Von Minutoli, in 1821.

b A pit unopened. It communicates with the passage discovered August 26th, 1839.

c The commencement of the inclined entrance-passage (unopened).

d A pit communicating with the gallery, discovered August 15th, 1839. It had been partially opened, but was afterwards closed up with sand, &c.

e The opening of the passage into the apartments.

f The opening of the gallery into the apartments.

g Loose stones sticking in the angle, and shewing the height, to which the apartment had been filled up by the stones and rubbish brought down from the roof. The rubbish was cleared out into the passages.

hh Holes, about two feet deep, apparently intended to receive the ends of beams.

i A shaft, which had been forced upwards into the masonry, and by which the interior construction of the edifice was discovered.

jjj Small chambers excavated from the large apartment. They are shewn more distinctly in Plate B, Fig. 2.

k A small passage.

l   A small passage, which connects the large apartment with the lower passages.

m A small passage, leading from one of the small chambers, *y*, to the main passage, and to the lower passages.

n A shaft formed in the masonry, with which part of the excavation is filled up. It connects the upper part of the excavation, which contains the principal passage, with the present entrance-passage.

o A passage, excavated in the rock, from the upper part of the shaft, to the present entrance-passage.

p An excavated communication from the above passage, *o*, to another, which connects the present entrance-passage with the excavation made for the principal passage.

r A passage, from the connecting passage, leading to a chamber to the eastward.

s A small chamber near the doorway.

t A small chamber or recess, wherein a body was probably deposited.

u, v, w,   Ditto,   ditto.

x A column, inscribed with the characters drawn in Plate D, Fig. 5. It is in the gallery discovered in August 1839.

y A beam across the large apartment, composed of oak, and measuring about 18 inches by 12. It had been strutted from each side by angle-pieces, but was broken in the middle. A similar one had also been broken down by the weight of the masonry, and had been removed.

z The remaining cross-bearers of the wooden platform, which carried the weight of the superincumbent masonry, and formed the ceiling of the apartment. Small portions of it were found; they appeared to be oak, larch, and cedar, and the larch was in the soundest state.

The Pyramid had been surrounded by an enclosure, within, and near the north-eastern angle of which, were two heaps of ruined masonry, about 120 feet in diameter, and 28 feet in height, apparently the remains of small pyramids (see Map). The rock within the enclosure to the southward had been cut down to a level with the base of the Pyramid.

On the western side beyond the enclosure, several tombs were placed, in lines parallel to the Pyramid, like those near the Pyramids of Gizeh.

PYRAMID No. 4 IN THE MAP.

It is situated a little to the southward of the last-mentioned Pyramid, and is surrounded with heaps of broken stone and of rubbish, formed by repeated attempts to open it, and also by the removal of the casing, which had consisted of compact limestone from the quarries at Tourah.

The base was so completely ruined, and encumbered with stones and with sand, that the extent could not be accurately measured, but it appeared to have been about 220 feet, and in height 62 feet.

The platform at the top was about 30 feet.

PYRAMID No. 5 IN THE MAP.

This is the only Pyramid built entirely with stone from the Arabian quarries. In all the others, that material was only used for an exterior casing, and for a lining to the rooms and to the passages. The good quality and convenient size of the stones employed in the building, have of course led to its destruction, and the inhabitants of the adjoining villages have removed most of them for their own purposes.

Present Base, about	250 feet.
Height	40 feet.

A causeway to the eastward may be traced, but it is nearly covered over by the sands of the desert.

PYRAMID No. 6 IN THE MAP.

This building is near the village, and is called "Haram é Showwaf," the Pyramid of the Watchman, because it was one of the stations where a look-out was formerly kept, to apprize the inhabitants of the approach of the Bedouins. It was built with unsquared stones, and had a casing of blocks from the Mokattam, which is, however, almost entirely removed. The remains of a causeway, about 36 feet wide, may yet be traced in the direction of the village; near the Pyramid it was formed by an inclined cutting in the rock, and afterwards by a masonry composed of large blocks. On each side of it, and at about 220 feet from the eastern face of the Pyramid, are the traces of two small buildings, which may have been appendages, like the buildings or temples opposite the eastern fronts of the three larger Pyramids of Gizeh.

Present Base, about - - - - 270 feet.
Height - - - - - 80 feet.

PYRAMID No. 7 IN THE MAP,

Is a small Pyramid, about 100 feet from the north-eastern angle of No. 6. It is entirely ruined, and the greatest part of the materials have been taken away.

Present Base, about - - - - 140 feet.
Height - - - - - 27 feet.
Top - - - - - 70 feet.

PYRAMID No. 8 IN THE MAP.

It is named by the Arabs, "Haram é Syadeen," the Pyramid of the Hunters, for which its situation may be supposed to account.

This Pyramid, and No. 6, are on the northern edge of a valley leading to the Faioum, on the southern side of which No. 9, and the Mustabet el Faraoon, are placed.[5]

The present appearance of this Pyramid is that of a square heap of rubbish.

Near it are the fragments of a former casing of stone from the Arabian mountains, and also broken pieces of granite.

A causeway runs obliquely into the valley to the southward of No. 6, and near a square enclosure, formed with walls of crude brick.

Present Base, about - - - - 240 feet.
Height - - - - - 87 feet.

PYRAMID No. 9 IN THE MAP.

It is called "Haram el Mustabet," from being placed near the building known by the name of Mustabet el Faraoon.

It is built in degrees, and with small stones, and both in the material, and its present condition, resembles No. 8, on the opposite side of the valley.

---

[5] The roads leading from the Faioum are often distinguished by Pyramids. Mr. Perring, however, does not consider that any connexion existed between the Pyramids and the roads, but that they were so placed merely because the entrances to the valley of the Nile afforded appropriate situations for their erection.

On the eastern side are several foundations, and beyond them, and towards the village, is a long causeway, constructed with stone.

Present Base, above	245 feet.
Height	75 feet.

MUSTABET EL FARAOON.

The Throne of Pharaoh, so called from an Arabian tradition, that an antient king of Egypt erected it for his seat.

It is a pyramidal building, composed of very large stones, and constructed in two degrees, or stories, the lower of which has consisted of five courses of masonry, each about 6 feet high; the upper story has also had five courses, each 5 feet 3 inches in height. On the northern and southern faces another course of blocks, about 4 feet in height, has been carried up, which forms at these fronts a sort of parapet, 23 feet in breadth.

The materials consist of coarse calcareous stone, in which are semi-petrified oyster-shells. The building has no doubt been a tomb. Attempts had been made to open the northern and southern fronts, but apparently without success.

	Feet.	Inches.
Original Base, North and South	309	0
.. East and West	217	0
Original Top, North and South	263	0
.. East and West	181	0
Original Height in Centre	56	3
.. at Ends	60	3

Near the eastern front are foundations, composed of compact limestone, and of granite, whence a causeway, made with crude bricks, extends due east for about 390 feet, and then inclines northwards towards the village of Saccara.

NOTES BY MR. BIRCH.

No. 3 IN THE MAP. PLATE C.

Some account of this Pyramid is to be found in a work of Signore G. Segato,[6] and in General Minutoli's "Reise zum Tempel des Jupiter Ammon."[7] The inscription over the architrave, and on the lintels of the

---

[6] Saggi Pittorici, &c. da G. Segato e Lorenzo Masi. Fas. Secondo. Fiorenze, 1827.

[7] Fol. Berlin, 1824, pp. 405–7, Tab. XXVIII. Fig. 4, a.

inner door, have been also published,⁸ and have been found to contain the titles and the standard of a monarch. The standard⁹ is of the usual shape, and is surmounted by the hawk of Harsiesi crowned with a pschent. The two symbols in the standard beneath it express the words ⲚⲞⲨⲦⲈ, "*divine*," and ⲢⲰⲦ, "*race*" or "*germ*," &c. The whole implies "*Horus the divine germ*," and is represented four times upon each lintel. The inscription on the architrave must be read, from the emblem of stability in the centre, to the right and to the left, and expresses —"*The king ruling over the upper and lower world, the divine germ, the sun, golden* (resplendent), *strong, and living.*" The sentence is closed by the abridged form of the determinative symbol of Ran¹ (*name*). As a cartouche containing symbols has not been found in this Pyramid, it is at present uncertain whether or not the symbols expressing the sun, *resplendent*, &c. (Renoubgom), form the prenomen of a king. The standard may belong to the founder of the Pyramid. It resembles that of the king Nepercheres,² and indeed those of all the monarchs in the Memphite dynasty; and, I have already observed, that a similar group of characters was found at Reegah, and also upon a tomb in the vicinity of the Pyramids of Gizeh.³

Fig. 10 shews the detached hieroglyphics inscribed upon the tiles.⁴ The subject of them is no doubt sepulchral, because a meaning may be deduced from them, which resembles that of other inscriptions copied from tombs in the neighbourhood of the Pyramids of Gizeh, as follows:— △ "*offering*" ⌂⏗ "*that he may give*" ⚬―― ⚲ ⏃ "*all true speaking and devoted to the great god*," which was at that time frequently added to the names of deceased persons, instead of the expression afterwards used—"*Justified* (truth-speaking, veridique) *to Ra, to Osiris,*" or "*to the great god.*" It is of course

---

⁸ Burton, "Excerpta Hier." Pl. XXVII. No. 6. Segato et Minutoli, loc. cit.

⁹ This standard has also been alluded to by Rosellini, "Mon. Stor." Tom. II. Pl. I.

¹ It has also been supposed to represent a signet; and in some instances it replaces the solar disc: thus both Isis and Nephthys kneel upon the symbol, *Noub*, and place their hands on this object, or on the solar disc. The vulture and hawk, when intended to represent Victory, hold it in their claws.

² Rosellini, "Mon. Stor." Tom. II. Part I. Pl. I. p. 15. Tav. Agg. I. No. 9.

³ Burton, "Excerpta Hier." Pl. XXVII. No. 5.

⁴ Some of these tiles were brought over by Mr. Burton, and are now in the British Museum. Hieratic numerals are inscribed upon their reverse sides, intended, most probably, as directions for their positions in the building.

impossible to determine to which deity the indefinite term "*the great god*" alludes. It has been applied to Anubis, who, as well as Phtah, was especially worshipped at that time.[5]

Fig. 11 was on a column in the gallery. It represents, in two places, a deceased person standing up, and presenting offerings to a deity seated upon a throne. The line of hieroglyphics to the left expresses—" ...... *Phtah Sochar, Osiris, resident in the centre of the tomb, may he give an abode, &c. to the royal scribe, attached to the silver abode of the lord of the world, and attached to the charge of the silver abode ...... mas*," &c. In the next line may be read—" *For the sake of the military chief* ......;" and in the line to the right,—" *For the sake of the bard of the gracious god,*" or "*of the person praising the gracious god, superintendent of the white (or silver abode) of the lord of the world, of the upper and lower hemisphere (?) ..... mas.*"

These inscriptions are also sepulchral, and appear to have been executed some time after the erection of the Pyramids, which were probably appropriated to persons of the royal family. They seem to belong to the eighteenth dynasty, because the title "*military chief*," or "*youthful chief*" (ⲣⲛⲉ ϩⲏ), although it occurs under the monarchs of the sixteenth and seventeenth dynasties, was not used during the reign of their Memphite predecessors.[6] Nor was the formula, "*royal scribe*," then known, but ⟨hieroglyph⟩ "*scribe of the white*," or "*silver abode*"[7] was employed. The expression in the dedication,—"*for the offering of,*" was seldom used towards the conclusion of the seventeenth dynasty, and was unknown at the time of the Memphite kings. The expression " .... *mas*" does not occur as a termination to any name till the close of the seventeenth dynasty.[8] For these reasons the inscription upon the column does not seem to have been earlier than the eighteenth dynasty, and must therefore have been made long after the decease of the antient

---

[5] Burton, "Excerpta Hier." Pl. XXVII. No. 35. Respecting Anubis, many sepulchral inscriptions from Memphis in the British Museum allude to the worship of this deity, and end with "*to the great god*." On some vases also in the Museum, which belong to the sixteenth and seventeenth dynasties, and were brought from Abydos, the name of Anubis replaces the expression "*the great god*," as "*devout to the great god*," "*devout to Anubis*."

[6] Cf. Tombs at Benihassan. Burton, "Excerpta Hier." Pl. XXXIII. The expression or title "*royal tutor*" was, however, often used at this epoch.

[7] Portion of the tomb of Onkhif, British Museum. Leemans supposes it to be a "*palace*" (or portion of some such edifice), "*salon blanche;*" but it is differently inscribed, with the group for silver, upon the statue of Pnahsi, British Museum, No. 43, and means "*the silver house.*"

[8] Aahmas, Oohmas, or Amasis, is the earliest.

monarch for whom the Pyramid was erected.⁹ The latter part of the inscription is obscure. It resembles a royal standard, in which the hawk is put for the uræus; but it is not easy to decide by the copy, whether in the original the "*world*,"¹ or the expression "*justified*," was inserted. It is hardly possible to suppose that this fragment, which is stated to have been built in, can be older than the inscription of the inlaid door.

We know that the tombs of inferior persons frequently became the sepulchres of other individuals; and history informs us that the memory of the monarchs, who erected some of the Pyramids, was not held in much veneration. But the desecration of these magnificent mausolea by the entombment of subjects, however high their rank, is a surprising fact, which cannot be now accounted for.

According to the following extract from the work of Signore G. Segato, characters were traced in black in the interior of the edifice:—
"Nella parte interna posteriore all' architrave si scorgono traccie di alcuni geroglifici lineati in nero, che non si puo rilevare, ma che sembrano ben posteriori all' edificazione della Piramide."²

This author's philological researches were not successful; indeed, hieroglyphics were ill understood when he wrote. The date of the monarch, upon whose standard "*divine germ*" is inscribed, has not yet been determined by any inscription, nor has it been ascertained whether he preceded, or was posterior to Cheops.

PYRAMIDS OF DASHOOR.

A MAP is given, and a general view, which was taken during the inundation from the neighbourhood of the village of Shinbab. The Pyramids are situated near the village of Mensheeh, and are about three miles from Dashoor, which is, however, the principal place in the neighbourhood. They consist of two large buildings of stone, of a smaller one of the same material, and of two of crude brick, and they are placed on a high undulating desert plain, covered with stones, with small pebbles, and with petrified

---

⁹ Mr. Perring has already observed that, as this stone is a fragment, the hieroglyphics must have belonged to a building more antient than the Pyramid; but Mr. Birch's opinion of them would seem to induce a belief that the passage in question, had been inserted upon the fragment long after the erection of the building.

¹ In some of the standards, belonging to the seventeenth dynasty, is the expression "*world*."

² Saggi Pittorici da Segato e Lorenzo Masi. Fas. Secondo. Fiorenze, 1827.

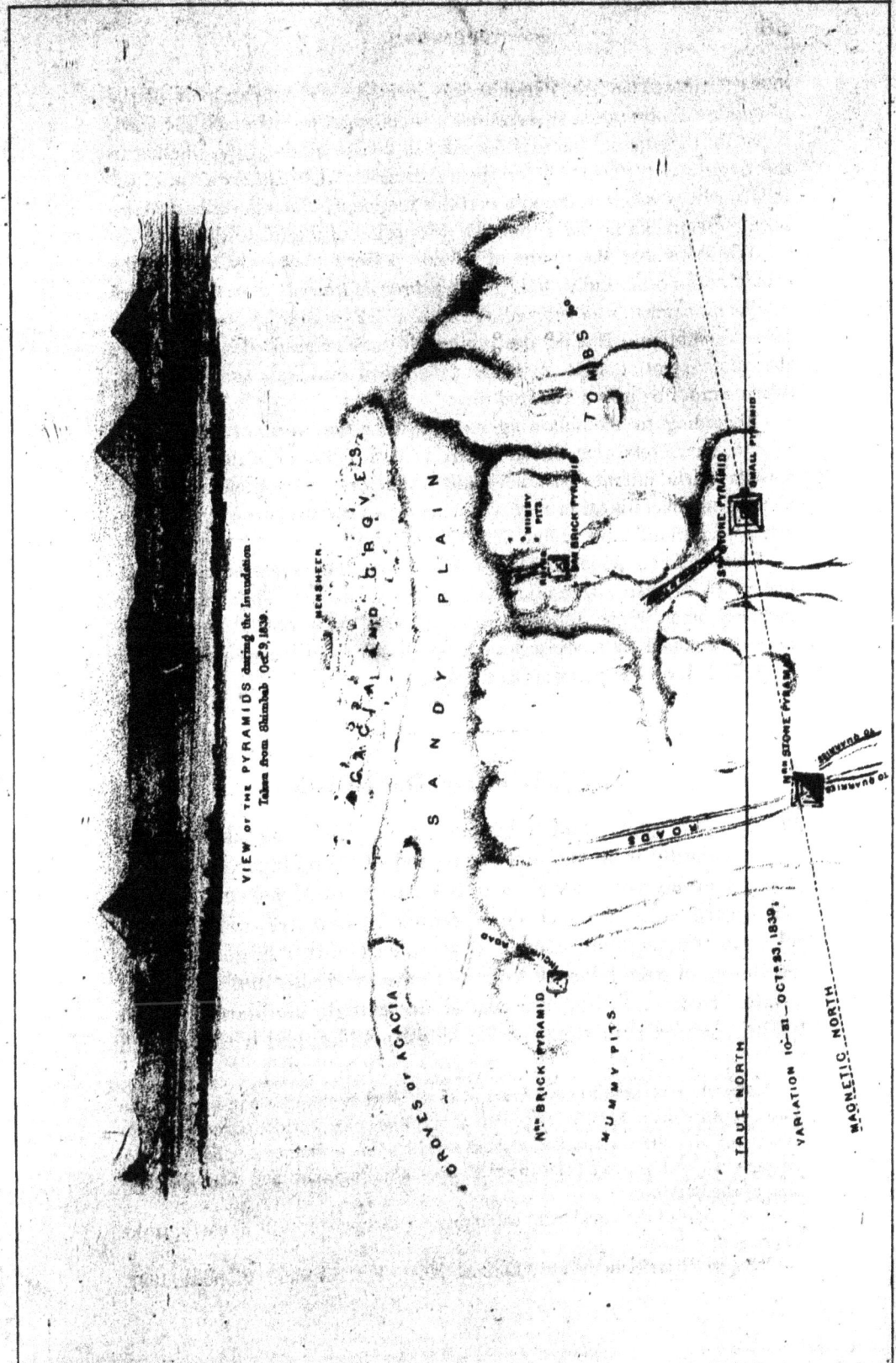

PYRAMIDS OF DASHOOR.

wood. But Mr. Perring observes that the place does not contain many shafts or tombs, although it formed part of the cemetery of Acanthus, the site of which is marked by considerable mounds, near the mountains to the north-westward of Zowyet el Dashoor.

THE NORTHERN BRICK PYRAMID.

On the 8th of September, 1839, Mr. Perring began to remove the rubbish and sand accumulated at the northern front of this Pyramid, which is called by the Arabs, "Haram Mekubbub," the Round or Flat Pyramid, as, from the effects of time and of the seasons, it has the appearance of a mound; but the materials had not been taken away, as they had been from the Southern Pyramid.

It is composed of crude bricks, and has been cased with stone from the Mokattam quarries, pieces of which were found near the base. The northern front has had the addition of a temple or portico, adorned with sculpture and hieroglyphics, like those said to be attached to the Pyramids in Ethiopia.[3] The casing and the portico had, however, been entirely removed, and their former existence was only ascertained by the operations carried on by Mr. Perring, in September and October 1839, in order to discover the entrance of the Pyramid; and in continuing the excavation to the eastward a hollow, about 6 feet deep, was found in the ground under the Pyramid, which was supposed to have been occasioned by the sinking in of a passage below it. It was therefore cleared out to the depth of 8 feet, but nothing was discovered.

The dilapidation of the Pyramid seems to have been begun at a very early time by the Egyptians themselves, as mummies were found in the ruins; and as many of the broken stones were inscribed with hieratic characters of a comparatively late period, by which it would appear that the persons who destroyed the edifice, probably for the sake of the materials, not only retained the customs, and the language of antient Egypt, but also used the spot as a place of interment; and the destruction of the masonry was no doubt accelerated by the facility, with which the stones could be removed to the neighbouring city, at one time the capital of the lower country. Indeed, the Arab historians have attributed the dilapidation of the Pyramids, and of the Tombs at Gizeh, to the establishment of Cairo in the vicinity of those monuments.

[3] See Caillaud, Waddington, and Hoskins.

According to Herodotus, Asychis, the successor of Mycerinus, added lofty propylæa to the eastern front of the Temple of Vulcan, and also, from a desire to surpass in magnificence his predecessors, constructed a Pyramid with bricks, upon which was this inscription:—"*Do not degrade me, by comparing me with the Pyramids built with stone, which I excel, as much as Jupiter excels the other gods; for those, who built me, thrust poles into the lakes, and, collecting together the mud, which adhered to them, they made bricks, and thus they constructed me.*" The Pyramid in question has been supposed by Mr. Hamilton, and by other good authorities, to have been built by Asychis; and, in support of that opinion it may be observed, that it is the most considerable Pyramid built with bricks, and that it is near the other Pyramids formed of stone, with which it might have been compared; and also that it is within a short distance of the Temple of Vulcan, which Asychis had so considerably embellished. The solidity of its construction is likewise remarkable. Not a single brick appears to have settled from its place; and, although the boasting terms of the inscription have excited much surprise, it is difficult to imagine a mass more solid, and also more durable, as long as it was protected, by an external casing of stone, from the effects of the atmosphere. It is certainly, therefore, as superior to those built with common stone rubble, as Jupiter may be supposed to have been to the other gods. The pre-eminence attributed to it may also have been enhanced by the grandeur of the portico or temple, by which it was distinguished, and which was probably adorned with sculpture and with hieroglyphics, executed with the greatest care and skill. As the whole of the bricks are not composed of alluvial soil, the latter part of the inscription can only refer to those formed of the mud or clay drawn out of one of the sacred lakes; and it is to be observed, that the Acherusia of Diodorus was at no great distance in the direction of Memphis, and that the boundaries of another lake are to be traced to the northward of the ruins, supposed to be those of the Temple of Vulcan, near that city. If it be urged that this Pyramid could not have been built by Asychis, because, from having been cased, it must have had the appearance of stone, it may be remarked that all the brick Pyramids at present existing in Egypt (which are four, exclusive of some small buildings at Thebes) appear to have been covered with stone; and likewise, that the above-mentioned inscription would have been unnecessary, had the material, of which the Pyramid was formed, been apparent. After a few days'

Nᴬᴺ STONE PYRAMID.
View of the Northern Front.

Nᴬᴺ BRICK PYRAMID.
View of the Northern Front.

PYRAMIDS OF DASHOOR.

labour a considerable quantity of the casing was found, which had been sawn up for removal. Most of the blocks were inscribed with red ochre, but the characters were generally illegible. In removing the rubbish, which was chiefly composed of the soil of the bricks washed down by the rain, and mixed with fragments of stone and with sand, a small part of a cartouche was discovered (see Fig. 8); also several pieces of cloth, a skull, an ornament composed of green earthenware, part of a cross-banded moulding, and blocks containing hieratic inscriptions, and hieroglyphics sculptured in relief. Two fragments adorned with stars on a blue ground, had apparently formed part of a coved ceiling. As the edges were imperfect, it could not be ascertained whether these stones had been inserted on the principles of an arch, but, as the grain was oblique to the curve, it was not probable. Part of a jar of brown pottery, with a remarkably handsome black border, was also dug up.

As stone had been used in the casing of the building, it might have been also employed in the construction of the apartments. But it was supposed that the interior of this Pyramid might possibly afford an additional proof of the antiquity of the arch, because ceilings of any extent could not well have been formed with bricks in any other manner. Mr. Perring, therefore, proceeded to examine it in September 1839, and for that purpose he first cut into the building, which he did with considerable difficulty, because the bricks continually fell in, as the sand, in which they were laid, was removed. He then laid open upwards of 90 feet of the northern front, and likewise the platform before it to the same extent: but he could not discover any entrance; and he therefore concluded that the apartments were excavations in the rock, and that the entrance was by a shaft, or by an inclined passage, at some distance from the Pyramid, and entirely unconnected with it. This he endeavoured to intersect, by sinking a trench 30 feet wide from the centre of the northern front; but, although he carried it in to the length of 160 feet, his attempts were unsuccessful. By these operations, however, he discovered that the building had been attempted to the eastward, and, as has been already mentioned, that there had been a portico, apparently connected by a stone platform with the casing of the Pyramid, and covered in by a roof, formed by the successive projections of the courses of the blocks. These courses had met at the summit in the centre, and their angles had been cut away, so as to constitute a curved line; a mode of construction by no means uncommon, and which would seem to imply an ignorance of the arch at the time when the roof was built, although it may have gradually led to the invention of it. Sir J. G. Wilkinson considers that the oldest stone arch, which had been discovered when he wrote his book containing Observations on Thebes, and a General View of Egypt (see p. 337), had been built in the time of Psammeticus II. (about 600 years before Christ), and the arch in Campbell's Tomb at Gizeh was of about the same date. There is said, however, to be an arch in the portico of a Pyramid at Meroe, inscribed with the cartouche of Tirhaka, about 700 years before Christ. The different methods, by which ceilings were formed, before the invention of the arch, have been already described, Vol. I. p. 219. Porticoes are said by MM. Caillaud and Waddington, to have been attached to the Pyramids in Ethiopia; but this is the only one hitherto discovered in Lower Egypt. Near this place, and at the depth of about 4 feet 6 inches, above fifty bodies were found, ten of which were mummies, embalmed and deposited in the usual manner. The others were much decayed, and had been buried in their clothes, and in some instances were bound round with common cord, and laid in wooden coffins, or amongst a few branches of date-trees. Some of the clothes were woollen, others coarse linen, with a fringed border of bright scarlet worsted. The heads were covered with bright red net-work. Mr. Perring imagined that these bodies had belonged to a pastoral people, probably to Bedouins, and that they had been interred, together with the mummies, at a very early period, before the introduction of Christianity. One of the embalmed bodies was in a decayed wooden coffin, and near it a reed flute was found. About a foot lower, a piece of cross-band moulding, slabs containing coloured and well-executed sculptures, which recorded the dedication of an offering, and part of a cartouche, were also dug up. Five or six bodies had been placed over these fragments, and one, enclosed in a coffin, was found in a small tomb constructed with the bricks of the Pyramid, in which had been placed a piece of glass like the bottom of a wine-glass, and a pair of brass armlets. Two mummies, handsomely decorated, and wrapped up, were laid in sarcophagi made of coarse earthenware, the ends of which were circular; and upon the lids, which were composed of two pieces, faces had been rudely painted. The mummies, upon exposure, crumbled into dust. They did not appear to contain the idols, and small figures usually found in Egyptians' tombs; but Mr. Perring collected some bronze nails, the bracelets and the earrings of a child, and, from the body of a female some beads, buttons, and bronze pins.

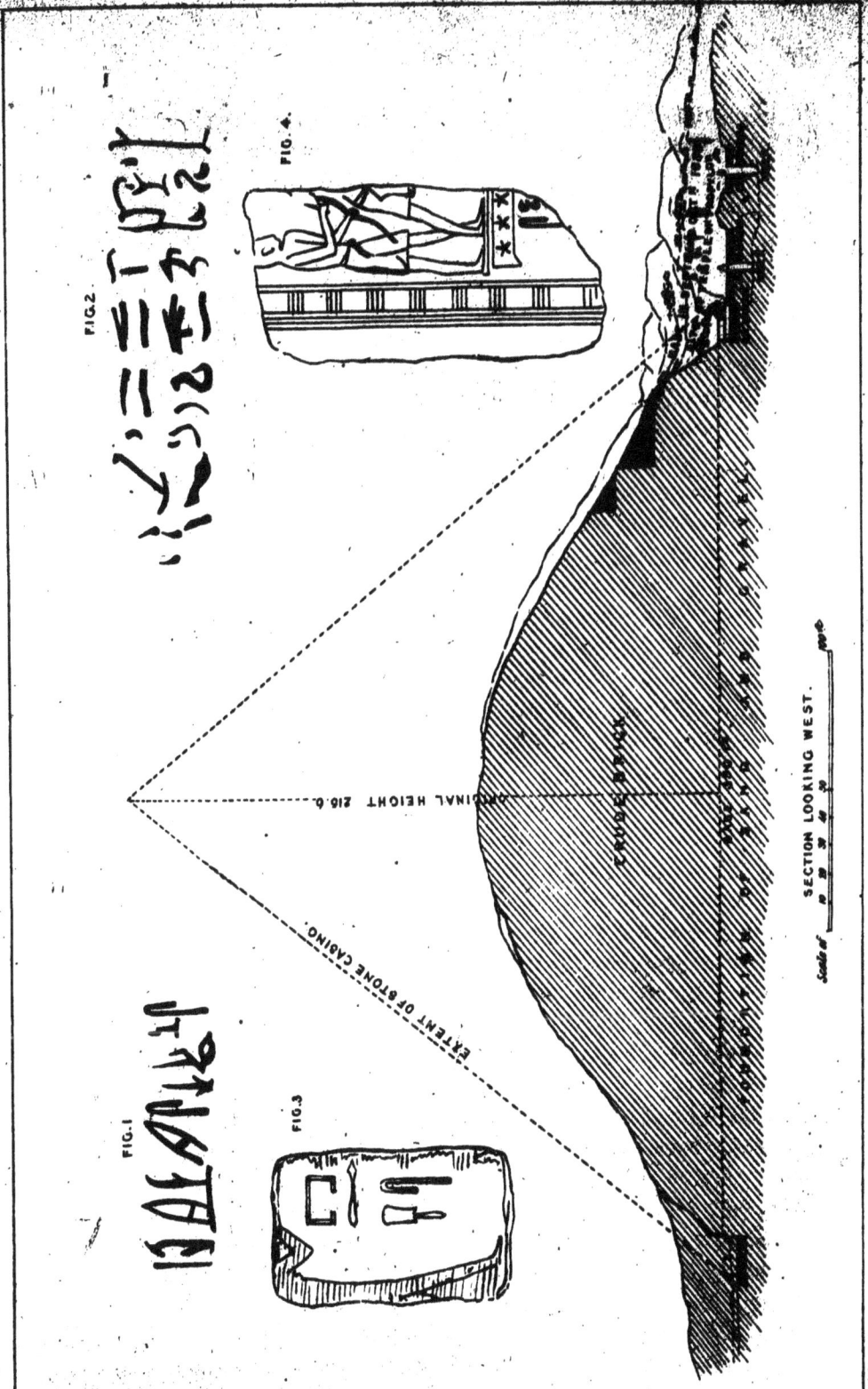

NORTH BRICK PYRAMID OF DASHOOR.

J.S. Perring.

APPENDIX. 61

The building was carried down much lower than Mr. Perring expected; he accordingly enlarged the excavation, and he found a wall of rubble-work, which appeared to be a protection to an entrance. On the 24th he arrived at the base of the building, 30 feet below the surface of the ground. He found a pavement composed of large stones, and towards the north a hollow about 2 feet 8 inches wide, which had been stopped up by a block, and had in some degree the appearance of an entrance to an inclined passage. The foundation was remarkable. The stony surface of the desert had been made level by a layer of fine sand, confined on all sides by a stone platform, 14 feet 6 inches wide, and 2 feet 9 inches thick, which supported the external casing; and the Pyramid was built upon the sand, which was firm and solid. Mr. Perring has met with other instances in Egypt where sand has been thus used;[4] and, provided it be retained in its place, it apparently may be depended upon. The blocks composing the platform were laid upon four courses of bricks.

Many of the stones, which belonged to the casing, are large. The dimensions of one are as follows:— Base, 8 feet 3 inches; vertical height, 1 foot 11 inches; and the face of it is above 6 feet in length. The blocks were not laid in regular courses of an 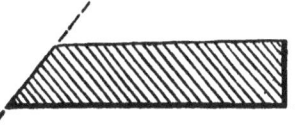 equal thickness, but each stone had been fitted to those adjoining, as in the masonry termed polygonal. Putlock holes had been cut into many of the blocks to receive the ends of the poles, upon which a scaffold had been placed, that the workmen might be enabled to finish, and trim off the casing to an even surface.[5] And these holes had been in every instance filled up with small pieces of the same stone, laid in cement or in gypsum, and so exactly worked, that many of them were not discovered until the stones had been broken. Several of the blocks, particularly in the lower part, were held together by stone cramps, thus. The base 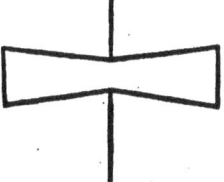 of the single stone, which formed the apex of the Pyramid, was about 6 feet 8 inches square. It had been fixed upon the course

[4] Namely, Campbell's Tomb at Gizeh, the Temple near the Pyramid of Reegah, the Platform of the Northern Pyramid of Abouseir, and some smaller tombs.

[5] These holes were probably intended for the above-mentioned purpose; at the same time a reference is made to Vol. I. p. 38.

below it (composed only of two blocks) by two of the above-mentioned cramps on each of the four sides. These cramps had been laid in cement composed of plaster of Paris. They were probably formed of wood or of stone, but none were discovered.[6]

The bricks, of which the body of the Pyramid was built, were 16 inches long, 8 inches wide, and from $4\frac{1}{2}$ to $5\frac{1}{2}$ inches thick. They did not afford any inscription, but had been marked on the upper surface, by means of the fingers, with different signs, apparently according to their quality; but varying according to their position, as the marks at the north-western differed from those at the north-eastern angle, and at the south-eastern angle only Mr. Perring observed ⌒ ═ . The greatest number were composed of alluvial soil, and were marked thus S. Those formed of sandy loam, or of sand mixed up with Nile earth, and a little straw, had this mark ⑃ . Others, with not quite so much sand in their composition, had merely been marked by a thumb thrust into the centre; a few, which contained a good deal of straw, had this ⌒ . The most usual mark, particularly on those near the base, had been made by two fingers, about an inch apart, having been drawn down the middle; and the bricks so distinguished were formed of a very dark tenacious earth, and without any intermixture of straw. They were all remarkably solid, and they had been laid principally in courses from north to south, occasionally intersected by courses running from east to west. The bricks were bedded in, and the interstices between them were filled up, with fine dry sand. In the operations already described, Mr. Perring had examined more than 90 feet of the northern front, and the platform, which supported the casing and the portico. He had also ascertained by two shafts, that the rock was 15 feet below the base of the building, and therefore, as the sand and rubbish had accumulated to a great height, that excavations in search of the entrance (in which he had already employed above sixty people more than a month), would be

[6] Similar spaces, in the blocks of the Great Temple at Karnac, were found to have been completely filled with cement, which, notwithstanding the great heat of the climate, still retained a degree of moisture. See Vol. I. p. 77.

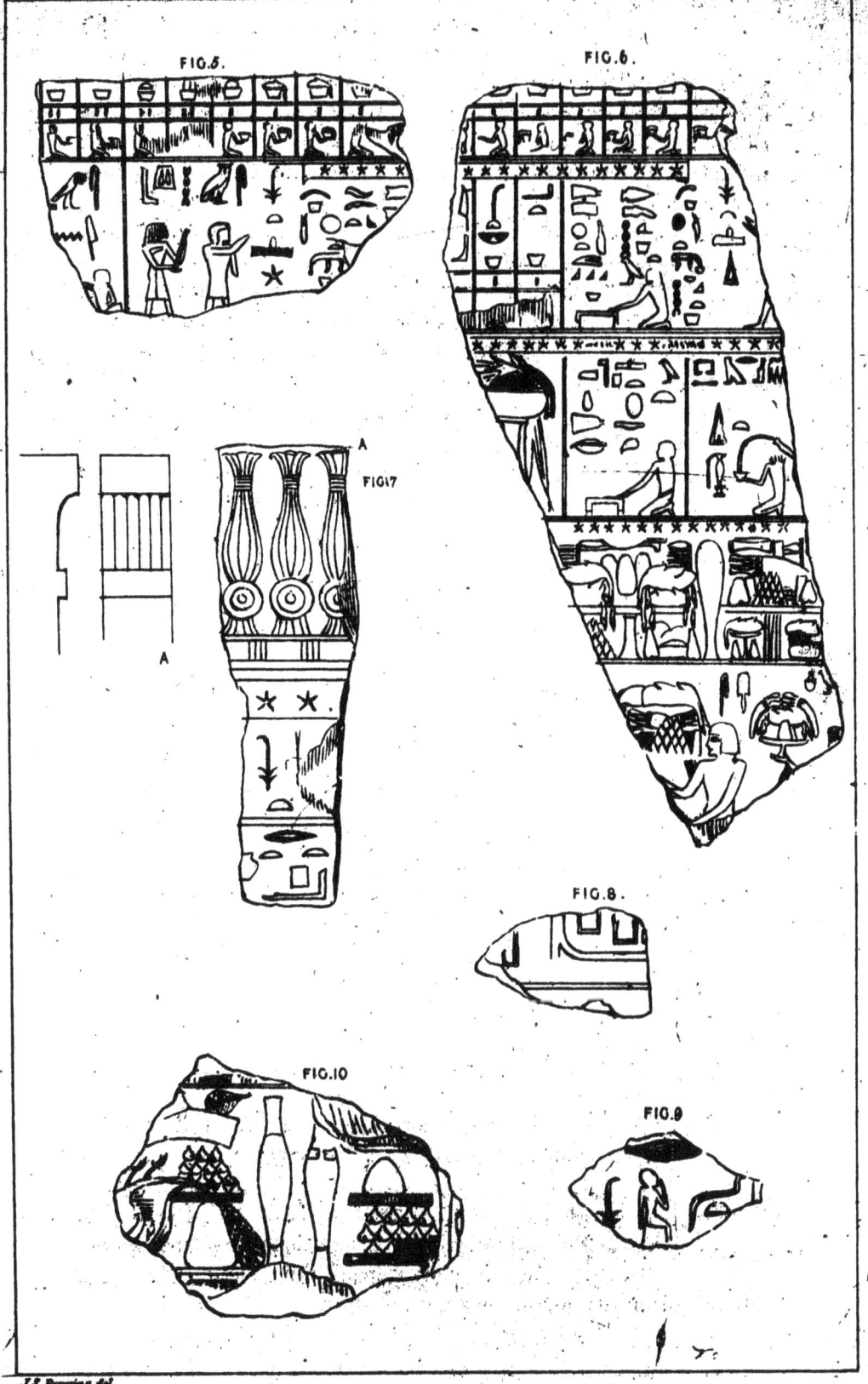

NORTH BRICK PYRAMID OF DASHOOR.

attended with great labour and expense, and with more time, than he had at his disposal. He therefore sent for the sheik of the village, and the reis, whom he had employed, and he offered them two purses (about 10*l.*) if they would discover the entrance by the time of his return from the Faioum; but they would not undertake the discovery at that price, notwithstanding the people of the village were unemployed.

The shafts A and B were sunk to ascertain the depth of the rock below the base of the Pyramid; it has been described to be 15 feet, and the intermediate space was filled up with compact gravel.

Figs. 1 and 2 were written with red ochre upon the blocks, which had belonged to the casing. Figs. 3 to 10 represent sculptured inscriptions found upon other blocks. Mr. Perring imagines that Fig. 3 formed part of the inscription mentioned by Herodotus.

		Feet.	Inches.
Original Base		350	0
Height		215	6
Angle of Casing	51° 20′ 25″		
Present Height above the Base, about		90 ft.	
above the surface of the sand of the Desert, about		82 ft.	

THE NORTHERN STONE PYRAMID.

It is built with stone taken from the adjacent mountains, and principally from quarries to the westward and south-westward of the edifice, which, like that in the Mustabet el Faraoon, is of a reddish colour, calcareous, and interspersed with semi-petrified shells, chiefly those of oysters. The exterior casing, and the linings of the passages, and of the chambers, are of white compact limestone from the Arabian mountains; and, were it not for a quantity of broken granite near an inclined road, which proceeds from the eastern side of the Southern Brick Pyramid, it might be supposed that these buildings were erected by kings, who possessed the lower country only, and who consequently had not access to the quarries at Es Souan; for that material does not appear to have been used in either of the stone Pyramids at this place.

Two causeways had been constructed from this Pyramid to the quarries to the westward, and two others also towards the valley of the Nile, for the conveyance of the stone, which was brought from the opposite side of the water.

In some places, particularly on the western side, the casing still remains. The top of the Pyramid was built entirely with Arabian stone. The apex had been formed of one block, and the course below it of four others, 4 feet 9 inches thick; but in general the courses towards the top were about 2 feet, and those near the base, about 3 feet in thickness. The stones are laid in horizontal courses, and the whole of the masonry is good, and resembles that of the Great Pyramid of Gizeh. The angle at the apex is nearly a right angle, and the building has on that account a handsome and solid appearance, and from retaining more of its original form than the others, it is called by the Arabs, "Haram Mesinee," the Pointed or Sharp Pyramid. It is also called "Haram el Wataweet," from the number of bats within it; and sometimes "Haram é Silsili," on account of a chain said to have been suspended from the entrance of the passage between the second and third chambers.

The centre of the entrance is 12 feet 6 inches to the eastward of the centre of the northern front, and the bottom of it is 94 feet perpendicularly higher than the base of the building. The passage is 3 feet 5½ inches in width, 3 feet 11½ inches in height, and has an inclination of 27° 56'. Its original length was 205 feet 6 inches, of which 4 feet 6 inches have been destroyed by the removal of the external casing. The lower part, and a horizontal passage, 24 feet 4 inches long, 3 feet 5½ inches wide, and 4 feet 5½ inches high, leading from the bottom of it to the first chamber, were much encumbered with rubbish.

The first chamber is 27 feet 5½ inches in length, north and south, and 11 feet 11 inches east and west. The floor is on a level with the base of the Pyramid. The four lower courses of the walls, to the height of 11 feet 8½ inches, are perpendicular; but each of the eleven courses above them sets over nearly 6 inches, so that the ceiling is only 1 foot 2 inches in width. The two lower projecting courses are 3 feet in thickness; the others rather more than 2 feet 6 inches; and the height of the chamber is about 40 feet 4½ inches.

A passage, 10 feet 4 inches long, 3 feet 5½ inches wide, and 4 feet 5½ inches in height, leads from the south-western corner of this chamber to another apartment, exactly similar, excepting that it is about two inches shorter from north to south. The pavement of this second chamber has been removed, and the room is full of rubbish. At the end of it, and at the height of 25 feet

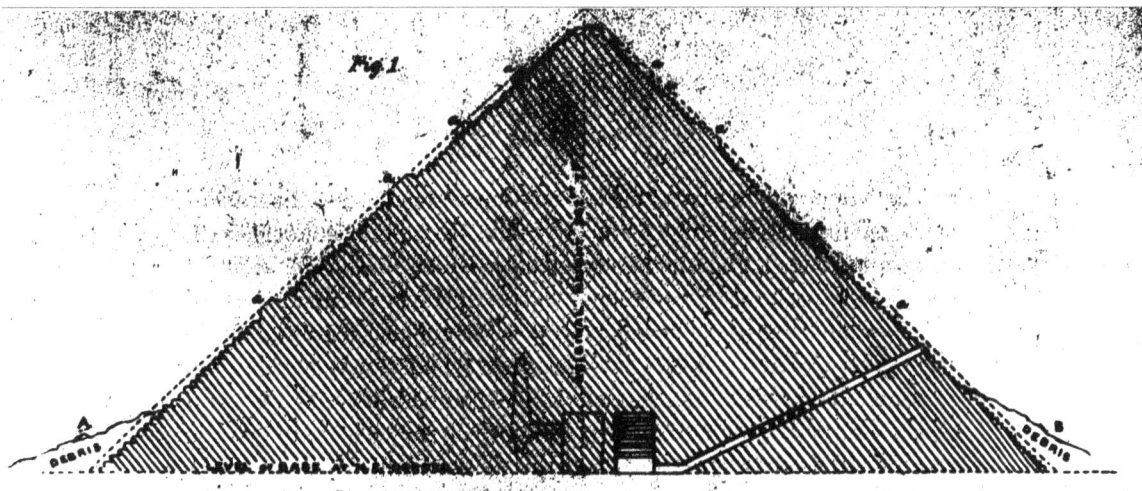

Fig. 1
SECTION THROUGH ENTRANCE PASSAGE
(LOOKING W.)

Fig. 2
PLAN THROUGH A B.

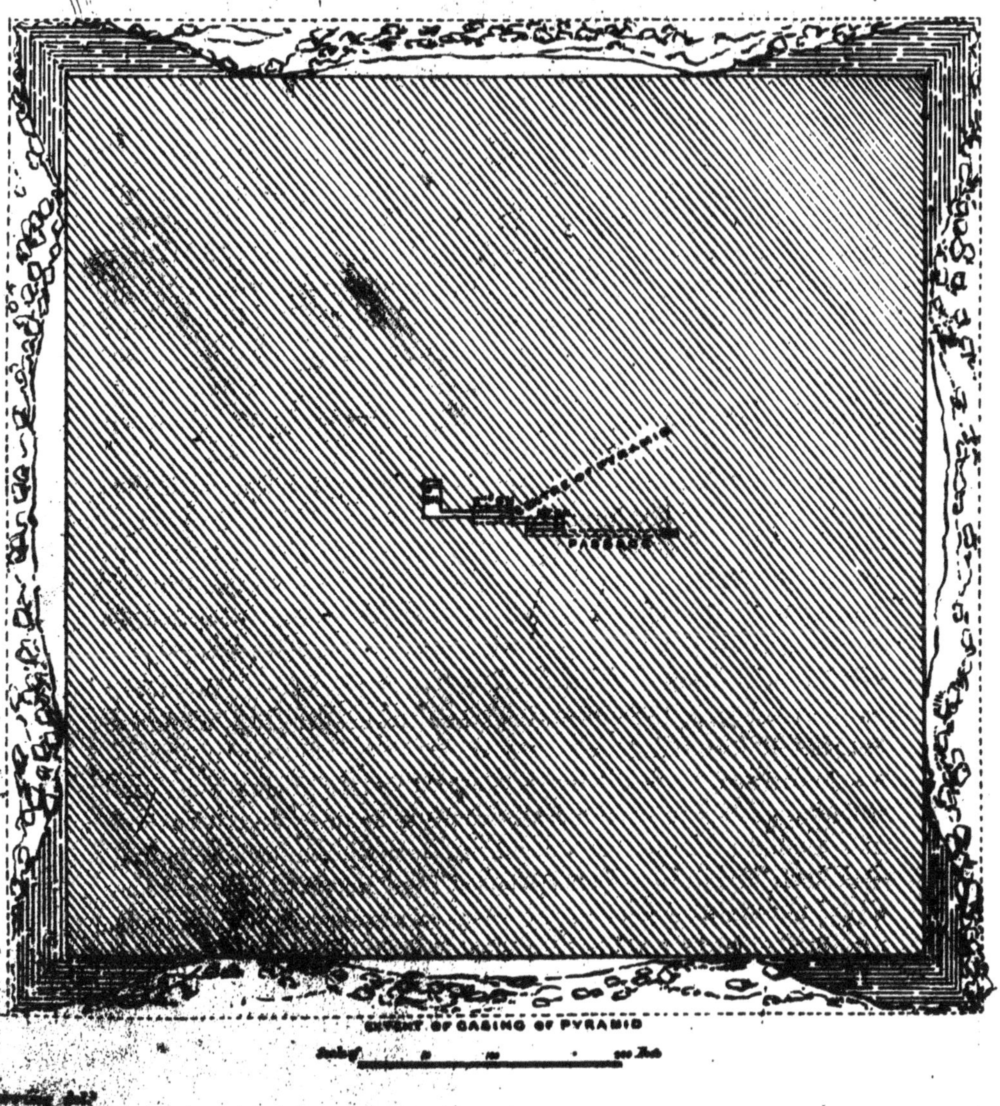

N. STONE PYRAMID OF DASHOOR.

N. STONE PYRAMID OF DASHOOR.

VIEW OF THE SOUTH STONE PYRAMID OF DASHOOR.

8¼ inches from the original floor, a passage, 3 feet 5¼ inches in width, runs southward, for 23 feet 11 inches, to a third chamber, the floor of which had been taken up to the depth of 14 feet. The floor of the above-mentioned passage (which was originally 8 feet 5¼ inches high) had also been taken up, in order, probably, to facilitate the removal of the large blocks from the inner chamber.

The third chamber is 27 feet 3½ inches long from east to west, and 13 feet 7½ inches wide from north to south. The sides are perpendicular for 12 feet 1 inch, after which fourteen courses project inwards, as in the other apartment; and the total height from the original floor to the ceiling is 48 feet 1 inch.

	Original.	Present.
Base	719 ft. 5 in.	700 ft. 0 in.
Perpendicular Height	342 ft. 7 in.	326 ft. 6 in.
Angle of external Casing	43° 36′ 11″	

Fig. 1 is a section of the Pyramid, through the entrance-passage and the first chamber, looking west. *a a a*, on the sides of the Pyramid, are parts of the casing.

Fig. 2 is a plan, through A B, Fig. 1, upon a level with the third chamber, and with the horizontal passage leading to it from the second chamber.

In another plate, Fig. 1, is part of the section on an enlarged scale.

Fig. 2 is a plan through E F in Fig. 1.

Fig. 3 is a section of the second and third chambers.

Fig. 4. A transverse section of the second chamber, looking south. It shews the entrance of the passage leading to the third chamber.

Fig. 5. Plan of the entrance-passage, and of the first and second chambers.

THE SOUTHERN STONE PYRAMID.

It is built in two inclinations, so that the lower part has the form of a truncated, and the upper that of a perfect Pyramid; which mode of construction, according to Sir J. G. Wilkinson, was probably occasioned by a desire to complete the building more quickly than it was at first intended: and it may be added, that this conjecture was in some degree confirmed by Mr. Perring's researches, by which it appeared that the upper part had been carried up with less care than the lower, and was also composed of smaller stones; but, whatever may have been the cause, the effect is unpleasant, particularly when compared with the fine proportions of the Northern Pyramid.

The beds of the casing-stones are not horizontal, but incline downwards towards the interior of the edifice, in order, probably, to obtain greater solidity, and likewise to save the materials, as less of the external faces of the stones thus laid, would require to be planed away to complete the exterior of the building. This incline, however, is not uniform, nor at right angles to the exterior, but it seems to be regulated by the shapes of the blocks; in the upper part it is generally at an angle of $3° 30'$, and in the lower part it varies from $6° 30'$ to $9°$. The casing-stones of the lower part are very large, some of the courses being 4 feet 8 inches in height; but they are often divided into two layers, and the joints at the sides, instead of being vertical, are cut to fit the adjacent stones. The courses in the upper part are seldom more than 2 feet in height. Although a good deal of the casing remains, the building towards the top is much injured by the weather, and most probably has never been completed. The masonry in the lower part has also been destroyed, principally, it is said, by the late Deftardar Mahommed Bey, to get materials for his palace near Cairo. Upon the exterior were several holes, in every respect like those observed in the casing of the Northern Brick Pyramid, and they had been concealed in the same manner.

The body of the Pyramid is built with stone from the immediate vicinity, and much of it seems to have been quarried near the northern and eastern faces; but the casing-blocks, and those immediately behind them, together with the linings of the passages and chambers, consist of stone from the Mokattam, which has induced a belief that the whole edifice is composed of that material.

The building has been surrounded by a stone wall; and a causeway, composed of blocks from the Mokattam, has led from the north-eastern angle of the enclosure to a small valley extending to the plain below. (See Map.)

	Feet.	Inches.
Base	616	8
Perpendicular height of lower part	147	4
... .. upper part	172	2
Total height at present	319	6

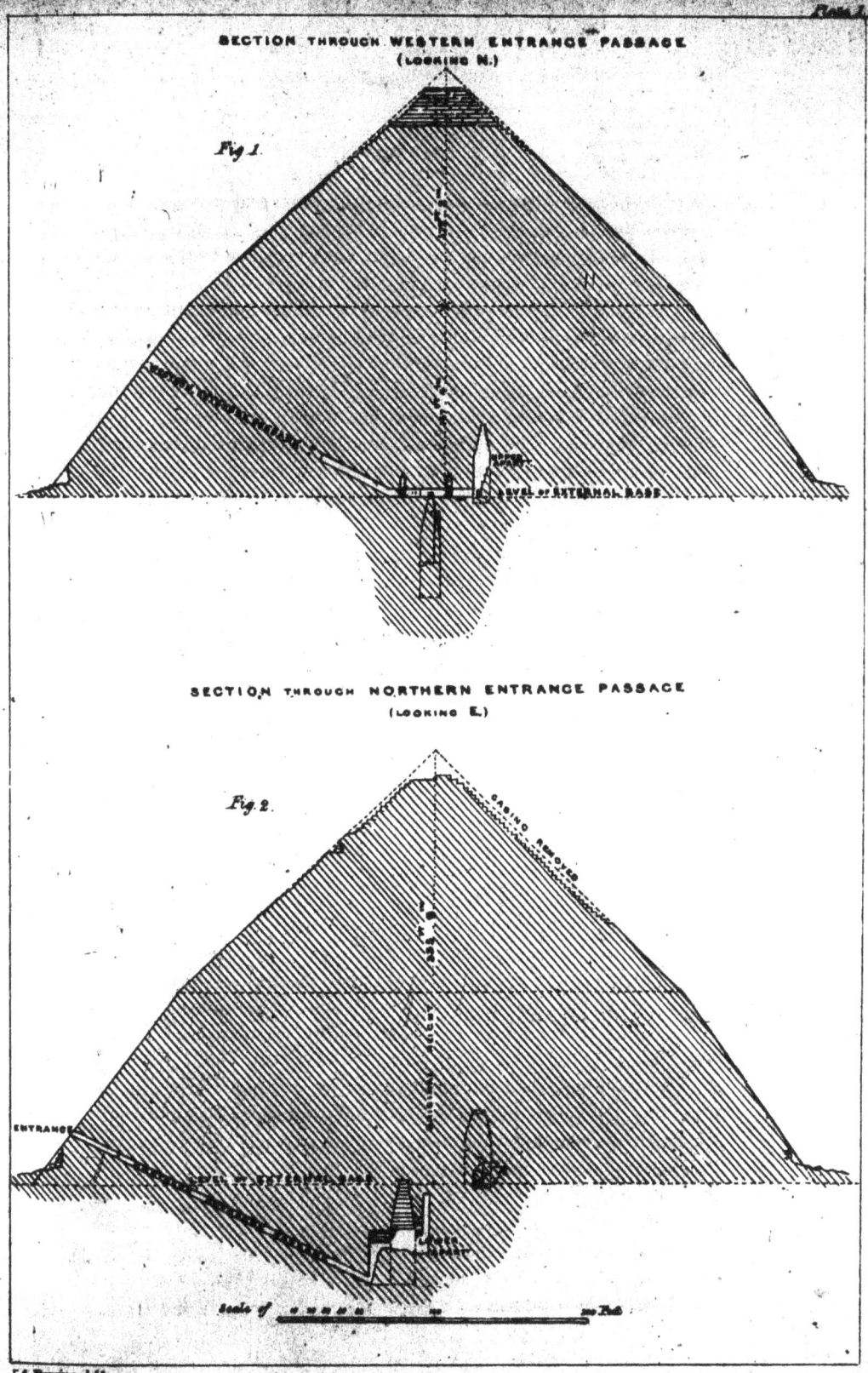

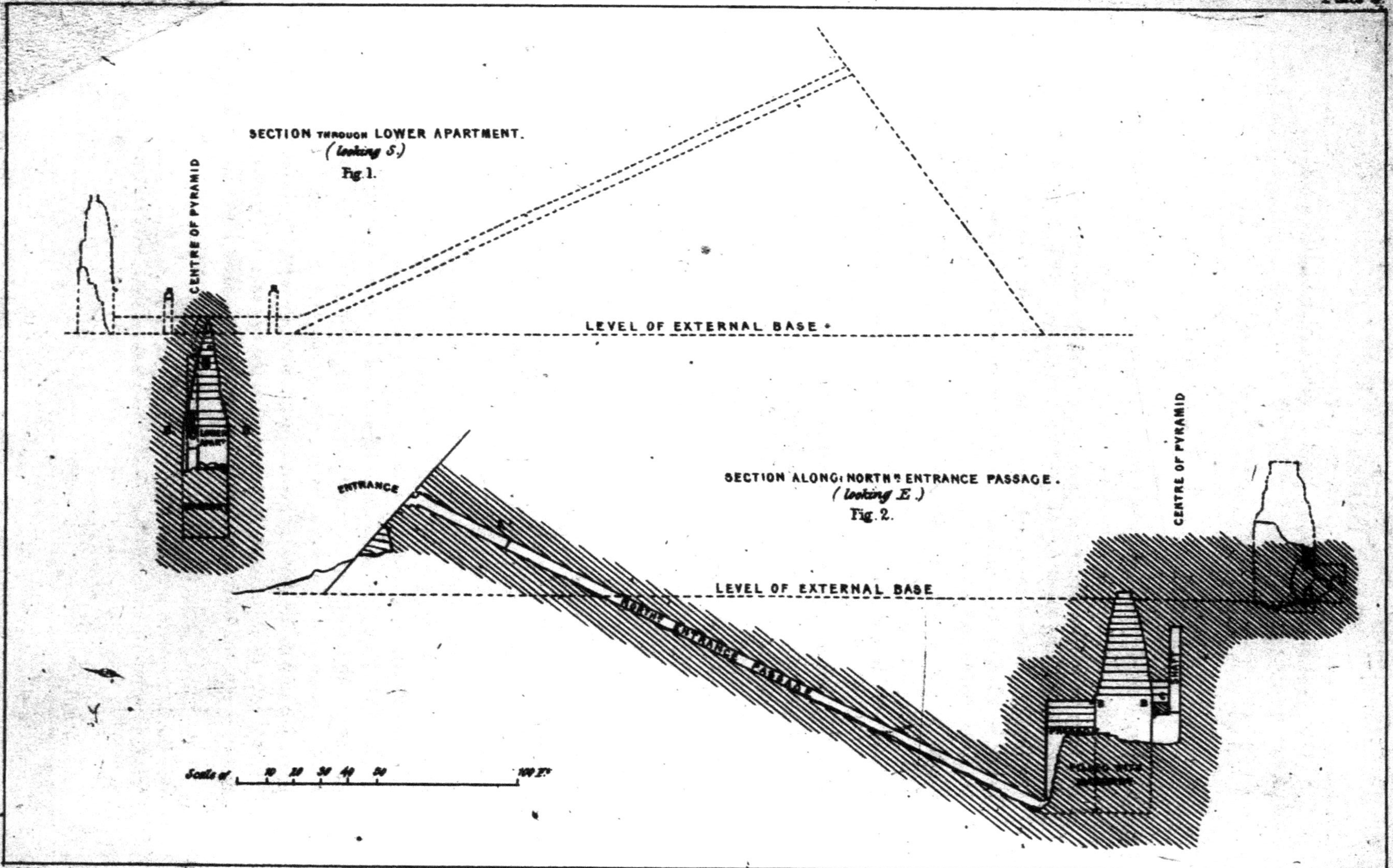
SECTION THROUGH LOWER APARTMENT.
(looking S.)
Fig. 1.
CENTRE OF PYRAMID
LEVEL OF EXTERNAL BASE
ENTRANCE
SECTION ALONG NORTHN ENTRANCE PASSAGE.
(looking E.)
Fig. 2.
CENTRE OF PYRAMID
LEVEL OF EXTERNAL BASE
NORTH ENTRANCE PASSAGE
Scale of 10 20 30 40 50 100 Ft.

J. S. Perring del:

SOUTHN STONE PYRAMID OF DASHOOR.

The original perpendicular height, if the casing had been completed, would have been 335 feet 9 inches.

Angle of the casing of the lower portion - 54° 14′ 46″
.. .. upper portion - 42° 59′ 26″
The platform at top is about 40 feet square.

Mr. Perring began to clear the passages on September 20th. There are two, and both of them are inclined. The one, which is open, is in the centre of the northern front, twelve courses above the present level of the ground, and 34 feet 10 inches perpendicularly higher than the base: it is difficult of access. The other is 44 feet 4 inches to the southward of the centre of the western front, and at a perpendicular height of 97 feet 8 inches above the base. It was discovered by Mr. Perring in October 1839, but it has not been opened. The first part of the northern passage, in length 41 feet 2 inches, at present descends at an angle of 28° 38′ on account of a settlement (shewn at A in the Section); but the original inclination was that of the remainder of the passage (26° 10′). Immediately at the entrance, the removal of the floor has increased the height of it to 5 feet 10 inches, but it is afterwards only 3 feet 5½ inches; the width is the same, and the total length is 256 feet 11 inches.

The Pyramid was entered in 1660, by Mr. Melton, an English traveller; and in 1680 by M. Le Brun, when a small apartment was discovered. It had also been visited by Mr. Pocock. It was examined by Mr. Davison, in 1763, by whom the passage was found to be blocked up. When Mr. Perring commenced his operations, it was only accessible to the length of 140 feet, and it had evidently been closed up intentionally, because stones detached from the upper part would have rolled over the mouth of the entrance; and because it was full of large stones, like those which are to be found in the adjacent desert. The removal of these obstructions has been said to have commenced on September 20th; but it could only be continued at intervals in consequence of the want of air, which on the 15th of October had nearly occasioned the work to be abandoned, when a rush of fresh air down the passage, consequent upon an opening being effected into the interior apartments, enabled the men to proceed, and in a few minutes to complete the operation.[7] The lower end

---

[7] Mr. Perring states that this current of air continued for two days, so that the lights could with difficulty be kept in. It would therefore appear that the apartments must have had some other communication with the outward air.

of the passage is horizontal for 2 feet 8 inches; after which, for 16 feet 2 inches, it is 40 feet 9 inches in height, and is constructed like the ascending gallery in the Great Pyramid of Gizeh. An apartment is then entered about 20 feet 6 inches in length, north and south, 16 feet 1 inch in width, and 80 feet in height. The walls are closed in on all sides, by the gradual projections of the fifteen upper courses, till the ceiling is about a foot wide. This is, probably, the apartment mentioned by Mr. Melton. It had been filled up with a masonry of small squared stones (see B B), to a level with the top of the passage, which had also been in like manner built up. This masonry had been partially removed, but it probably now conceals a sarcophagus, or the entrance to a secret apartment. The Pyramid, however, appeared to have been exposed to great violence, and many of the stones were broken; but the walls had not been blackened by smoke.

From another passage, 10 feet long, in the southern side of the room, and opposite to the entrance, is a shaft 42 feet 6 inches in height, which again communicates, by the opening C, with the apartment, at about half its height; but the shaft does not appear to be connected with any other place, unless it be continued downwards. Many of the stones in this apartment have given way under the superincumbent pressure, and the settlement must have taken place whilst the building was going on, because most of the faulty places have been covered over with plaster. After a great deal of trouble wood and ladders were introduced; and by means of a scaffolding the aperture on the southern side of the apartment was examined, from which a decayed cord formed of papyrus was suspended. The masonry was found to have been cut through, in order to connect the apartment with a horizontal passage, which communicated with the western entrance. (See Plate.) This cutting, 61 feet 8 inches in length, was not straight, nor regularly formed, but was slightly inclined upwards. The right-hand corner of the upper end (marked x) had been rounded, and a small recess had been cut out on the opposite side of the horizontal passage, apparently for the conveyance of a long solid body into the lower apartment.

The entrance from the western front of the Pyramid was by a passage 222 feet 8 inches long, 3 feet 4 inches wide, and 3 feet 4 inches high, and laid at an angle of 26° 36′. The greater part of it was closed up with large blocks, which had only been removed for about 60 feet at the lower end. The entrance on the outside of the Pyramid was so well concealed as to have escaped the closest examination, and the blocks within it appeared

SECTION OF WESTERN ENTRANCE PASSAGE
AND UPPER APART.T LOOKING S.
Fig. 1
LEVEL OF EXTERNAL BASE
W. ENTRANCE PASSAGE
PLAN OF WESTERN ENTRANCE PASSAGE &c.
Scale of 10 20 30 40 50 100 Feet
Fig. 2

J. S. Perring del.t

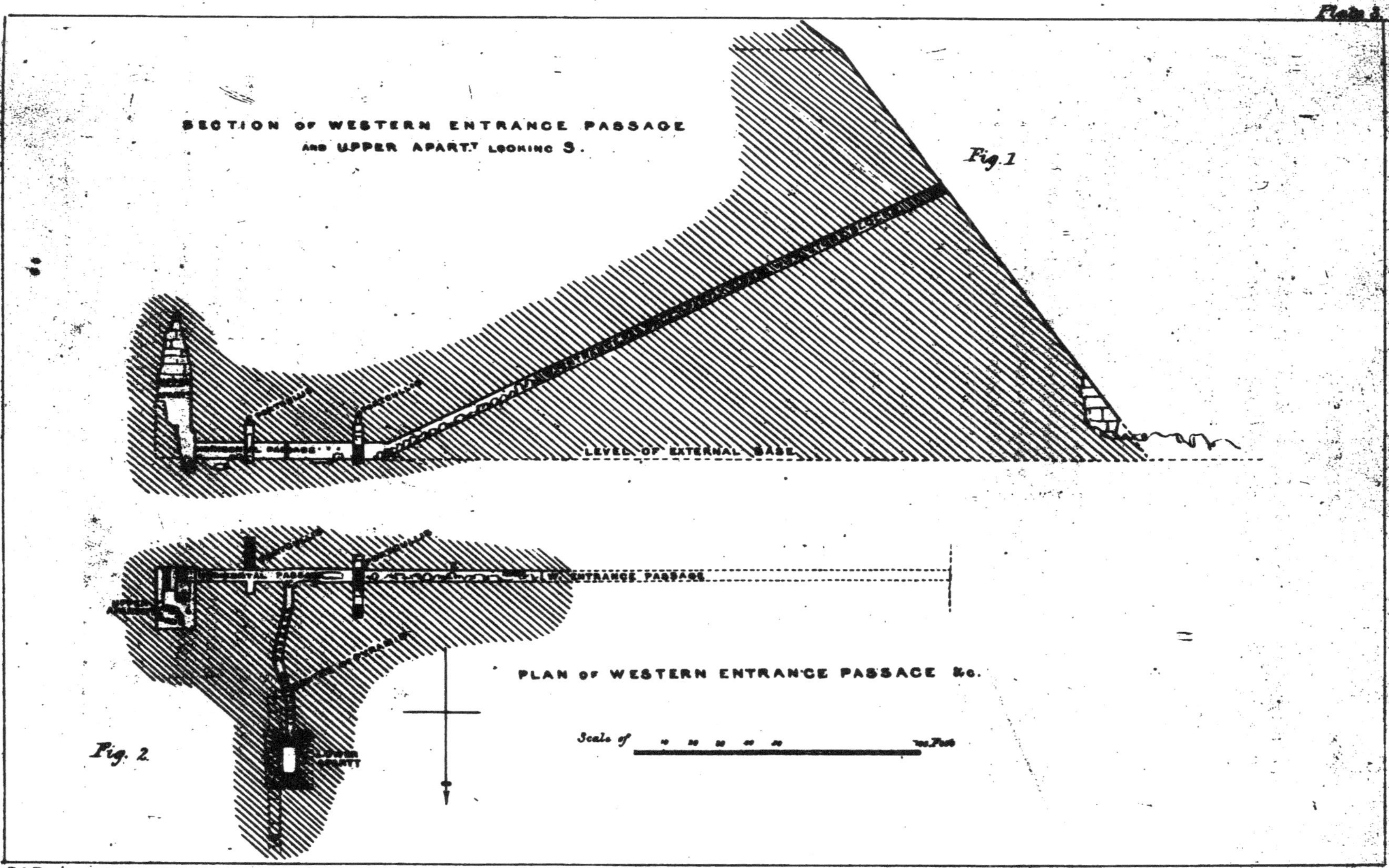

S. STONE PYRAMID OF DASHOOR.

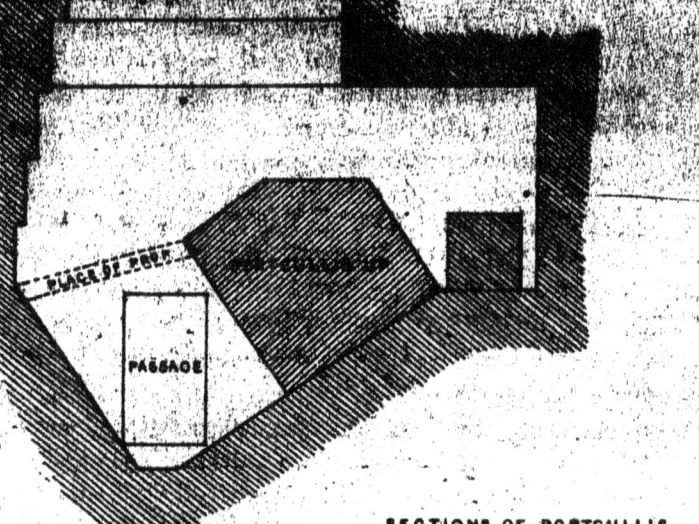

SECTIONS OF PORTCULLIS.

to have been fitted with the greatest accuracy. In one place, E, on the southern side of the passage, two upright pieces of wood had been let into a recess in the stone-work. The horizontal passage at the end of the incline was on a level with the base of the Pyramid. It was remarkably well constructed, and was 3 feet 4 inches wide, 5 feet 4 inches high, and 65 feet 6 inches in length. It contained two portcullises of a peculiar construction, see Plate, Figs. 1, 2, and 3. Fig. 1 shews the position of the slab, which, during the building of the Pyramid, had probably been propped up, and, upon the removal of the support had slid down the incline, and had closed the passage, as shewn in the other figures. This portcullis was found in its place, but the upper part had been broken away to allow of an entrance. The portcullis must have been let down when both of the entrance-passages were open, as it had been plastered on both sides. The eastern end of the horizontal passage communicated with an apartment 21 feet 6 inches long, 13 feet 6 inches wide, and 52 feet 6 inches high. It had been constructed like the other, and had been built up to a great height with small stones. An excavation had been carried on, to the length of about 12 feet, into this masonry near the floor, and the apartment had been entirely ruined. This is the only inclined entrance hitherto discovered in a Pyramid from any other quarter than from the north, for the passage from the southern front of the Pyramid of Saccara is horizontal; and it seemed to be the principal entrance, for the northern was constructed with inferior masonry, and had not the defence of a portcullis.

Fig. 4 represents some rude characters near the mouth of the northern entrance. In Sir J. G. Wilkinson's opinion, they were inscribed at a comparatively late period, in which case the passage must have been accessible when hieroglyphics were still in use; and according to Zoega, "De Obeliscis," that mode of writing, together with idolatry, gradually disappeared, when the Christian religion was introduced, about the third century. Cordage, and antient baskets formed of the papyrus, were found in the passages of this Pyramid; and the operations carried on at the Northern Brick Pyramid seem to prove, that in some instances, the Egyptians themselves broke open and destroyed these antient tombs.

Plate I. Fig. 1, is a vertical section of the Pyramid along the western entrance-passage, looking north.

Fig. 2. Ditto, along the northern entrance-passage, looking east.

Plate II. Figs. 1, 2, and 3. Details of portcullis, in the upper passage.

Fig. 4. Hieroglyphics in the northern entrance-passage.

Plate III. Fig. 1. Section along the western entrance-passage, and the upper apartment, discovered October 20th, 1839, looking south.

Fig. 2. Plan of ditto.

Plate IV. Fig. 1. Section of lower apartment.

Fig. 2. Section along the northern entrance-passage, looking east.

THE SMALL PYRAMID.

It is situated at the distance of 180 feet, and immediately opposite the centre of the southern face of the preceding one; and it is inclosed by the same peribolus.

It is built with roughly hewn blocks, and has had a casing of stone from the Mokattam, which is, however, destroyed.

	Original.	Present.
Base	181 ft. 0 in.	
Height	106 ft. 9 in.	68 ft.

Angle of Casing, 50° 11′ 41″
Platform at top, about 40 feet by 30 feet.

THE SOUTHERN BRICK PYRAMID.

It is called by the Arabs, "Haram é Sodah," the Black Pyramid, and is now much destroyed, as it has afforded materials for the houses and tombs of the neighbouring village of Mensheeh. Mr. Perring did not discover any traces of the chamber, the roof of which is stated by Dr. Richardson, and by others, to have fallen in; nor did he perceive any considerable settlement. It is built in the same manner, but not so carefully, as the other Brick Pyramid. The bricks contain a greater quantity of straw, and are of unequal sizes; from $15\frac{1}{2} \times 7\frac{3}{4} \times 5\frac{1}{2}$ to $13\frac{1}{2} \times 6\frac{1}{2} \times 4\frac{1}{2}$ each. Most of them have been made of rubbish, containing broken pottery and pieces of stones, like that which at present forms the mounds near the modern villages in the country. It might be supposed that this Pyramid was the one built by Asychis, as shells may be observed in some of the bricks, the upper surfaces of which are distinguished by various marks made with the fingers, of which the principal are

Mr. Perring was very anxious to discover the interior of one of the Brick Pyramids, but, on account of the vast quantity of sand and rubbish, which encumbered the base of this Pyramid, he did not venture to undertake the operation.

The ruin is at present about 400 feet square; but the original base did not, probably, exceed 350 feet.

Like the other Pyramids, it had been cased with stone from the Mokattam. One of the blocks had been worked to an angle of 57° 20′, which, although steep, in some degree corresponds with the present shape of the ruin; and Mr. Perring observes that the angle would depend on the position of the blocks, as one block gave an angle of 57° 25′, and therefore, that the beds of the blocks were no doubt differently inclined according to the shape of the building.

The remains of considerable buildings, composed of stone from the Djebel Achmah, near Cairo, and also a good deal of broken granite, are to be found near an inclined road, which proceeds from the eastern side of the Pyramid, towards the village.

	Feet.	Inches.
Original Base	342	6
Height, perpendicularly	267	4
Present Height	156	0

Angle of Casing, 57° 20′ 2″

The defeat of the Pasha's army in Syria rendered the country between Gizeh and the Faioum unsafe for travellers, and during his residence at Dashoor Mr. Perring's tents were attacked by a party of Bedouins. He was, however, well armed and prepared for their reception, and the Bedouins at length withdrew, without any other ill consequences, excepting the loss of a red cap, which they stole from an Arab, whom they rode over in their retreat.

NOTES BY MR. BIRCH.
THE NORTHERN BRICK PYRAMID.

These inscriptions were found upon blocks of calcareous stone, which had belonged to the propylæon erected before the northern front of the Pyramid. From the specimens sent by Mr. Perring to the British Museum, the hieroglyphics appear to have been executed with a purity of style, which distinguished the intervening period between the Memphite dynasty, and the expulsion of their successors to Abydos; and may on that account, without impropriety, be assigned to the era of Asychis, by whom the Pyramid has been by some persons supposed to have been built; but the fragments of a royal prenomen, discovered amongst the ruins, are too imperfect to admit of identification: and the other inscriptions are similar to those often found upon coeval sepulchral monuments, and do not possess any distinct peculiarity. It is, therefore, a point yet undetermined, which of the brick Pyramids at present existing is the work of Asychis. Considerable illustration of the general design of this propylæon is afforded by the sculptures on the propylæon of the Pyramid at Mount Birkel.[8]

The inscriptions are at all events sepulchral. They represent tables of provisions deposited as offerings to the dead; sacerdotal and other functionaries performing acts of adoration and of consecration; and officers of state presenting funeral gifts. Similar tables have been almost exclusively found upon monuments executed before, or during the seventeenth dynasty. Several have been discovered; those, upon the entrance of a tomb, in the possession of Signore Athanasi; upon the stele Anastasi, No. 36, in the British Museum; upon a rectangular sarcophagus, purchased of Mr. Sams, and now placed in the British Museum; and upon the sarcophagus of a person named Savaknaa, or Souchinaa, belonging to Signore Athanasi, may be cited as instances. No doubt can exist respecting the character of these offerings, because, in the beginning of the inscriptions over the tables upon Signore Athanasi's sarcophagus, the title "*Osirian (deceased)*," is inserted. It is to be remarked that, besides these tables of provisions, other articles, such as mirrors, collars, and their counterpoises,[9] bracelets, armlets, crowns, pillows, shentis, daggers, bows, arrows, and various kinds of sceptres, are sometimes inscribed, which do not appear upon the fragments from Dashoor.

The provisions are usually placed in baskets, by which they are counted, and the greatest number here appears to have been four.

---

[8] Caillaud (Fred.), "Voyage à Meroe," fol. Paris, 1823, Pl. LIII. LIV.

[9] By counterpoises are meant the objects shaped like this ⌓ or ⌓ worn behind, to counterbalance the collars or tippets of the Egyptian kings.

These tables are not seen upon tombs or stelæ coeval with the Pyramids of Gizeh, although the same articles of food are found in inscriptions of a later date.

The inscriptions at Dashoor appear, therefore, to shew that the Pyramid was constructed at a period intermediate between the dynasty, which built the Gizeh Pyramids, and their successors at Abydos, and at Thebes.

On a fragment, Fig. 6, chamberlains, and other officers in the service of the court, perform adoration, consecrate royal offerings, and carry various provisions; other processions, see Figs. 3, 4, 5, are composed of members of the family of the deceased, and of persons connected with his household, who bear articles of furniture and of food.[1]

Quarry-marks, in linear or hieratic characters, Figs. 1 and 2, have also been discovered; but, as they do not contain a royal name, they cannot establish the date of the building.

From Mr. Perring's account of the stone casing of these Pyramids, they may be supposed to have been constructed in imitation of the magnificent Tombs at Gizeh, and to have been formed with bricks on account of their comparative cheapness. This conjecture is more probable, because great political difficulties are said to have occurred in the time of Asychis. The manner in which the sculptures are executed, and the style of the hieroglyphics, although they do not afford a positive proof, yet seem to indicate that they belonged to a time prior to the sixteenth dynasty, and consequently, to the invasion of the Shepherd kings. Indeed, it may be remarked, that, immediately after that event, the Egyptian monarchs could not have possessed either resources, or leisure for the erection of such colossal structures; but that, on the contrary, affected either by want of power, or by change of taste, or of habit, instead of engaging in such gigantic undertakings, they were evidently contented with the elaborate detail, and finished embellishments, which decorate the interior of the excavated tombs in the Biban el Molook.

Fig. 3. The hieroglyphics, before the figure walking, signify his titles — ⲚⲀⲀ ⲤⲀⲢⲞⲚⲬ, "*the great house, the fabricator.*" During the reigns of the early dynasties, deceased persons were styled "*functionaries attached to the great house or palace;*" and this title occurs over a male figure in the Tomb of Trades, and is also seen on sculptures taken from another tomb at Gizeh, and now in the British Museum.

Fig. 5. The lines immediately above the figures express the numbers of the several objects in the baskets. The eatables presented upon the tables have been already mentioned. Other objects, although not clearly

---

[1] The female relations, including the ⲀⲖⲞⲞⲚⲈ, or nurse, are also frequently represented in sculptures executed under the sixteenth and seventeenth dynasties.

designed, are articles of food, such as a cake, the ribs and the shoulder of an animal, grapes, &c. represented in baskets; and the hieroglyphics, before the man dressed in the skin of a panther, signify "*a royal offering.*"[2] Behind him, and above another figure, holding in both his hands the roll of a manuscript, are the words ⲈⲂⲀⲒ, "*priest,*" and ⲤⲈⲖⲖⲤⲒ, "*approved minister, officer;*" and behind these figures a person is represented in a kneeling position, with one arm lifted up, and with the other placed upon his breast, as if in the act of adoration.[3] There is also an imperfect inscription, which has consisted of two lines.

Fig. 6 resembles No. 5. The inscription above the figures enumerates the number of the different offerings, and the termination of the table, in which the objects have been phonetically inserted.

Part of the same table occurs in the second division, with characters signifying "*water,*" or "*libations,*" and with another tropically employed to denote "*plants;*" which represents a young plant shooting from a clod of earth, and, as the symbol for "*all*" is beneath it, "*a basket filled with every young vegetable*" may be signified. In the next division a kneeling figure is apparently employed in grinding, and in the area are various articles of food, with their names; and amongst them are ⲈⲒⲔ, "*cordials or refreshments;*" ⲈⲖⲎⲖ, "*grapes;*" and a material called ϢⲦ or ϨⲦ.

Behind is the arm of a figure in the act of making a royal offering.

In the third division the flowers and buds of the lotus are placed upon an altar or stand, with a figure, like that in the second division. And in the area is an inscription in hieroglyphics:—ⲚⲞⲨⲦⲈ ⲰⲠⲦⲞⲨ, "*the divine bread,*" together with cakes of bread, the shoulders of victims, &c. In the next compartment an inscription expresses "*attached to the hall of audience,*" "*charged with the care of the great house,*" or "*palace;*" and below it a figure pours a libation from a vase into a cup held by another person, and in the area are inserted "*the gift of a libation,*" and two tables covered with offerings, consisting of waterfowls, vases, cakes of bread, onions, together with joints of meat.

The traces of two figures may also be made out, bearing, upon small trays or stands, different offerings; and before one is inscribed "*the architect;*" and before the other, two symbols, frequently found in family registers, apparently expressive of some relationship.

Fig. 7, A, is part of a cornice, taken from the upper part of the propylæon. It contains hieroglyphics, and also the insignia, which are

---

[2] A figure in a similar attitude occurs upon a stela of the seventeenth dynasty, in the British Museum; and upon it is inscribed—"*He makes a royal offering,*" or "*He performs an act of adoration.*" Champ. "Gram. Egypt." p. 66. And below is a star, which, besides other significations, as glory, adoration, &c. expresses the name of the god Siou, or Seb, Chronos.

[3] A similar figure is inscribed in the quarries at Tourah.

often inserted above the representations of deities. Below them is part of the starry heavens, and an inscription, containing " *the royal chief*," a title conferred upon the highest officers, and, in this instance, written in a more ample form than usual, and most probably accompanied by the figure of the person to whom it belonged. According to M. Rosellini, the phonetic group ⲡⲛⲉ is analogous to ⲡⲟⲛⲧⲩ, and indicates that the individual was young, and probably, also, that he belonged to the military caste. The same title was, however, frequently attributed to queens and princesses, and, when applied to men, was often accompanied, as in the present instance, with feminine attributes. Its exact meaning, however, is not ascertained.

Fig. 4 contains fragments of two compartments. In the upper, a man clothed with a shenti round his loins, inclines forward; and another holds in his right hand a club or scimitar, and in his left a bow. In the lower compartment, the sides of which have been ornamented with a border in a rectangular pattern, are traces of the starry heavens, and also of an inscription in hieroglyphics, of which, however, only one (the back of a chair) can be made out.

Fig. 8. Part of a royal prenomen appears in a horizontal line of hieroglyphics, but, unfortunately, the fragment contains little more than a quarter of the cartouche. Like that of Mencheres, it has evidently been composed of three groups of uplifted arms, of another symbol apparently rectangular, and of the disc of the sun, or of the hawk. From such imperfect remains, it is impossible to tell to what monarch the cartouche belongs, for it can scarcely be assigned to Mycerinus; and the only other cartouche, with which it can be compared, is a disputed reading.[4] It may also be remarked, that, from the position of the characters in the lower part of the cartouche, there was probably another symbol, besides the disc of the sun, and those, which are contained in this fragment; and in that case, it would be unlike any cartouche hitherto discovered. It may, however, from its general resemblance, be referred to the sixteenth or seventeenth dynasties.

Fig. 9. This fragment consists of the remains of two horizontal lines of hieroglyphics. In the upper, a bundle of papyrus, of an unusual shape; and in the lower, the phonetic symbols ⲥⲝⲧ may be traced, and also the figure of a child, with his hand to his mouth, and a peculiar branch, which forms the initial to the word ⲧⲧ, or ⲥⲟⲧⲧⲛ.[5]

Fig. 10. In this are represented the eatables commonly used in

---

[4] The one engraved in Rosellini, " Mon. Stor." Parte Prima, Tom. II. Tav. XV. 11; and Laborde, "Arabie Pétrée," Tab. Hier. It reads Ⲡⲉ or ⲉⲁⲡ ⳓ .... ⲕⲁ. The name accompanying it has been read Osterot. Rosellini, loc. cit.

[5] These two pieces are in the British Museum.

sepulchral offerings placed upon a table or stand in the presence of individuals of high rank. In the centre of the table are two vases, which, as they end in a point, like the antient amphoræ, are placed in small cylindrical stands. They are painted in different colours, to denote the materials of which they were formed; red for earthenware, green for bronze, and yellow for gold. These vessels may be supposed to have contained wines and other liquors. To the right of them are the haunch of a deer, coloured red; a goose, coloured yellow; a cake of bread, two bunches of grapes, and a basket of yellow figs.

THE SOUTHERN STONE PYRAMID.

Plate XV. Figs. 7 and 8, are hieroglyphics traced upon the sides of the northern entrance of the Southern Stone Pyramid at Dashoor; but they do not appear to have a reference to the original design of the building.

The inscription on the eastern wall, Fig. 7, seems to have been as follows:—

"*The bearer of the feather standard of the god Phtah, Periphtah justified, son of Penamoun justified.*" It is to be observed that the feather sometimes represents the feather standard, and that the above-mentioned title does not seem to have been used before the eighteenth dynasty, and then to have belonged to the officers of various kings, and also to the priests of Phtah, and of other gods.[6] The pat sceptre is usually put before the sceptre in the form of a feather, or of a fan; and, although it sometimes phonetically replaces the bird, as Ϥ or Π, yet, it is also frequently used as the determinative of the word ϣορπ, and apparently signifies "*to lead,*" or "*to precede.*"[7]

The meaning of the inscription upon the western wall, Fig. 8, is not so easily determined, on account of its imperfect state, and of its laconic style. It may, however, be remarked, that, if the first four characters are correctly copied, they express "*in all her tribunals;*" but that, if the third character, instead of representing the basket, neb, or nibi, "*all,*" be the symbol which may be found in Champ. "Gram. Egypt." p. 45, No. 219, it will, in conjunction with the fourth and fifth, represent the word ϩεмсι, "*to sit.*" The next symbol is a stream of water poured out from a vase upon a man's leg, and expresses ογλβ,

---

[6] Pedestal, British Museum, No. 42.
[7] Pap. Sallier, No. 2, *passim*. Peyron. Lex. Ling. Copt. voce.

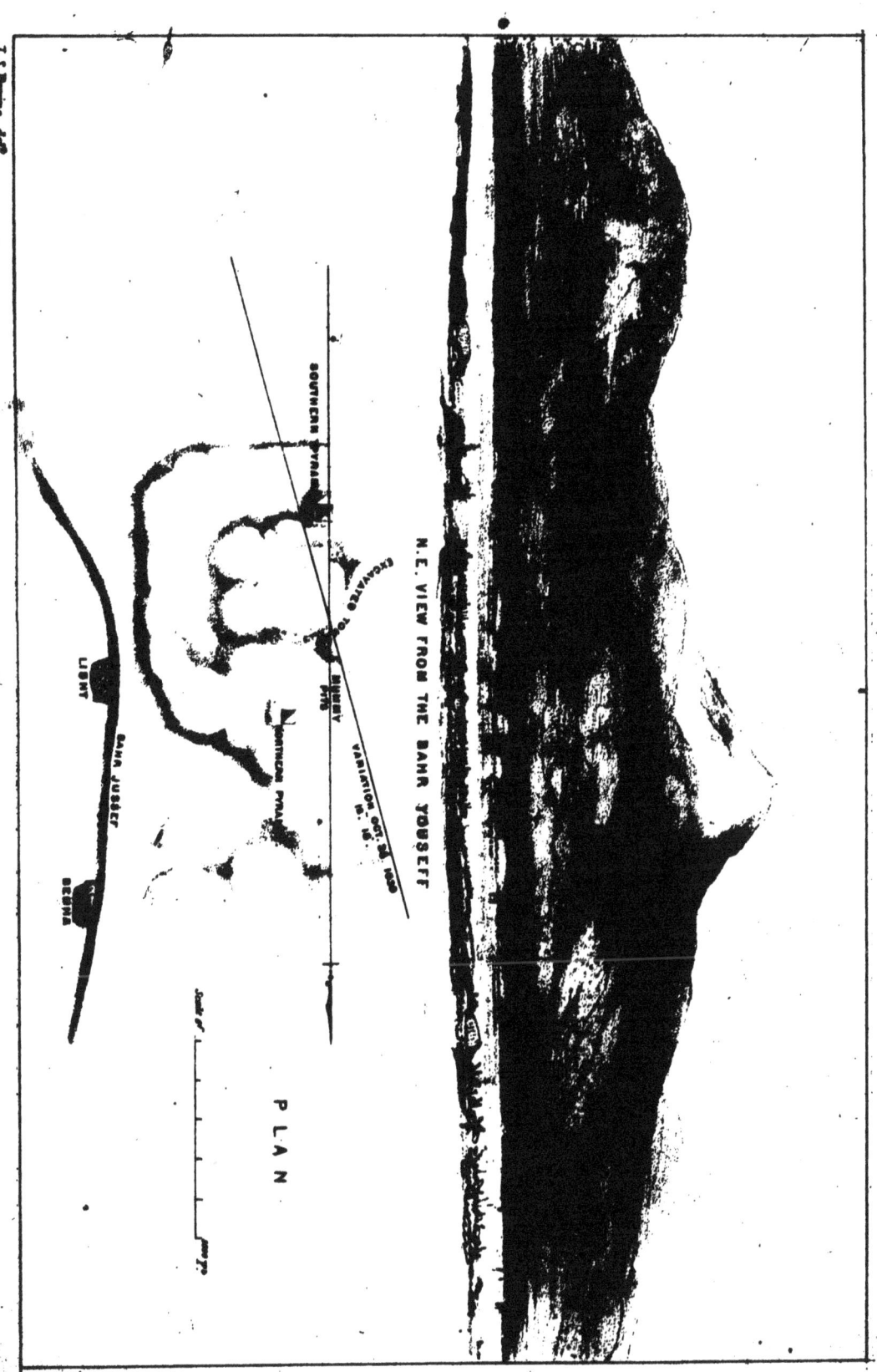

"*pure.*" It is followed by three undulating lines, a scarabæus, and the figure of a man sitting. Although the two lines are not connected, they seem to have been executed at the same time, and, from analogy, not to be more antient than the twenty-sixth dynasty; and if the line contains the unexplained titles used during the era of the Psammetichi and Ptolemies, it should precede Fig 7.[8]

The Pyramids in Ethiopia appear to be less antient than those of Gizeh, and many of the smaller were, probably, of a comparatively recent date, and were erected in imitation of the original buildings. These imperfect inscriptions cannot, however, be considered as a positive proof of the age of the edifice.

PYRAMIDS OF LISHT.

Mr. Perring went to Mensheeh on the 21st of October, to await the arrival of a guard from Cairo, which the disturbed state of the country made essentially necessary. On the 25th four soldiers arrived from Ali Bey, the sub-governor of Cairo, to say that Mr. Perring could not with any degree of safety proceed by land, even with a guard. He accordingly procured a boat, and leaving Mensheeh on the 27th, went across the inundation to Dashoor, round the northern and eastern sides of which place, the canal, known by the names El Bainhee, El Menhee, and Bahr Youseff, runs in a circuitous course, so as to avoid the site of the antient town. Beyond Barnasht the canal is evidently artificial, and marks the limits of the cultivated ground. Mr. Perring passed the night at Tahmé, whence the principal road crosses the Desert to the Faioum, a little to the northward of the Pyramids of Lisht, where Mr. Perring arrived about twelve o'clock on the 28th.

They are usually distinguished by this name by the Arabs, but they are also called the Pyramids of Metanyeh, or of Bemha. Metanyeh is about two miles and a half to the eastward; but Bemha,[9] although still farther off to the north-eastward, occupies an antient site, probably that of Peme, or Pemeau, and has, therefore, of the two, perhaps a better claim to the Pyramids.

---

[8] A figure dancing is also seen in titles upon Stèle, in the United Service Museum.

[9] This does not appear on the Map.

Both these monuments are entirely ruined. The space between them (rather more than a mile) contains excavated tombs and mummy-pits, most probably belonging to the antient cemetery; but neither sculpture nor hieroglyphics are to be observed near them.

In the Plate is a section of the Northern Pyramid. It is situated near a canal, and is placed upon an elevation of about 60 feet above the plain. Many of the blocks have been taken away to build a bridge at Tahmé, and their removal has disclosed its construction, which is very irregular, and consists of differently sized stones, put together with Nile earth instead of mortar, and arranged in walls of unequal thickness, so as to form steps or degrees (as in the Great Pyramid of Saccara); and over the whole a Pyramid appears to have been formed with bricks, and then covered with a stone casing.

	Feet.	Inches.
Present Base, about	360	0
Height	89	8

A section of the Southern Pyramid is also given. From having been built with a soft limestone, it has crumbled away until it has the appearance of a round hillock; and, in fact, many of the adjacent desert hills are much more pyramidal. It is, however, more advantageously placed, is larger, and has been constructed with greater masses of stone, and apparently with more care, than the Northern Pyramid.

	Feet.	Inches.
Present Base	450	0
Height	68	6

The view of these Pyramids was taken from the Bahr Youseff.

PYRAMID OF MEYDOOM.

On the 29th of October Mr. Perring sailed to the Pyramid of Meydoom, having been delayed by his boat getting aground on the ruins of a bridge, where the water ran with great force. The boat could not be got afloat without taking every thing out of it. Luckily a number of Arabs were upon the spot, but their assist-

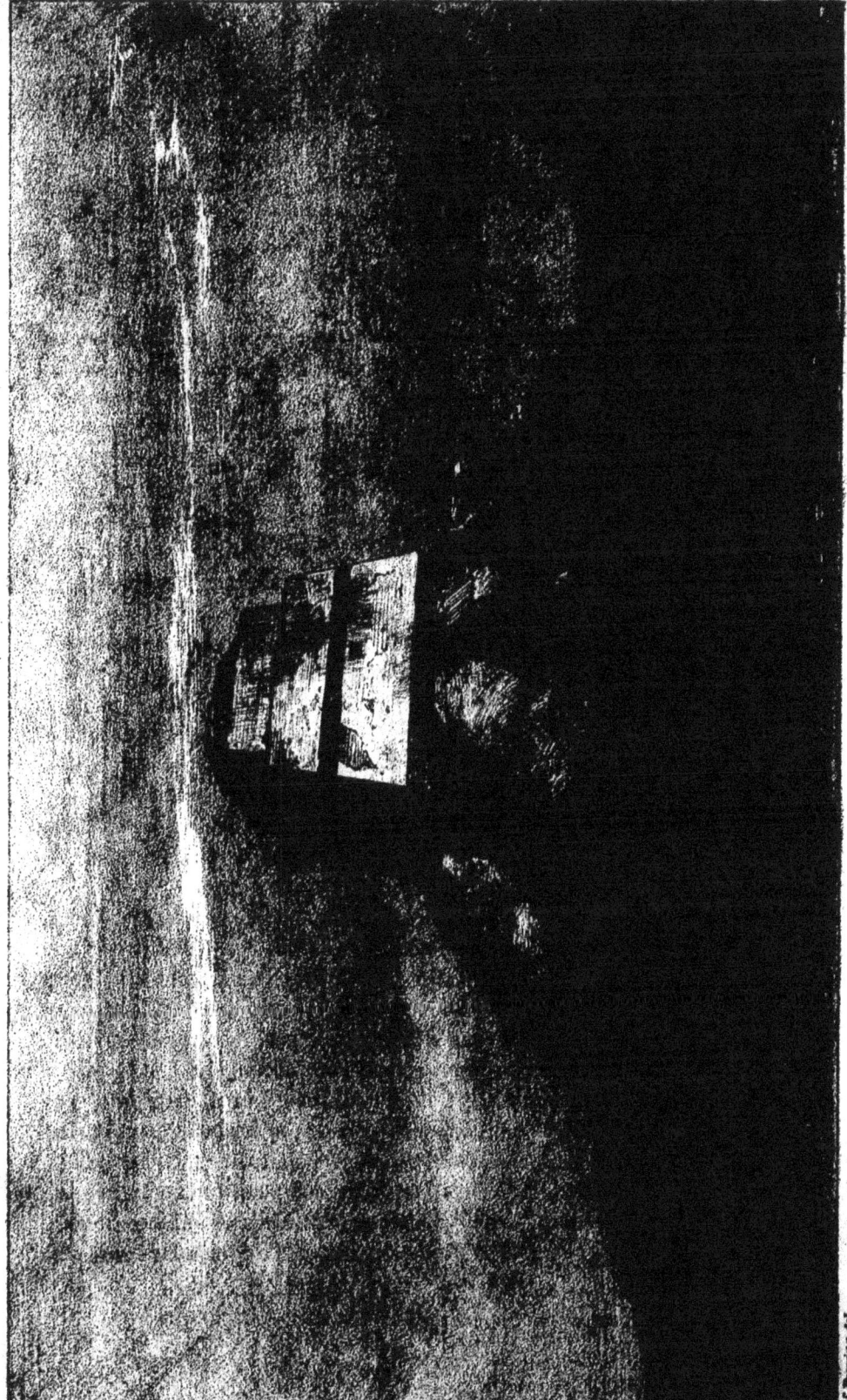

"S.E. VIEW OF THE PYRAMID OF MEYDOON, DURING THE INUNDATION."

ance could not be procured till a remuneration had been regularly settled. He could not, therefore, examine the Pyramid till the following day.

This monument is near the limits of the cultivated ground, and about two miles to the north-westward of the village, from which it takes its name.

The Plate shews its present appearance, which is peculiarly striking when seen from the river.

It is called the "False Pyramid," because the base is supposed to have been formed out of a knoll of rock, and it certainly has that appearance. To ascertain the fact two excavations were made, one at the north-eastern angle, and the other on the western side, but the rock was not discovered. Owing, however, to the want of assistance and of leisure, the operations were not satisfactorily concluded. The supposition, therefore, may be well founded, and the exterior only may consist of masonry, as a large tomb, near the north-eastern angle, is evidently constructed in that manner.

The base, about 530 feet square, is much encumbered with rubbish, and is at present of an irregular form. The superstructure is in three degrees, each having the form of a truncated Pyramid, with an angle of 74° 10'. The lower degree has a base of 199 feet, and is 69 feet 6 inches in height; the second, a base of about 127 feet, and is 32 feet 6 inches in height; the third, or upper degree, is entirely ruined, and is at present only about 22 feet 6 inches high. The actual height of the Pyramid is, therefore, about 124 feet 6 inches.[1]

The blocks consist of compact limestone, are about 2 feet thick, and must have been brought from a considerable distance. They are laid at right angles to the external face, and have been worked, and put together with great skill; indeed, the excavation made by the removal of the stone for the bridge at Tahmé, shews that the masonry is of a superior description, and that it has been continued into the mound, upon which the edifice is built. The whole has probably been covered with large unsquared blocks, so as to complete the shape of a regular Pyramid.

On many of the stones, writing in red ochre may be traced, but it is in general scarcely legible. The characters here given, however, were observed in two places. The entrance was not

---

[1] Accidentally inserted in the Plate, 224 feet 6 inches.

discovered, but previous attempts in search of it were evident, as the rubbish had been removed from the centre of the base of the northern front, into heaps on either side. The smooth surface, and steepness of the building rendered an ascent to the summit impracticable without artificial assistance.

There had been a peribolus of stone masonry, and near the north-eastern angle a large tomb had been constructed on a knoll of rock.

About a mile to the northward were other ruins, apparently of tombs, which had been supposed by the French[a] to be the remains of Pyramids; but their oblong shape, and the nature of the materials (small crude bricks) of which they were composed, did not support the supposition.

PYRAMID OF ILLAHOON.

Having finished the Pyramid at Meydoom, Mr. Perring proceeded to the southward, and in doing so his boat again grounded, and was obliged to be unladen before it could be hauled over a bank. On the 31st of October he met with the Gebalee, a powerful tribe of the Bedouins. The sheik was absent, but his son received him hospitably, offered a house, and sent down large trays, containing a roasted lamb, wheaten bread, stewed dates, and abundance of other provisions. Mr. Perring was informed that the Bedouins had agreed with the Pasha to remain tranquil, and to furnish a body of cavalry, upon consideration of an annual payment, and of permission to occupy productive ground at a very small yearly rent.

The tribe appeared to have availed itself largely of this privilege, and to have taken possession of a considerable quantity of ground, which afforded a refuge to the Fellahs, or stationary Arabs, who had escaped from the adjacent country, for fear of conscription, or on other accounts. These Fellahs, however, appeared to be better satisfied under the authority of the Bedouins, than under that of their native sheiks,—possibly from the effect of change. From twenty to thirty of them were em-

---

[a] "Description of Egypt," Vol. IV. Chap. xvi. Sect. 3.

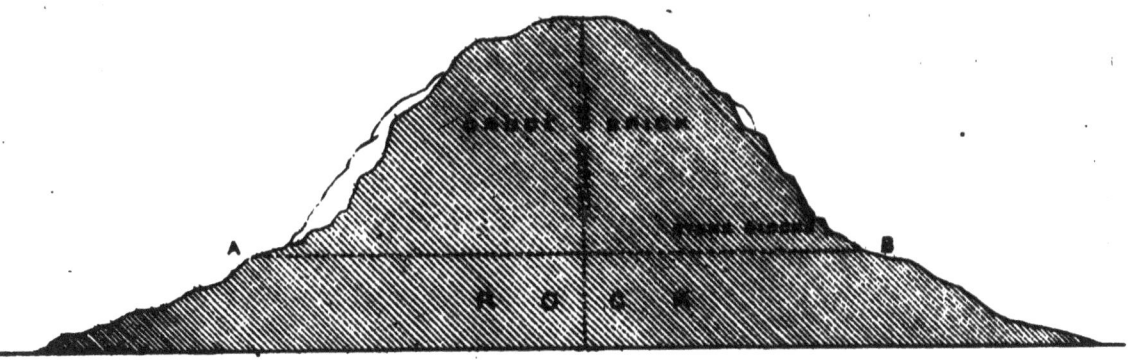

SECTION LOOKING WEST.

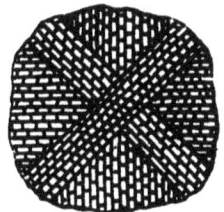

ARRANGEMENT OF BRICKS IN CENTRE

PLAN. THROUGH A B.

J. S. Perring, delt.

PYRAMID OF ILLAHOON.

ployed in cultivating the ground, with wooden hoes, under the direction of a single Bedouin, like blacks under a slave-driver.

The boat was drawn over a bank into a canal, and arrived opposite the Pyramid of Illahoon on Nov. 1st. This building is situated about two miles to the northward of the village, and at no great distance from the cultivated plains, which extend to the banks of the river. It is also near the commencement of a strip of land, along which the principal road passes to the Faioum, and which is rendered productive by the admission of water through a lock, erected about five or six years since, apparently upon antient foundations. The arrangements of the water at this place, and particularly those at the Lake Mœris, are important, because they regulate the inundation of the whole country. The water is brought down by the Bahr Youseff; and by means of a sluice, the remains of which are visible near the entrance of the canal, the current was originally turned through a lock, and through several smal sluices to the westward of it, into the Faioum. A bank or dyke, composed of antient masonry, and now called Gisr e Sultanee, confined the inundation between the river and the mountain, and was furnished with various small sluices, for the occasional passage of the water, necessary for the cultivation of the country below it; by which means, the water could be regulated with the greatest accuracy, and the dangers, which might have resulted from an accidental failure in a larger work, were avoided.

The Pyramid is built round a knoll of rock, which is nearly 40 feet higher than the base. The rock towards the base has been faced with crude bricks, and a superstructure has been erected above it, composed of the same material, and supported by walls of stone, which proceed from the centre of the edifice, and which, until they are minutely examined, have the appearance of masses of rock. (See Plate.)

The Plate also shews the mode of construction. The bricks are laid in a mortar formed of Nile earth, as high as the walls extend, and above them in dry gravel. They measure $16\frac{3}{8}$ by $8\frac{3}{8}$, and about $5\frac{1}{4}$ inches in thickness; are well worked, and are formed of Nile earth, mixed up with various proportions of chopped straw. They have also been marked with the fingers on the upper surface, in the same manner as those in the ruins at Dashoor.

The Pyramid has had an external casing of stone, and also

a peribolus of the same material. There are mummy-pits in the adjacent ground, and grottoes amongst the desert hills,[a] which, in Mr. Perring's opinion, formed part of the cemetery of Ptolemais. The Pyramid of Howara is visible, but does not appear to have had any relative connection with this building.

Present Base, about - - - 360 feet.
Height - - - - 130 feet.

The view in the accompanying Plate is taken from the Bahr Youseff.

PYRAMID OF HOWARA.

On the following day Mr. Perring proceeded to Medeénet el Faioum by the Bahr Youseff, which is also called Bahr el Faioum. It is from 80 to 120 feet in breadth; but near the village of Howara el Gusab it flows in a narrow channel, which has been cut through the rock, and at one place is of small dimensions, adapted for the application of a bridge, or else of a sluice, by which the waters may have been directed into an adjacent ravine, which Mr. Perring supposes to be the canal, called by Pliny "Fossa Grandis," and said by Strabo to have been connected with the lake. A large village occupies the northern bank of the ravine, which near Howara el Gusab is crossed by a bridge of ten Roman arches; the arches are, however, built up with masonry. The bottom of the ravine contains a small stream, and is also covered with a grove of palm-trees, which proves that for many years past no great body of water can have flowed through it.

The actual distance from the village of El Gusab to the Pyramid of Howara, is a mile and half; but, owing to the inundation, Mr. Perring found the road extremely intricate, and nearly four miles in length; and he had great difficulty in obtaining a guide.

The Pyramid is situated on a desert plain (bounded by the above-mentioned ravine, which connects the Bahr Youseff with

---

[a] These grottoes, when partially examined in 1837, appeared to be natural, and not to have been worked, or used as places of sepulture. (See "Operations carried on at Gizeh," Vol. I. p. 10.)

VIEW OF THE RUINS AT BIAHHMOO.

VIEW OF THE PYRAMID OF HOWARA.

J. S. Perring, delt.

the lake), near the spot where the Faioum may be said to begin, and at the termination of the strip of land, near the other end of which the Pyramid of Illahoon is built.

The Pyramid of Howara is constructed with crude bricks, which contain much straw, measure $17\frac{1}{2} \times 8\frac{3}{4} \times 5\frac{1}{4}$, and are laid in fine gravel. The remains of a stone casing are to be seen near the base, but it has been entirely removed. On the northern front is a large chasm, supposed to have been made about the year 1815 by a M. Jaques Riffaud, in search of an entrance; and several small buildings have been constructed with the bricks, which have been taken down.

In the great French work an account is given of the discovery of an interior apartment, but it appears to want confirmation.

The state of the country, and other causes, prevented a more exact examination of this monument.

Present Base, about - - -   300 feet.
Height - - - - 106 feet.

The ruins of extensive buildings (by some people supposed to have been the famous Labyrinth) are to be seen to the southward of this Pyramid. They occupy a space of about 800 × 500 feet; but they were, perhaps, originally of greater extent, as they seem to have been intersected by the above-mentioned canal. This space is covered with large fragments of compact limestone, which bear a high polish, and also with broken columns and capitals of granite, executed in the best style of Egyptian art. See "Thebes, and General View of Egypt," p. 355.

In the Plate is a plan of the ruins, and a vertical section of the Pyramid.

The Governor of Medeénet offered to receive Mr. Perring in his house, but he preferred the accommodation of a tent. It was pitched near the house, and owing to the unsettled state of the country, a guard was constantly necessary.

PYRAMIDS OF BIAHHMOO.

These remains are about five miles from Medeénet el Faioum, and about half a mile from the village of Biahhmoo. They consist of two masses about 30 feet in height, and in length and breadth about 30 feet by 22, and likewise of a few smaller heaps, of well-constructed masonry composed of large blocks of compact limestone.

A plan is given in the Plate. The original bases appear to have been squares of about 120 feet, with a space of the same dimensions between them; and, at the height of about 4 feet 6 inches, Pyramids, 114 feet square, seem to have been erected upon them.

The inclination of the sides was 63° 30′, and the appearance of the building when complete, is shewn in the section. (See Plate.)

According to Pocock, and to other writers, these ruins were formerly called by the people of the country, "Rigl Faraoon" (the Legs of Pharaoh); but that name is not at present known, and the ruins are styled "El Senem" (the Statue), or "Mustahmel" (the Bathed); and Mr. Perring imagines, that, as antient names and traditions were probably preserved in the secluded province of the Faioum, long after the occupation of the rest of the country by the Mahometans, these names indicate that the ruins mark the site of the Pyramids described by Herodotus (B. II. c. 149) to have been surmounted by colossal statues, and that the Pyramids were not built in the Lake, but in the waters of the inundation; for he saw near Senhoris the artificial dyke, which M. Linant had observed, and which was evidently intended to retain the waters, notwithstanding the elevation of the ground above the level of the lake; and indeed he considers that the exaggerated accounts of Herodotus respecting the lake itself, may in this manner be accounted for. He also remarks, that Sir J. G. Wilkinson appears to be of the same opinion ("Thebes, and General View of Egypt," p. 354); and at all events, that these are the only remains, which in any degree answer the description of the antient author.

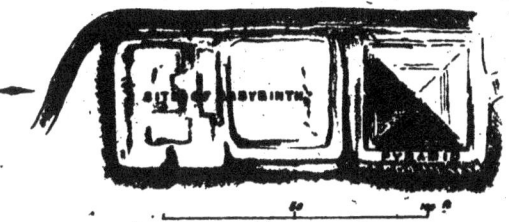

SECTION LOOKING N

PLAN OF RUINS.

PYRAMID OF HOWARA.

SECTION OF PYRAMID
PRESENT   SURFACE

PLAN OF THE
PYRAMIDS OF BIAHMOO

THE BIRKET KHAROON.

Mr. Perring proceeded to the Birket Kharoon, which he believes to have been the Lake Mœris, and he employed the four following days in visiting the lake; and the other parts of the Faioum. Wretched as he had found the general condition of the people of Egypt, he was surprised at the miserable state of this once most fertile province. Out of sixty-six villages, twenty had been entirely deserted within the last two years. Cultivation was carried on by forced labour, and the distress naturally increased in proportion as the population diminished. The repairs of the dykes and canals, essentially necessary for the cultivation of the country, depended on the same means, and were consequently so much neglected, that in less than twenty years the province would probably be either a desert or a marsh. The soil, an extremely fertile loom, is capable of constant irrigation, and, by its position, is completely sheltered; but, notwithstanding these great advantages, and the fineness of the climate, the cultivation is carried on, as has already been observed, by compulsion, and the inhabitants are not only exposed to the conscriptions and levies of the government, and to the tyranny and extortion of each individual sheik, but also to the depredations of the wandering Bedouins, who turn their cattle into the crops, live at free quarters amongst the villages without distinction, and who were prevented from laying waste the country only by the authority of the Pasha. (See Vol. I. p. 131.)

PYRAMID OF EL KOOFA.

In lat. 25° 10′, near the village of Bisaleh, between Esneh and Edfoo, is a Pyramid called "El Koofa." It stands upon a mountain, at the verge of the cultivated land, and about two miles from the river. The present base is 59 feet 6 inches square, and it does not appear to have been much larger. Twenty-seven courses of blocks, built in three stories or degrees, remain, and are 38 feet 6 inches in height above the rock which forms the base. The stones composing it have been taken from the adjoining mountain, and consist principally of petrifactions: they are small, and have been roughly hewn into a quadrangular form.

Several pyramidal structures have also been found amongst the tombs in the western mountains of Thebes. (See Vol. I. p. 91.)

THE MUMMY-PITS AT SACCARA.

MANY of these pits are entered by shafts in sepulchral apartments, excavated in the eastern side of the rock, upon which the Pyramids are placed, and which has supplied the greater part of the building materials; the apartments are frequently connected by doorways, and have been adorned with painted hieroglyphics, and with sculpture, now, however, much defaced, but still retaining this cartouche [4] ⟨cartouche⟩

In other instances the shafts, from 20 to 80 or 100 feet in depth, are sunk in the ground, which is covered with bones, broken pottery, rags, and the remains of mummies, and of their cases. The shafts communicate, at various depths, with sepulchral chambers, in the largest of which, and frequently in a recess, a sarcophagus is generally found, which, from its position, size, and peculiar decorations, may be supposed to have contained the body of the individual, for whom the pit was excavated; the different members of his family having been also deposited in sarcophagi, whilst the other chambers are filled with the remains of persons apparently of less consequence, but evidently of various ranks, because some of them are only wrapped in linen bandages, and piled up in heaps; and others are carefully placed in wooden coffins, or in cases formed of layers of linen cloth stuck together with glue.

It would appear, by Mr. Grey's papyrus now in the British Museum, that tombs were sold, and that money was paid for interment, and for the performance of funereal rites.

Notwithstanding the prohibition of the Pacha, many of the

---

[4] Mr. Perring is of opinion that considerable information respecting the antient dynasties might be obtained by a careful examination of the hieroglyphics in the tombs at this place, and at Gizeh. He conceives that the superior antiquity of the Pyramids of Gizeh is proved by the total absence of the hieratic character, and in the use alone of hieroglyphics in the quarry-marks.

He was anxious to discover whether pyramids were restricted to the tombs of monarchs, or whether they were sometimes appropriated to those of their subjects, and observes that he found in two tombs to the southward of the seventh, eighth, and ninth Pyramids at Gizeh, a representation of the end of a sarcophagus closed with a lid, which resembled the sarcophagus found in the Third Pyramid. The hieroglyphics were indistinct, but he discovered this cartouche ⟨cartouche⟩, which has been given by Sir J. G. Wilkinson. ("Manners and Customs of the Antient Egyptians," Vol. III. p. 280.)

inhabitants of the villages near Saccara are frequently employed in collecting the various antiquities deposited in these pits. Small articles of gold are sometimes found on bodies enclosed in sarcophagi; but on those in wooden coffins the ornaments are composed of stone, or of earthenware; and, indeed, from mummies less carefully prepared two or three scarabæi are only obtained. According to Sir J. G. Wilkinson, the idols of Phtah Sakari[5] (stated by Herodotus to have been the peculiar deity of Memphis) are exclusively found in the tombs at this place, and at Gizeh. The other articles consist of small figures, of vases, of scarabæi, and of amulets composed of various materials, and workmanship according to the rank of the deceased. Models of furniture, arms, and papyri, which are frequently found in the tombs at Thebes, are sometimes discovered at Saccara; and, as these objects are inclosed within the linen wrappers, frequently about the chest of the mummies, the bodies are always broken up in search of them, and of the gums, and resinous substances used in the process of embalmment, which are now sometimes esteemed to be medicines, and which were formerly in great repute.

The catacombs containing the birds are entered by the shafts, A, B, and C, in the Map, of which A and B were open, but the most considerable, C, was closed up. The mummies are deposited in galleries irregularly excavated in the rock, if that term can be applied to a soil composed of indurated clay and of shale; and the material, which was removed, was no doubt ground up, and employed in the manufacture of the coarse vases, which contain the birds. They are of a conical shape, rounded at the ends, and usually contain the mummy of an ibis,[6] wrapped up in

---

[5] From which Mr. Salt derives the name of Saccara.

[6] Mr. Perring observes, that in Egypt the Ibis was a sacred emblem of the god Thoth, who, as the regulator and dispenser of time, had a reference to the influences and phases of the moon; that, according to Plutarch, the Ibis was adored on account of a fancied relation between the blended tints of its plumage and the appearance of the moon. He adds, that Diodorus Siculus described Thoth to have been the inventor of calculation, of numbers, and of letters; and that, upon the authority of Ælian, the Ibis was sacred to Thoth because its steps were exactly a cubit in length. He also remarks that Thoth is denoted in hieroglyphics by an Ibis; and that Hermes, likewise supposed to have been the inventor of letters and of figures, and the teacher of wisdom, is styled Ibiform. Mr. Perring considers that Herodotus is mistaken when he asserts that all the mummies of the Ibis were preserved at Hermopolis, although it is probable that some may have been collected in that nome, as in the "Itin. Anton." an Ibium is stated to have been situated thirty miles distant from Oxyrynchus, and twenty-four from Hermopolis.

various ways; some being merely tied up in a linen rag, whilst others are carefully bandaged, as is well described in the plates of the great French work.[7]

Jars of earthenware, containing eggs, beetles, and, in a few instances embalmed snakes are concealed under heaps of sand near the shafts. The snakes had not been very carefully preserved. They appeared to Mr. Perring to be either the cerastes, said by Herodotus (B. II. c. 74) to have been consecrated to Ammon, or the species sacred to Knef, and emblematic of royalty. Most of the beetles were about 1½ inch long (scarabæus sacer), considered to be the mysterious emblem of Phtah, or Vulcan: the species is not at present generally found in Egypt, although it is common in the more southern countries. Upon some of the jars, which contained eggs, Mr. Perring observed hieratic inscriptions in black characters. The jars varied in shape, and also considerably in size, as they were calculated to contain from one to six hundred eggs. They had been closed up with a linen cloth, fastened by a string, or with a covering of clay; the impression of a seal, however, was not observed. The eggs belonged principally to geese, and in almost every instance they contained birds just ready to break the shell. They appeared to have been preserved by means of bitumen: some had been separately wrapped up in a piece of linen, and others were placed in ashes. Mr. Perring conceived that they were offerings to the deities in order

---

[7] These pits were examined on the 15th of January, 1836, by climbing over the layers of vases, with which the galleries were filled nearly to the top. The extent of the excavations was surprising, as was also the immense number of the vases, which were laid in rows, with the large and small ends in alternate directions, so as to form a solid mass of unknown extent, and to all appearance of the same antiquity. The means, by which this extraordinary collection could have been made, is therefore as surprising as the motive which induced it. It has been already said that, with few exceptions, each vase contains an Ibis. The bird is not at present to be found in Egypt, although it is to be met with higher up the river; but such astonishing numbers, even if the bird had been common, the whole country could hardly have afforded, unless the breed was particularly attended to, and preserved. For although the pits were probably open in the time of the Romans, and even in that of Cambyses, and have been exposed to continual and unlimited depredation, yet the vases seem comparatively undiminished, and inexhaustible. It is also remarkable, that, from the various ways, in which the birds are inserted in the vases, they appear to have been held in veneration by all ranks of people. In examining the contents of a number of these vases, which were brought up from the shafts, in one near a sarcophagus a hawk was found, of which the beak and legs, and also the feathers upon the thick part of the wings were perfect.

to insure the increase of the flocks, and that they had been deposited in these places on account of the sanctity of the tombs.

Under other heaps of sand, at no great distance from the former, together with jars containing eggs, a quantity of sea sand, and of ashes had been placed, and also small parcels of natron tied up in linen: natron is also found in the tombs.

At D is the entrance to other catacombs. They also consist of galleries, on each side of which the bones of oxen are placed in wrappers, with the heads upon them: the remains, probably, of sacrifices, which seems to correspond with the account given by Herodotus.[a]

The entrance to the catacombs, where the mummies of dogs were deposited, is marked by E, but most of them had been destroyed apparently by fire, which, upon the authority of Plutarch, Mr. Perring supposes to have taken place in consequence of the sacrilegious attack made by the dogs on the entrails of the bull Apis, after he was slain by Cambyses.

The catacomb containing the mummies of cats is at H in the Map, and many fragments of them were scattered about the entrance. The cats were sacred to Bubastes (the Diana of Memphis), and their remains were consequently preserved with great care. These mummies are covered with fur, well preserved, and of a red colour — the effect, probably, of the embalmment. Bronze images of cats were found in the bandages, which had been very carefully applied. This Mr. Perring considers to agree with the antient account of the high estimation, in which these animals were held. He adds, that, as their mummies are to be found at this place, at Thebes, and at Beni Hassan, the account of Herodotus, which states that they were only entombed at Bubastes, is not to be trusted.

---

[a] Mr. Perring observes, that in the sands at this place the bones of sheep were found intermixed with those belonging to oxen, but that the remains of those animals were not found in the catacombs; and he conceives that this agrees with the tradition that sheep were not held in peculiar adoration at Memphis. He adds, that the heads of sheep are found in almost every mummy-pit, and he supposes that the heads of the animals killed for food were so disposed of, because Herodotus says that the inhabitants did not eat them, and because it was not likely that the Egyptians would defile the sacred waters of the Nile (the only fresh water in the country) by throwing into them the heads of slaughtered animals, professedly held to be unclean. The imprecations stated by Herodotus to have been pronounced upon the heads of animals, in Mr. Perring's opinion, applied only to those, which had been sacrificed.

DISCOVERIES AT TOURAH.

The following account is drawn up from a letter received from Mr. Perring, and dated September 14th, 1838.

The sarcophagi, and other antiquities were chiefly excavated from a range of sand-hills, or, rather, from a bank of sand, which begins near the village of Massara, and extends about half a mile beyond Tourah. It skirts a narrow slip of cultivated land at the edge of the desert, and, as it corresponds in length with the antient quarries, it was no doubt the cemetery of the people employed in them. The length of it was about two miles, and it was only interrupted by the village of Tourah, and in one or two other places by roads leading from the quarries to the river, till it was cut into by Mr. Perring in carrying on the level, and in searching for materials for the construction of a railroad, which was made by the orders of the Pasha, for the conveyance of stone to the river.

When the antiquities in question were first discovered, Mr. Perring imagined that they might lead to important results respecting the history of the Shepherd Kings, because the cartouche of Amenophis, who, acccording to Manetho, reigned soon after the expulsion of the shepherds from Egypt, is inscribed in one of the quarries.[9]

Mr. Perring was not at the time resident at Tourah, he therefore requested his friend, Mr. Holroyd, who was living upon the spot, to attend to the discoveries; and the following details are the substance of a communication from Mr. Holroyd, dated Dec. 23d, 1837:—

One hundred and fifty sarcophagi were found: they were composed of compact limestone. Most of them were perfect, and were closed with lids.[1] They did not afford any inscriptions, and were evidently in their original positions, but in

---

[9] See Josephus against Apion.

[1] The lids were not fastened, but were let into a recess, as is shewn in the annexed figure:—

VIEW OF THE TOURAH QUARRIES.

J.S. Perring, del?

TOURAH QUARRIES. (View of the Interior.)

various directions, chiefly north and south. The cavities of fourteen of the sarcophagi were rectangular, one was in this shape, and five in this, Several of them contained perfect skeletons; but the bones were brittle, and crumbled, when they were handled. The fourteen rectangular sarcophagi were of different sizes, as if for children, as well as for other persons; but the others, from their dimensions, were evidently intended for adults. Some of them were furnished at the corners with projections, which were probably used as handles. A sarcophagus made of one piece of earthenware, with a lid, was also found; likewise another, composed of four pieces of that material fastened together with strings and pegs. It was, unfortunately, broken in taking it out; but upon the upper part the form of a female face could be traced, intended, no doubt, to be a portrait of the deceased. It had been painted, and the eyes were shewn to have been ornamented with khol, and it contained a few rude hieroglyphics. Within the sarcophagus were some bones, a round plate of earthenware, and, across the feet, a small jar of the same substance containing the bones of a fœtus—the offspring, most probably, of the woman, who may have died during parturition. The feet of the woman were towards the west, those of the fœtus towards the north: these skeletons had not been embalmed. At the distance of about two feet from this sarcophagus, a small figure cut out of limestone, and inscribed with a row of hieroglyphics down the centre; and in other places a number of jars,* of various forms and sizes, containing, in many instances, black pulverised earth, were dug up; remains of walls, and of bricks composed of the mud of the river mixed with small pebbles, likewise pieces of copper greatly corroded, and the fragments of a small jar or bottle, were also found near the sarcophagi. Other skeletons had been inclosed

* The jars, and part of this sarcophagus, were in the possession of Mr. Holroyd. Many of the former resembled the crockery at present used in Egypt. The most common shape was this, in which the mummies of cats are frequently inclosed.

in wooden coffins, with wrappers of coarse woollen stuff. None of these bodies had been embalmed, or prepared with bitumen, but they appeared to have been salted, as a quantity of salt was found on the skeletons, and in the sarcophagi, and was collected by the Arabs for culinary purposes. Many skeletons without sarcophagi or coffins were also discovered, generally near the above-mentioned walls.[3] These bodies appeared to have been buried in their clothes; one in particular, which had four or five dresses, and an outer garment of bright red, seemed by the hair to have belonged to a female. The skulls and bones were less decayed than those in the sarcophagi; the hair in one instance was finely curled, and was of a red colour, which was supposed to have been held in abomination by the Egyptians.[4] All the wrappers were composed of coarse woollen cloth, similar to that found in the Third Pyramid of Gizeh. A very large sarcophagus was also discovered. It was 7 feet 10 inches in length, was rectangular, and had a heavy lid. Several indistinct characters had been scrawled in red on the inside—

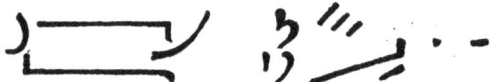

A number of heads of oxen, with the horns pointing upwards, and slightly covered with sand, recalled to Mr. Holroyd's recollection the account given by Herodotus; and every circumstance connected with these antiquities impressed him with the idea that they belonged to the sepulchres of the poorest of the Egyptians, excepting the woollen cloth,[5] and that, he supposes, was only considered impure in reference to the priests, and to those persons, who were connected with the service of the Temple.

Several hundred additional bodies were soon afterwards dug up. Most of them were inclosed in sarcophagi, but a few were in wooden coffins. Three or four tombs, constructed with large slabs of calcareous stone, were likewise opened. In these the

[3] Mr. Holroyd quotes a passage from Diodorus Siculus, B. I. 92:—"If any one has a tomb for his sepulture, his body is placed in it; if not, a chamber is constructed in his house, and his bier is placed close against the most solid part of the wall."

[4] It is to be observed that the bodies of Jacob and of Joseph were embalmed, and that the Hebrews appear in many instances to have adopted the customs of the Egyptians.

[5] Scarcely any of this cloth could be preserved, but some of it, and a skull, have been deposited in the British Museum.

TOURAH QUARRIES. (View from the Interior.)

PLAN OF THE QUARRIES AT TOURAH and MASSARA.

bodies were preserved with bitumen, and with linen wrappers painted in the usual manner; but had not the protection of coffins: they were laid parallel to each other upon the floor, with the heads towards the north. Eight bodies, of various ages, placed in this manner, were found in the largest tomb, which had probably belonged to one family. A number of jars, and other small objects, were also discovered; the most interesting of which were two figures of crocodiles, rudely sculptured, and about 1 foot 3 inches in length; small statues of deities; the model of a pyramid of calcareous stone, 2 feet 2½ inches square at the base, and of about the same height, but which had not any inscription, or hieroglyphics; also two pieces of bronze, apparently the unfinished heads of hatchets.[6]

From the proximity of these tombs to the quarries, and from the extreme probability that they contained the bodies of the people employed upon them, it was naturally expected that the remains of tools would be found, by which the nature of the metal antiently used in quarrying stone might have been ascertained. Nothing of the kind was, however, observed in these excavations, nor in the quarries.

TABLETS FOUND IN THE QUARRIES AT TOURAH AND MASSARA.

NOTES BY MR. BIRCH.

These inscriptions are extremely interesting, because, although they have not been exactly copied on the Greek and Roman tablets of later times, they prove that the same devotional expressions were at all times used, and that the same adorations were offered to the local divinities, whenever works were undertaken in the quarries.

That the hieroglyphical tablets, executed during the seventeenth and eighteenth dynasties, were the originals of those drawn up under the Roman authorities, may be seen by comparing them, particularly No. 2 from Tourah, with an inscription upon a granite cippus found by M. Belzoni in the quarries a few miles south-eastward of Es Souan, and published by MM. Belzoni, Caillaud, Letronne, and Labus.[7] It appears

---

[6] The above dimensions are in English feet and inches.

[7] Cf. Lib. Ent. Kn., Eg. Ant. Brit. Mus. i. 361. Letronne, "Rech. pour servir à l'Histoire de l'Egypte," p. 361. Belzoni, "Voyage," Vol. I. p. 270. Labus, "Di un Epigr. Latin." Mil. I. p. 26. Dubois, "Descrit. des Ant. de la Coll. de feu M. J. F. Mimaut," 8vo. Paris, 1837, p. 85. Belzoni's copy is almost quite correct, and only wanted properly dividing.

that the person, under whose superintendence, and the object, for which the works were carried on, are stated in both the inscriptions; that the name of the monarch forms the first part of the hieroglyphical, and the second of the Latin record; and that the tutelary deities are placed in compartments above the hieroglyphical text. Considering, therefore, the difference of idiom, and the time, which had elapsed between the respective dates, the inscription upon the cippus represents the devotional formularies, which had been adopted in the earliest times.

The relative positions of these tablets, and the progressive enlargement of the quarries, are shewn in the ground plan. No. I, the most antient, and executed towards the end of the reign of Amonemhe IV. is at the entrance of the excavation, which appears to have been worked under Amenophis II. and III., by an imperfect tablet, to have been continued to the time of Necho, and according to a demotic inscription, traced in black, even to a later period. The tablet of Necho, indeed, warrants a conjecture that the works were carried back again towards the entrance of the quarry.

The Latin inscription on the cippus is as follows:—

"To Jupiter, the highest and most excellent Chnubis; to Juno, the queen; the tutelary deities of this mountain; under the dominion of the Roman people, and in the propitious era of our lords and emperors, Severus and Antoninus, the most pious Augusti; of Geta, the most pious Cæsar(?); and of Julia Domna Augusta, the mother of the camp; new quarries were first discovered near Philæ; and many large rectangular columns and pillars were taken from them under Subatianus[a] Aquila, the prefect of Egypt; the care of the imperial works being under the superintendence of Aurelius Heraclides, decurio of the Moorish division (ala) of the army."

TOURAH QUARRIES.

No. 1.—This tablet, although imperfect, is of considerable importance, because it contains on the cornice a date, "the 43d year." It does not exhibit the figure of any deity, excepting that of Hat, "the good demon," and the words "celestial sun," together with the names, and titles of the monarch, are written in large characters under the architrave. The prenomen, which would have determined the name of the individual king, is wanting, but the name proves that he belonged to either the sixteenth, or seventeenth dynasty. The titles are "*the son of the sun, Amonemhe,[b] beloved of Phtah, the rampart of the south,*

---

[a] M. Dubois supposes that it is "Atianus," and that "Sub." is a repetition.

[b] The earliest date connected with this name in Sir J. G. Wilkinson's "Mat. Hier." agrees with the forty-first year of Amonemhe IV, according

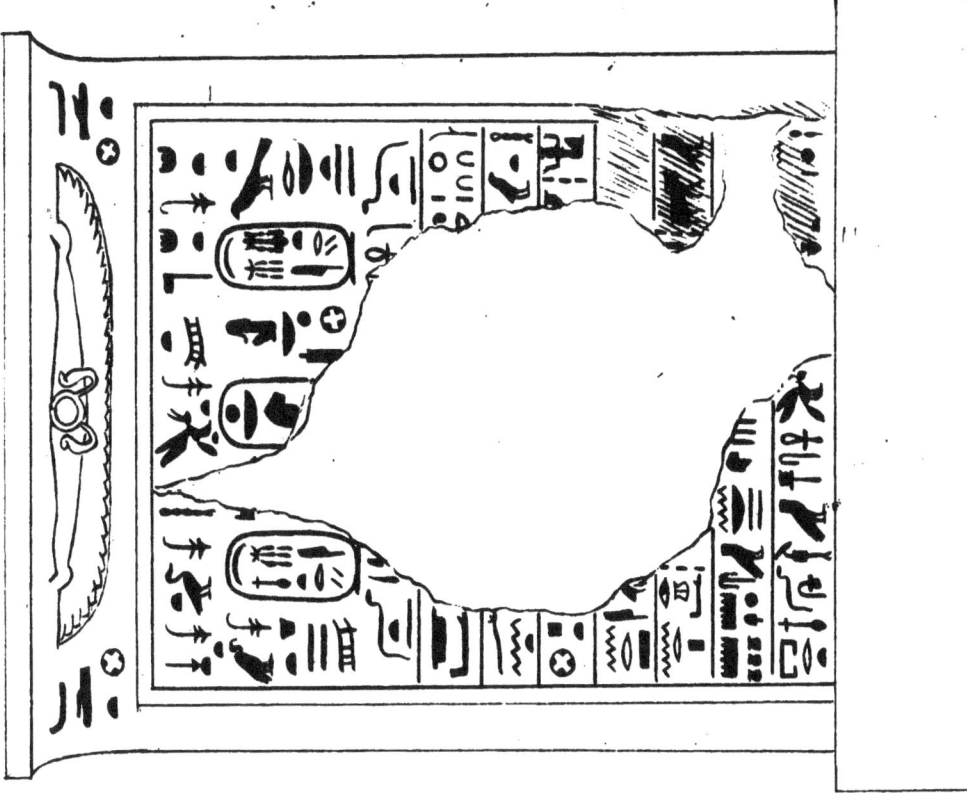

MAASARA QUARRIES.
TABLET Nº 8.

TOURAH: QUARRIES.
TABLET Nº 1.

and *of Anubis.*" The titles of "*Athor, mistress (of the fields of the sun?)*" also appear; and "*giver of life, of stability, and of power, like the sun for ever.*" At the upper corner is the name "*Hat.*" The three horizontal lines express "*the opening of the* (quarries) *to cut the good and white stone* (calcareous stone) *of the precincts, for the temples of the pure god of the lands of the south, under the arm of the military chief, attached to the charge of the signet* (?) . . . ." The lower part of the tablet is erased, but the inscription is amply illustrated by other tablets, containing similar formulas. They usually terminate with the name of the officer, under whose charge the excavation took place, and who probably cut the inscription as a record of himself, as well as of his sovereign, and of the quantity of stone taken away. Parts of the inscription are obscure, especially the end of the second, and the commencement of the third line; but it is possible to read "*the priest of the lands of the south.*" (?) I have already observed, however, that the term, which at an earlier period signified a "*god,*" was afterwards used to express "*priest,*" "*prophet-priest.*" Several of the symbols, especially the larger, do not appear to have been correctly copied, and their forms are unusual, and cannot be made out; but, by a reference to other tablets, in the upper line, the "*caves* (quarries) *of the rock,*" "*in order to draw forth,*"[1] may be deciphered.

No. 2.—This tablet is in the shape of a propylæon, and a long inscription round the lintels, although partially effaced, records on the left side, that Amenophis II. under the titles of "*the mighty Horus, the greatly vigilant, the king, the sun, the chief of the worlds, has paid devotions to the gods and goddesses, and has opened the quarries to take away the good and white stone, for the temples* . . . .;" and on the right side, "*make him a giver of life like the sun.*" In the upper compartment the monarch is represented offering water and incense to a train of deities, Amoun, Harsiesi, Souchis, Anubis, Athor, and Pasht. In the second he adores Phtah, Osiris, Penterotei,[2] Ashtaroth, Pasht, Athor, and Sate. The five lines beneath are, "*In the fourth year of the sanctity of the king, he the king, the sun, the ruler of the world, the son of the sun, Amonophth, the giver of life, commanded the opening*

---

to the arrangement of M. Rosellini; but this author also ascribes a reign of forty-four years to Amonemhe V., which at all events is not impossible. The absence of a prenomen makes it uncertain to which of the above-mentioned monarchs this tablet belonged; but it was probably to the immediate predecessor of Amasis. Cf. Wilkinson (J. G.), "Mat. Hier." Dynasty I. Pl. I. Rosellini, "Mon. Stor." Tav. IV. 96, p. 198.

[1] If the "great god of the land of the south" means Osiris, or Amon, the stone was probably required for the repairs of the temples at Thebes, or at Abydos.

[2] A form of Horus.

of the abodes (supposed of the gods); *to draw the good and white stone for the repairs of the temples for a period of years. Before the king opened the abodes by these excavations, the appointed adorations were made in the quarries, in the presence of his majesty, who was entitled the giver of life, and of power like the sun: done under the arm* (by the authority) *of the military chief, who was attached to the heart of the king by the fabrication of his constructions* (on account of his skill in architecture), *who adorned the head of the temples, who erected tablets in the lands of Naharaina* (Mesopotamia), *and of Karoei* (a province in Lybia), *who was attached to the bearers* (a title analogous to our bricklayers) *of Egypt, of all the gods of the north and of the south the royal scribe, Saph.*"

This tablet is, therefore, an historical document, and commemorates a public act, performed in the fourth year of the reign of Amenoph II., connected with the repairs of the edifices erected by that monarch. The beginning of the third line is not clear, but the meaning of the first two, and of the last two lines is evident; and the important functions held by Saph are similar to those recorded in the tombs at Benihassan, and have a reference to the progressive conquests of an Egyptian king. Saph appears to have been a royal scribe, an architect, or surveyor, engaged in the erection of the temples, and likewise of the stelæ, and tablets, which are phonetically, and ideographically described in the fourth line by the onion and pullet, the initials of the Coptic words ⲰⲈⲒⲦ, "*white*," and ⲞⲨⲈⲒⲦ, "*stele or column*." According to M. Champollion he must have been employed in Lybia and Mesopotamia, which countries had been conquered by Amenoph II. or by his predecessors.[3]

No. 3.—The upper part of this tablet is erased, but Amenoph III. or Memnon, appears to stand before three deities; Amoun-ra, whose form can be with difficulty made out; Harsiesi, "the lord of Sahatem," crowned with a pschent; and Chnoumis, or Chnouphis-ra, the "great terrifier, lord of Souten rot." The monarch is in the act of presenting a symbolic eye on a basket, which he holds in both hands. Behind the monarch, and on the right, is an imperfect vertical line of hieroglyphics, in which the titles of Chnouphis only remain. The end of the inscription is as follows:—". . . . . *astonisher of the gods.*[4] *That they will give thee all life, all force, all power, for ever.*" The four horizontal lines beneath contain—"*the year of the sanctity of Horus, the bull, the mighty* (victorious), *ruling with truth; the lord of the upper and lower worlds, the establisher of the houses of stone, the tranquilliser of the*

---

[3] These tablets probably recorded important conquests, like that supposed to have been left by Sesostris, at the Nahr el Kalb.
[4] A title of Noum.

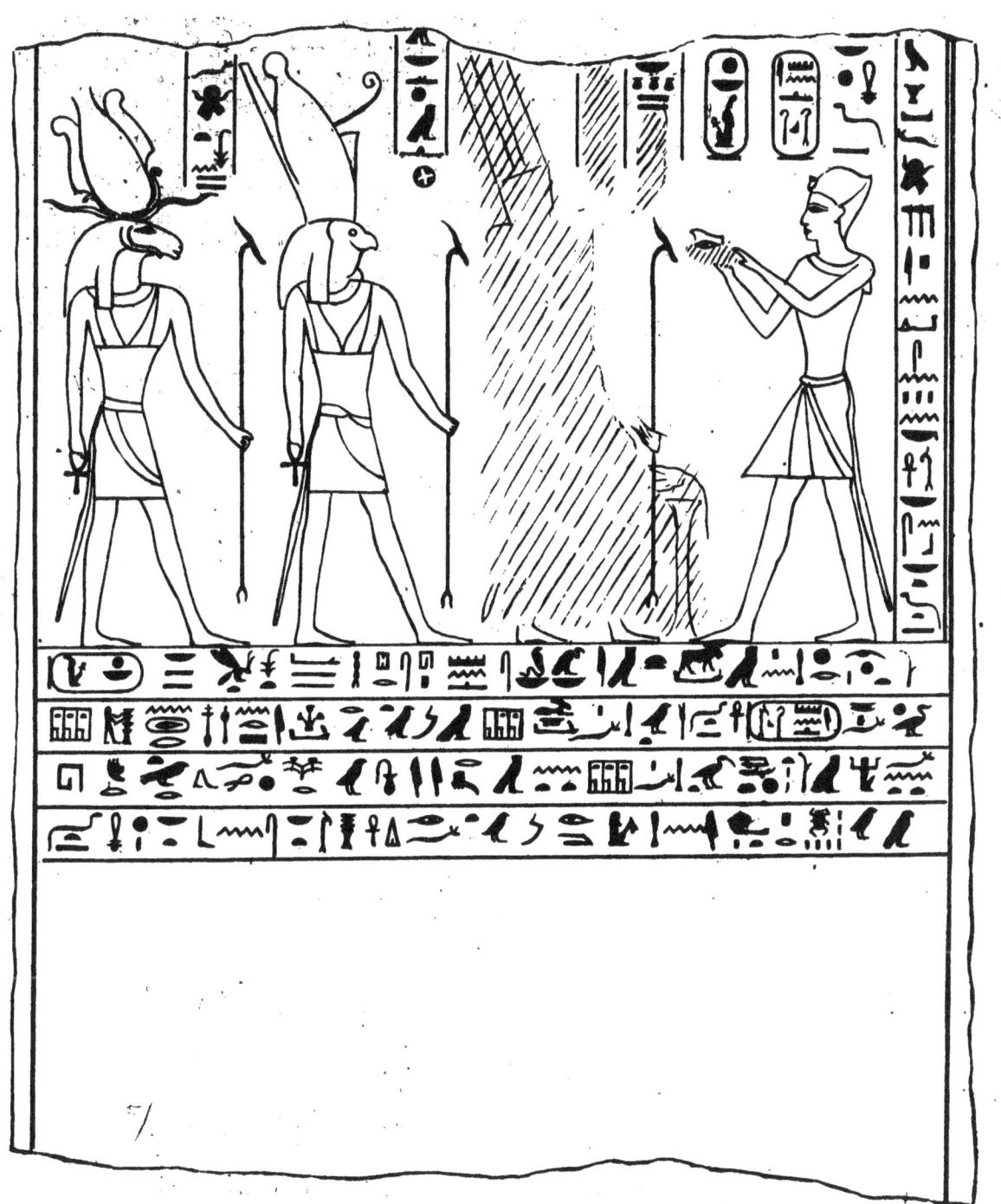

TOURAH QUARRIES.

TABLET No 3.

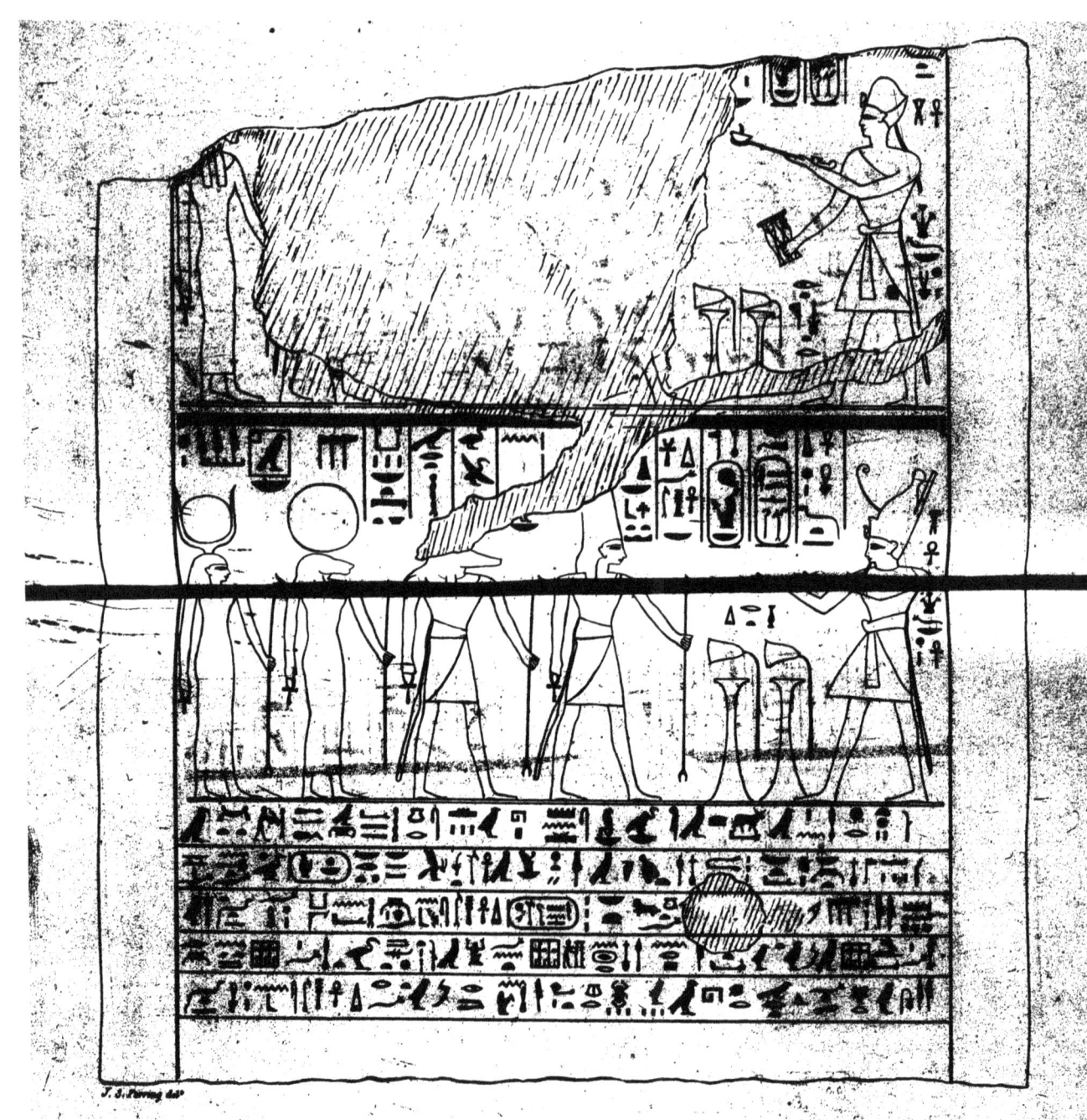

TOURAH QUARRIES.

TABLET Nº 4.

world, the king, the lord of the two worlds, the sun, the lord of truth, the son of the sun, loving him, Amenophth, ruler of the land of power (of Egypt), *living for ever. The commands of his sanctity were to open the abodes of stone* (the quarries?), *in order to procure good and white stone for the repairs of the temples for a period of years; before his majesty destroyed the existing abodes* (of the gods of the quarry) *by lengthening the paths, the appointed adorations were made on the rock, in the presence of his majesty* (?) . . . . . *that he may be made the giver of all life, of stability, of power, and of all strength, like the sun, for ever."* This inscription, which belongs to the reign of Amenoph III. (or Memnon), has probably commenced with a date, which, however, does not appear, nor, indeed, any place, where it could have been inserted. All that remains is, "*year . . . . . . month of the sanctity* (or of the purity)." The intermediate parts between "*years*," and "*fixed*,"[5] are so imperfect, that they cannot be made out; but as the other tablets commemorate excavations, which were carried on under the arm (the authority) of a great officer, it may be presumed, that this was of the same nature.

No. 4.—In the upper compartment, Amenoph III. of the eighteenth dynasty, (Memnon), is represented in the act of offering incense in an amshoir, and of pouring out libations from a triple vase, before two altars, to a train of deities; but they are almost erased, excepting part of the last, which is a female with a lion's head. As the monarch's titles are enumerated below, it is unnecessary to advert to them. An inscription before the king states "*he offers gifts and incense.*" In the second division he appears in the pschent, and holds in each hand a vessel full of fresh milk, the vapour of which appears to ascend. He is styled—"*the gracious god, the sun, the lord of force, Amenoph, the ruler of Egypt, the giver of life, like the sun for ever; surrounded* (?) *with all life and power, like the sun.*" Two altars are also before the king, and the following specification of his offering:— "*he gives milk.*" The first deity seems to be Moui (?), "the lord of the east." The next is uncertain, as both the name, and the head in the form of that of an animal, are partially erased; but from an undulating line, signifying "n" in Anoup, apparently indicates Anubis. The third is Oerihek, "*the great avenger,*" a type of Pasht, and of the Egyptian Nemesis, "*mistress of the heaven, and regent of the gods.*" The last is Athor, "*mistress of the fields of the sun.*" The five horizontal lines of hieroglyphics below the figures, contain an account of work carried on in the quarries, in the second year of the reign of Amenophis III. It runs thus:—"*In the second year of the sanctity of the mighty Horus, ruling in truth; the lord of the upper and lower worlds, the establisher of the*

---

[5] See Page 96.

abodes of stone; the tranquillizer (according to Champollion) *of the world, the hawk of gold, the lord of strength, the conqueror of eastern* (?) *foreigners; the gracious god, the lord of dilated heart, the lord of diadems, ... gracious, in the oeit,* (the crown of Upper Egypt), *bearing* (?) *the pschent with life, and with power; the king, the lord of the world, the lord giving light,*[6] *the sun, the lord of truth, the son of the sun, the beloved son of his race,*[7] *beloved of the gods . . . .* (in) *his tribunal, the lord of diadems, Amenoph, the king of Egypt, the giver of life, of stability, of power, and of victory; of dilated heart, with his offering* (?)[8] *. . . . like the sun for ever. The commands of his majesty were to open the rock, and to excavate the good and white stone, in order to repair the temples for a period of years, when his majesty,"* &c.

No. 5.—This tablet is also in the shape of a propylæon, and had probably a frieze and a cornice, with the representation of Hat, "the good demon." The sculpture is almost effaced; but, it appears by the name in the compartment, above the monarch, and below the emblem of heaven, that Pharaoh Nechô, who is styled " *the lord of the world, the sun strengthening the heart, the giver of life like the sun,*" is represented in the act of making an offering of wine (for the word " wine" can be made out, where the offering is usually mentioned) to two divinities. The deity (in a shrine to the right) is Phtah, or Khons, and he holds in his hands a sceptre, often assigned to the Egyptian Hephaistos, and composed of the gom, the symbol of life and of stability. The other deity, Atmô, or Athom, is crowned with a pschent, and also bears the gom.[9] The word " *eternal*" is legible in the centre; and lower down were evidently several horizontal lines of hieroglyphics; they are effaced, but, doubtless, referred to works carried on in the quarries during the reign of Nechô.

[6] This expression has been translated by M. Rosellini, "*lord over the rest.*" It is here apparently in an abbreviated form, but it is written with its full complement of characters upon one of the obelisks at Luxor, ⲛⲉⲃ-ⲓⲡⲓ-ⲟⲩⲃⲁϣ, "*the lord making light,*" (?) which would coincide with the solar epithets of the monarch. Cf. Rosellini.

[7] There is an ellipse here of "*makes,*" "*gives,*" or "*places.*" The term "*gods*" may be put adjectively for "*divine,*"—"*his divine constructions.*"

[8] Two arms upon an ensign; which often appear borne behind the monarch.

[9] This deity has been called Tôm, Thom, Tmou, Atmou, &c. The final vowel is paragogic, and the reed, often prefixed, is probably an ⲁ. But the term ⲙⲟⲩⲥⲉ, "Athom," is the proper name of a man. Cf. Quatremère, "Recherches sur la Langue de l'Egypte." 8vo. Paris, p. 128. Tattam, "Lexicon Linguæ Copticæ," voce Athom. MS. Vaticanus. Tablet of Wood in the British Museum, Case LL. No. 2.

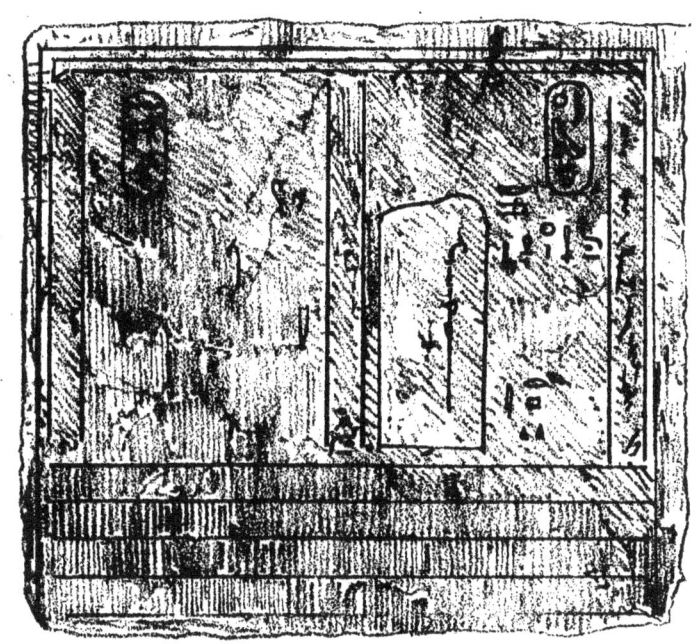

TOURAH QUARRIES Nº 5.

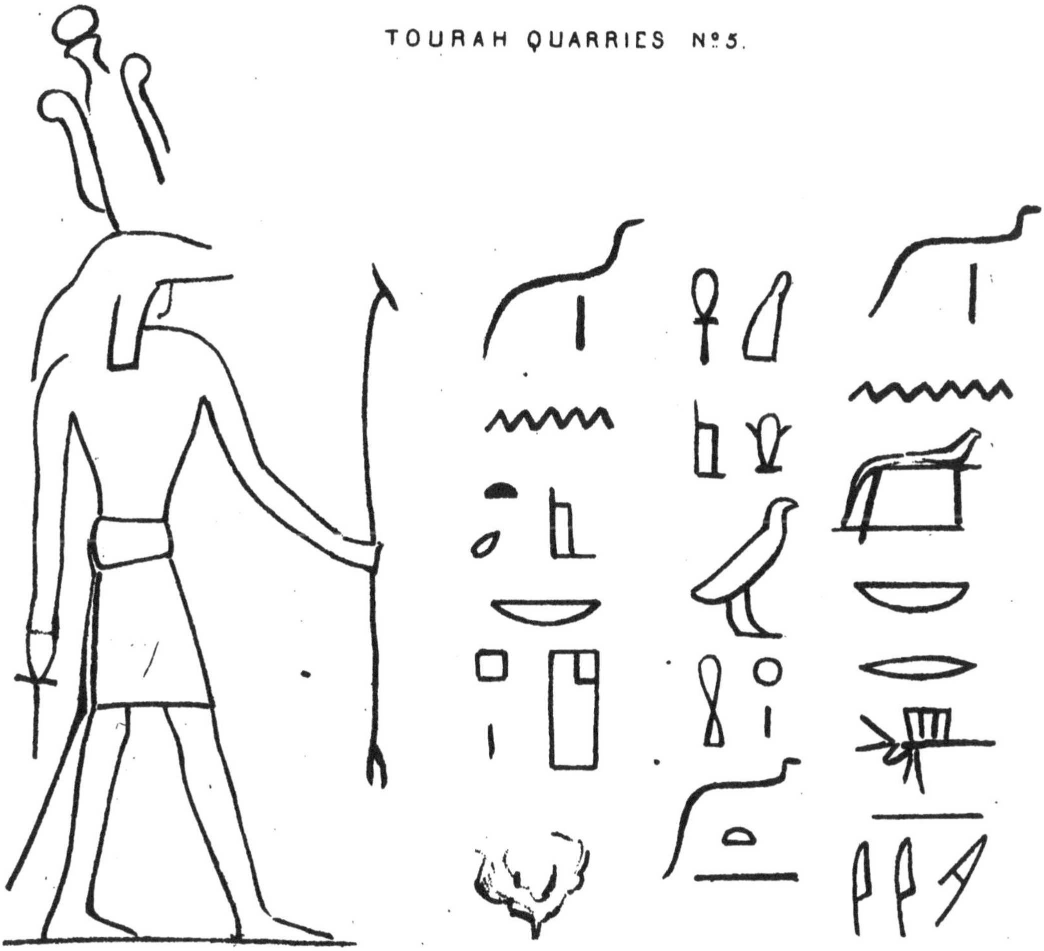

MASSARA QUARRIES Nº 7.

MAASARA QUARRIES.

TABLET No 6.

MASSARA QUARRIES.

These quarries appear also to have been worked from north to south. The earliest tablets, Nos. 6 and 7, are of Amasis, but his immediate successors are not noticed; although the names of Psammetichus II., and of Hakoris, are inscribed on the cartouches to the southward. The remainder of the tablets belong to the Ptolemies.

No. 6.—The upper part contains the names and the titles of Amasis,[1] and those of his wife, Amasis Nofreareh. The royal prenomen, with the usual titles, is in the centre. On the left is expressed—"*beloved of Athôm, lord of Poni;*" on the right —"*beloved of Phtah, who is the southern rampart.*" Further to the left are the titles, &c. of Nofreareh, the queen of Amasis, "*the royal daughter, Aahmes Nofreareh, the giver of eternal life, the royal sister, the chief;*" and to the right is written — "*the royal wife, the great royal mother, the mistress of the world.*" Below these titles are eight horizontal lines of hieroglyphics. It will be seen by the Plate, that they are imperfect, but that they refer to excavations in the quarries. " *In the twenty-second year of the sanctity of the king, the son of the sun, Aahmos, the giver of life, the caves . . . . . filled with good and white stone of the precinct (?) were opened for the abodes belonging to . . . . abode, the abode of Phtah, the gracious god of Amon in Thebes . . . . . his sanctity made . . . . . the stone by oxen(?) . . . . Done under the arm* (the authority) *of the chief . · . . the chief of the lord of the world constructing . . . . of the gracious god the guardian of the signet . . . . .*" Beneath this inscription, a block of stone, drawn on a sledge by six oxen, and attended by three drivers, is represented. The tablet records the fact, that the quarries, which had been begun in the forty-third year of Amonemhe, probably the fourth, were worked in the twenty-second of Amasis, apparently for the same purpose, viz. the building of the temples of Phtah, and of Amon in Thebes; which probably were begun by Amonemhe, because the inscription mentions that the stone was intended for the temples of the gods of the south, and for the temple of Amon in Thebes. It therefore appears that the monarchs of the sixteenth and seventeenth dynasties (whose capital seems to have been Abydos, from the recurrence of their names upon monuments brought from that place) had regained complete authority over the whole country, especially towards the close of the seventeenth dynasty. These tablets

---

[1] A tablet of the same import, and referring to the same monarch, has been published by M. Rosellini, "Mon. Stor." Teste. Tav. last of Vol. I.

seem to be the earliest records at present known respecting Thebes, which city acquired importance in proportion to the conquests of the Egyptian kings; and superseded Memphis, as the capital of the whole country, on account of the comparative superiority, and security of its situation. The deficiencies of this tablet may be in some degree supplied by a reference to No. 8.

No. 7.—The figure to the left represents the deity Sebek,[2] Savak, or Souchi-ra; which appear to be varieties of the same name. He has the head of a crocodile, wears the crown called otf, and holds in his left hand a gom, or koucoupha sceptre, and in his right hand the symbol of life. The inscription, which is in three vertical lines of hieroglyphics, is

—"*the invocation of Savak, lord of Rogal* (?) [ ] *beloved, the giver of life in his tribunal, like the sun, for ever;*" and the final line is—"*an invocation to Isis, mistress of the abode of the sycamore.*" These inscriptions are evidently imperfect, and are also in an unusual form. If the expression "*beloved,*" at the end of the first line to the right be correctly copied, which from the accompanying royal titles appears to be the case, it means that the invocation or address is that of the Pharaoh, or monarch, "*the beloved of Souchi-ra, of the lord,*" &c. In other respects the inscription is complete. The characters are red, the colour usually employed by surveyors, and by the persons, who were engaged in executing the sacred inscriptions.

No. 8.—This tablet contains in the cornice, Hat, "the good demon," and, with some slight variations, and with the omission of the representation of the blocks drawn by oxen, resembles No. 6. The rank of the officer seems to be exactly the same as that in No. 6: his name, in the left-hand corner, is Nofreheri, and a second excavation, made in the twenty-second year of Amasis, is probably recorded.

No. 9.—This magnificent tablet is unfortunately much defaced. It is in the shape of a doorway with a double cornice, on both of which is the winged symbol of the good demon, and at each end of the lower cornice are the titles of Hat, "*the great god, the lord of the heaven.*" On the sides are plants of the papyrus and of the lotus,[3] emblems of the upper, and of the lower hemispheres; and above the one to the right, which is perfect, is an uræus, crowned with the white crown, the ouobsh or oeit, the emblem of dominion over the upper regions, of Soaven, or Suen, the Egyptian Eilethyia,[4] and likewise of Maut, or Mouth, the Hera or Juno of

---

[2] Cf. Wilkinson, "Mat. Hier." Pl. XXXV. Champollion, "Panth. Egypt." *Sabak.* Peyron. "Lexicon Linguæ Copticæ," p. 219, by the inhabitants of Arsinöe crocodiles were called *Souchis.*

[3] Cf. Rosetta Stone, l. 5, Hier. Part. Champol. "Gram. Egypt." p. 9.

[4] Champol. "Pan. Egypt." Soaven. Wilkinson, "Mat. Hier. Pan." same deity. Ser. X. Pl. XXXVIII. p. 47, who hypothetically allies her with Sate.

MAASARA QUARRIES.

TABLET Nº 10.

the Theban system. On the lower part of the tablet are alternate rows of the flowers, and of the buds of the papyrus. The upper part of a standing figure, crowned with an otf, represents Ptolemy Philadelphus, adoring a train of deities; slight indications of the heads, only remain: but they appear to have been "*Ra, or Re, the lord of the . . . . . region, fixed for ever* (?); *the great god, the father* (or the statue); . . . . *Moui, the son of the sun, the lord of the . . . region; and Tafne . . . of the sun, the mistress of the . . . region, the daughter* (the eye) *of the sun, the mistress of heaven, the regent of the gods.*" If the tablet was ever completed, the respective titles and addresses were no doubt prefixed in vertical lines before these figures; but, under the Ptolemies, many of these works were left unfinished. In the centre is the name of the " Queen *Esi-Arsinoe,*" the sister, and the wife of the king; and she appears to offer incense to " *Amoun-ra,*" and to " *Khons* (or Shons), *the son of Ra, the lord of the two worlds, the great god, the lord of . . . region, illuminating his son* (?), *resident* (?) *in the symbolic eye.*" The head-attire of the deity (Khons) is that usually assigned to Pnebto,[5] the son of Horus; it consists of three vertical, vase-shaped ornaments, surmounted by discs, and supported by the horns of a goat. The name of the region, repeated among the titles of the deities, probably indicates the place, from which the stone was procured. Like those on the other tablets, the inscription was a prayer to the local divinities on the occasion of the quarries being opened during the reign of Ptolemy Philadelphus. It refers to a triad, consisting of Ra, the sun; of his son Moui, (splendour), the Phaethon of the Greeks; and of his daughter, Tafne, twin-sister of Moui, and equivalent to the Gemini in the Zodiac, the eldest of the Heliades; and also to the Theban triad, Amoun, or Jupiter; Muth, Hera or Juno, whose figure is erased; and Chons or Khons, Hercules or Deus Lunus.

No. 10.—On the cornice of this tablet is Hat, "the good demon;" and below it is the figure of a king, who holds in his hands the emblem of fields, and who wears a flowing head-dress and an uræus. The lines immediately before him contain a cartouche, and the titles,—" *all life, all power, and all dilated heart* (?), *like the sun, for ever ;*" but they do not express his name; and the other lines exhibit the name, and the titles of the divinity, and the benefits conferred by her. The king is in the presence of two deities, the first of whom holds in her hands a lotus sceptre, and the symbol of life, and wears upon her head the vulture claft, surmounted by a disc, by goat's horns, and by two plumes. An inscription before her contains her names and titles, among which are

---

[5] Cf. Champol. "Pan. Egypt." "Mon. Egypt." fol. Paris, Pl. IV. 1. Pl. LVIII. Horus, in a similar attire, is called " *Har,*" or " *Hor, the sun, the great god, the great and first (born) of Amon-ra.*"

—" *Oerihek,*[6] *Pasht, and Athor, the guardian of* .... *the daughter of the sun."* Behind her is " *Thoth, the lord of the divine writings, resident in the abode of Monkh,*" he holds in his hands the symbol of life, and the gom, and wears upon his head the otf. As there are not any traces of an inscription, the tablet was probably unfinished.

Near No. 10 are the prenomen, and the name of Psammetichus. The cartouches are surmounted by a disc, and by two feathers.

No. 11.—This represents an act of adoration (Ⲉⲱⲟⲧ)[7] to the Theban triad, Amounra; Maut (Mouth); and Khons. The monarch's name is erased, and also his figure, excepting the hands, which apparently hold the symbol of fields,[8] which, in this instance, signifies that a portion of the produce of the soil, upon some particular occasion, was dedicated to the local deities. Before the king's cartouche are the titles —" *the good god, the lord of the world.*" The two perpendicular lines before the first deity express —" *the speech of (A)moun* .... *the great god, the lord of the two abodes of the sun, of the upper, and lower hemispheres, and of the region of Ouabsh, or Oeit-sbe,*" the " white wall," (λευκὸν τῦχος,[9] the Memphite Acropolis.) Before Maut (who bears upon her head the upper and lower part of the pschent, the oeit, and tcahr, the red and white crowns of Egypt, and the vulture-shaped head-dress) is — " *the invocation of the great mother, the mistress of the land of Eshor, and of the region of the white wall.*" To Maut succeeds the hawk-headed type of Khons, with an inscription containing " *the invocation of Khons the son of Hor,* (or *of Ra*), *the great god, the lord of the region of the white wall.*" The characters on the architrave, and in the centre of the cornice, refer to Hat, " the good demon." The fact that the Theban triad presided over quarries excavated in the neighbourhood of Memphis proves that the monarch, whose name is erased, must have belonged to the Diospolitan line, for the tutelary deities of Memphis were Phtah, Merephtah or Pasht, and Nofre-Athom. The region mentioned in the text was either in Upper, or in Lower Egypt. In a ritual in the British Museum, this group, together with a star[1] suspended from heaven, expresses " night,"—the Ⲉϫⲱⲣϩ of the Memphite, and the Ⲥⲱⲣⲁϩ of the Theban dialect. On the coffin of Soter, in the British Museum, the

---

[6] It is to be observed that, at a late epoch, deities frequently bore all the names, of which they were personifications. Oerihek, the great avenger, and Pasht, Diana, or Artemis, and also Athor, or Aphrodite, were types of the same deity. On a ritual in the possession of the University of Dublin, a hippopotamus erect, with female breasts (*Te-oër*), was identified with Athor, and was placed before the goddess, when she came out of the Syenite mountains; but the prayers of the deceased were addressed to Athor only.

[7] Champol. "Gram. Egypt." p. 387.   [8] Ibid. p. 39, n. 64.
[9] Salvolini, "Analyse Gram." p. 96.
[1] Ritual in British Museum, pp. 79, 97. Champ. "Gram. Egypt." 643, n. 186.

MAASARA QUARRIES.

TABLET Nº II.

Written in Red Ochre.

in Black Ochre.

in Red Ochre.

in Black Ochre.

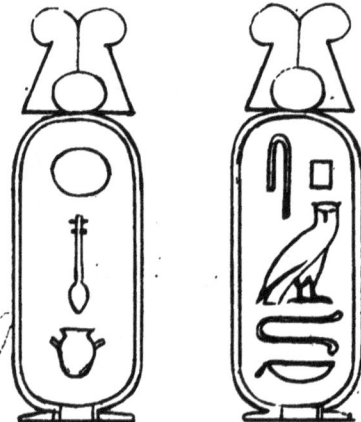

CARTOUCHE OF PSAMMETICUS, 2ⁿᵈ

CARTOUCHE Nº 12.

INSCRIPTIONS FROM MAASARA AND TOORAH QUARRIES.

hieroglyphical[a] symbol for 𐦯 is substituted for the pool used for ⳁ; indeed, ⳁ[3] and 𐦯 are indifferently used, as ⲗⲗⲁⳁⲓ for ⲗⲗⲁ𐦯ⲓ, "*an axe;*" ⳁⲏϥ and 𐦯ⲏϥ, "*to lay waste,*" &c. The name of the region may consequently be read Eshor, or Ejor. In many instances, particularly in the sacred dialect, a vowel is affixed to words in Coptic, the radical elements of which are contained in the consecutive consonants. Thus, ⳁⲉ,[4] ⳁ, and ⲉⳁⳁⲉ, are equally used in both dialects to express "*powerful,*" "*able.*" ⲇⲟⲩⲗⲗ, and ⲑⲟⲩⲗⲗ,[5] are names of the god hitherto called Thmou, Atmou, or Atmoo. Now, as the determinative is expressed by three waving lines, which also signify water, the word may be ⳁⲁⲣⲓ,[6] which was applied by the Egyptians to the Red Sea, in the form of ⲫⲓⲟⲙ ⲛⳁⲁⲣⲓ, "*the sea of Shori, or of Shari;*" a term which has excited much controversy.[7] In the sacred dialect of Egypt it would be "*Eshormoou,*" or "*Eshoriom, the dark waters or sea;*" a term not applied to the Nile, which is styled ⲓⲁⲣⲟ, "*the river.*" By a reference to the stele of Tiberius, in the British Museum, it may mean "*darkness*" or "*extinction.*" These conjectures, however, are by no means conclusive. The lines in the lower part, if any were inserted, are entirely erased; but, from the tenor of the other inscriptions, the tablet was no doubt executed in honour of the gods when a fresh excavation was undertaken for sacred purposes.[8]

No. 12.—"*The lord of diadems, Hakr (Acoris).*" The name of the monarch Acoris, or Akoris, of the twenty-ninth dynasty of Mendesians.[9]

---

[2] Champ. "Gram. Egypt." Salvolini, "Analyse Gram."

[3] Peyron, "Lex. Ling. Copt." 4to. Turin, 1835, p. 279.

[4] Peyron, loc. cit.

[5] Journal, "Tourah Quarries," No. 7, n. 2.

[6] Peyron, "Lex. Ling. Copt." &c. p. 304.

[7] Peyron, loc. cit. According to Akerblad it means "*the sea of the fallen,*" in allusion to the miraculous defeat recorded in the Exodus; but this opinion appears to be erroneous, for, even if the etymology be right, the expression does not seem to have been used till after the introduction of Christianity into Egypt. Σαρι is "*a reed;*" and Cf. Tattam (H.) "Lex. Ægyptiaco-Latinum," contends at some length that it signified "*the reedy sea.*"

[8] The monarch was probably one of the Ptolemies. The term "*white wall*" seems indeed to have been as old as Rameses III. (Cf. Burton, "Excerpt. Hier." Pl. LVI. l. 8), but it was not commonly used before the time of the Ptolemies. Cf. Monuments, Stelæ, &c. *passim.*

[9] Cf. Champ. "Précis du Syst. Hier." 2d edition, 1828, p. 243. Pl. Tabl. Gen. 124. Rosellini (Hipp.), "Mon. Stor." Teste, Tom. II. Tav. XIII. p. 153, n. Wilkinson (Sir J. G.), "Top. Thebes," and "Mat. Hier." Kings.

REMARKS ON THE MEASURES, BY WHICH THE PYRAMIDS WERE BUILT,

TAKEN FROM MR. PERRING'S OBSERVATIONS.

It appears, that there were various sorts of cubits, but that the length of the ordinary cubit (as the name implies) was the distance from the elbow to the end of the middle finger, and was supposed to contain six hands' breadths, each of which was subdivided into four fingers' breadths. The uncertainty of the measure, unless reduced to some positive standard, is evident, and may have given rise to the above-mentioned varieties.[1] But, as Sir J. G. Wilkinson very properly observes,[2] the Egyptians adhered strictly to their antient customs, and preserved most accurately their accustomed measures, particularly those, which were used for the regulation of the waters of the Nile, as any uncertainty would in that instance have produced the greatest confusion.

Mr. Perring found that the dimensions of the Pyramids agreed with a cubit, described by Ezekiel, chap. xl. ver. 5, to have been a cubit and a hand's breadth, and therefore to have contained seven hands' breadths.[3] He assumed for the antient measure a mean taken between a cubit in the Royal Museum at Paris, one from

---

[1] The modern Egyptian "drah belladee," although rather longer, probably represents one of these measures. The cubit was expressed in hieroglyphics by ⟨hieroglyph⟩ ⟨hieroglyph⟩ equivalent to the Coptic word ⲙⲁϩⲉ, or ⲙⲁϩⲓ, "mahe," or "mahi."

[2] "Manners and Customs of the Antient Egyptians," second series, Vol. I. p. 28.

[3] This cubit, therefore, appears to have been used by the Hebrews; and, notwithstanding the cities, which had been built, and the civilisation, which had taken place in Syria, it is, indeed, probable, that, before their arrival in Egypt, the sons of Jacob, owing to their pastoral habits, and to the little intercourse, which existed between them and the Philistines, had few, if any, opportunities of acquiring scientific knowledge, which had then attained a great perfection in Egypt; whence, like the Greeks, the Hebrews subsequently derived a knowledge of architecture, and of the other sciences, by which mankind was civilised and refined.

the Nilometer in the Island of Elephantine, and another found in a propylæon at Karnac; and the following figures will shew how nearly it coincides with a cubit stated, in Sir Isaac Newton's "Treatise on Antient Weights and Measures," to have been calculated from the proportions of the King's Chamber in the Great Pyramid of Gizeh:—

	English Feet.
Cubit in the Museum	1·707
from the Nilometer	1·712
from Karnac	1·720
	3) 5·139
Mean Cubit	1·713
Sir Isaac Newton's	1·719

According to Sir J. G. Wilkinson, the cubit in the Nilometer contains 20·6250; that at Karnac 20·6500 inches; and the Hebrew cubit 1 foot 8·24 inches, or 1 foot 9·888 inches.[4]

This measure does not exactly agree with the buildings in their present state; but Mr. Perring considers, that the difference may be attributed to dilapidation, and to other accidental causes, and that a general agreement is obvious. He also observes, that the cubit calculated from the King's Chamber proves, that that apartment was constructed with the greatest accuracy; and he conceives, that the dimensions of the different chambers and passages were originally exact, but that they were in some degree enlarged by the blocks having been afterwards trimmed down to a polished surface. He adds, that Pliny appears to have been the only antient author, who actually measured the Pyramids, and that the contradictory statements respecting the dimensions of these monuments were owing to the rubbish and sand, with which they had been encumbered, probably, from very early times. The late surveys were, therefore, taken with considerable advantage, because the pavement at the base of the Great Pyramid was uncovered in three places on the northern front, and because the interiors were in general well examined.

As the assumed cubit is reduced to English measure, it can be easily applied to the plans in Mr. Perring's large work. The several details are, therefore, omitted; and the following obser-

---

[4] See "Manners and Customs of the Antient Egyptians," second series, Vol. I. pp. 30, 32, and 27.

vations by Mr. Perring are only inserted. He remarks, that the perpendicular height of the Great Pyramid was to the base, as 5 to 8, and that the inclined height was to the base, as 4 to 5;[5] that the eight plethra, stated by Herodotus to be the square of the base, were measures of fifty-six cubits, eight of which formed an Egyptian juger; that, according to Pliny, the whole building occupied eight jugera, which measures must therefore have been nearly three times larger than the Roman acres; that the height from the base of the Great Pyramid to the floor of the Queen's Chamber, the height from the floor of the Queen's to that of the King's, and thence to the top of Campbell's Chamber, were equal (about 40 cubits); also, that the space from the ceiling of Campbell's Chamber to the top of the Pyramid was 160 cubits, and therefore exceeded the three above-mentioned distances by 40 cubits; and likewise, that the space from the roof of the King's to that of Wellington's Chamber, and thence to the roof of Lady Arbuthnot's Chamber, were the same, and that each of them was equal to the height of the King's Chamber.

Mr. Perring found that the incline of the roof-blocks in the Queen's Chamber, and of those in Belzoni's Chamber in the Second Pyramid, was one-third of the width of the respective apartments; and that the incline of the roof, in the lower chamber in the Second Pyramid, was one-fourth part of the width of that room.

He also endeavoured to ascertain whether any relative proportions were observed between the angles of the exteriors of the Pyramids, and those of the entrance-passages, but they appeared to have been merely determined by the proportionate extent of the base and of the perpendicular height of the building. He observes that the entrance in the Great Pyramid inclines about one foot in two, but that the ascending passage seems to have been regulated by the height of the King's Chamber above the base, which was 80 cubits. Mr. Perring also remarks, that, as the buildings were not intended for astronomical purposes, but for tombs, their exterior forms were no doubt adapted for duration and for grandeur, and their internal arrangements for strength and for security, according to the facilities, which the rocks, over which they were erected, and their positions, afforded.

[5] A reference to the dimensions will shew the general accuracy of these observations.

VIEW OF THE SPHINX DURING THE EXCAVATIONS.

THE SPHINX.

AN ACCOUNT OF M. CAVIGLIA'S EXCAVATIONS IN 1818, TAKEN FROM THE PAPERS OF THE LATE MR. SALT.[6]

"This monument, so imposing in its aspect, even in the mutilated state, to which it has been reduced, has always excited the admiration of those who possessed sufficient knowledge of art to appreciate its merits at a first glance; for, though to an untutored eye there remains so little of the features as scarcely to give more than a general idea of the human head, yet, by repeated and accurate observation, the several parts may be sufficiently traced to afford a tolerably complete idea of its original perfection.

"The contemplative turn of the eye, the mild expression of the mouth, and the beautiful disposition of the drapery at the angle of the forehead, sufficiently attest the admirable skill of the artist, by whom it was executed.[7] It is true, that no great attention has been paid to those proportions, which we are accustomed to admire, nor does the pleasing impression, which it produces, result from any known rule adopted in its execution; but it may rather be attributed to the unstudied simplicity of the conception, to the breadth, yet high finish, of the several parts, and to the stupendous magnitude of the whole.

"Such are the sentiments, which a repeated view of this extraordinary work has inspired. At first, I confess, that, like many other travellers, I felt that the praises lavished upon it by Norden, Denon, and by others, were exaggerated; but, the more I studied it at different hours of the day, and under different effects of light, and of shade, the more I became convinced of their having barely done justice to its merits: it must indeed be allowed, that the drawings by both these gentlemen but faintly accord with their encomiums, but, after having repeated the same task myself with little success, I must admit, that the difficulties, which attend the undertaking, are sufficient to baffle the efforts of any one not professionally dedicated to the arts.

[6] Part of this paper has been printed in Hall's "Life of Salt," and in one or two other publications, but the plates, taken from Mr. Salt's drawings, have never, I believe, been published. I have great pleasure in making known the successful results of M. Caviglia's labours, which I am enabled to do by the kindness of the Earl of Mountnorris, and I beg leave publicly to express my acknowledgments to his lordship.

[7] The monument has probably been much defaced since 1818, for these beauties are no longer visible.

"Before I proceed, I must premise, that the general impression, made upon me by this monument, has been produced by a deliberate contemplation of it, when laid open to its base, with the fragments of a beard resting beneath the chin, with its paws stretched fifty feet in advance, and with the temple, the granite tablet, and the altar, represented in the accompanying sketches, spread out on a regular platform in its front. These interesting objects, which no one for ages had had an opportunity of seeing, have undoubtedly tended to exalt it in my estimation; and, in order that I may endeavour to convey something of the same feeling to others, I shall proceed to a detailed account of what was discovered by Capt. Caviglia; which, together with the several sketches taken on the spot during the progress of his operations, may remain as a record of his labours, when the objects themselves are destroyed, or again entombed in the moving sands.

"From various reports in circulation in Egypt I was given to understand, that the French engineers had made a considerable excavation in front of the Sphinx, and that they had just discovered a door at the time, when they were compelled to suspend their operations. This account was confirmed by the repeated assertions of the Arabs, several of whom declared, that they had been present at the discovery; and said, that the door led into the body of the Sphinx; while others affirmed, that it conducted up to the Second Pyramid. Though little stress could be laid upon such statements, yet they rendered Capt. Caviglia very unwilling to give up his researches without at least doing all in his power to ascertain the fact.

"To this end he first began to open a deep trench on the left, or northern, side, opposite the shoulder of the statue; and, though the sand was so loose, that the wind drove back frequently during the night more than half of what had been removed in the day, yet he managed, by the aid of planks arranged so as to support the sides, to dig down in a few days to the base. (See view of Sphinx.) As the trench, however, was not more than 20 feet across at the top, and not above 3 feet wide at the bottom, the situation of the workmen evidently became dangerous; for, if any large body of sand had fallen in (and the planks were very weak), it must have irrecoverably smothered those, who were employed below; it was therefore found necessary to abandon this part of the attempt. By what had been done, however, the height of the statue from the top of the head to the base, was ascertained; and it was also found that the external surface of the body was composed of stones, of various sizes, but put together

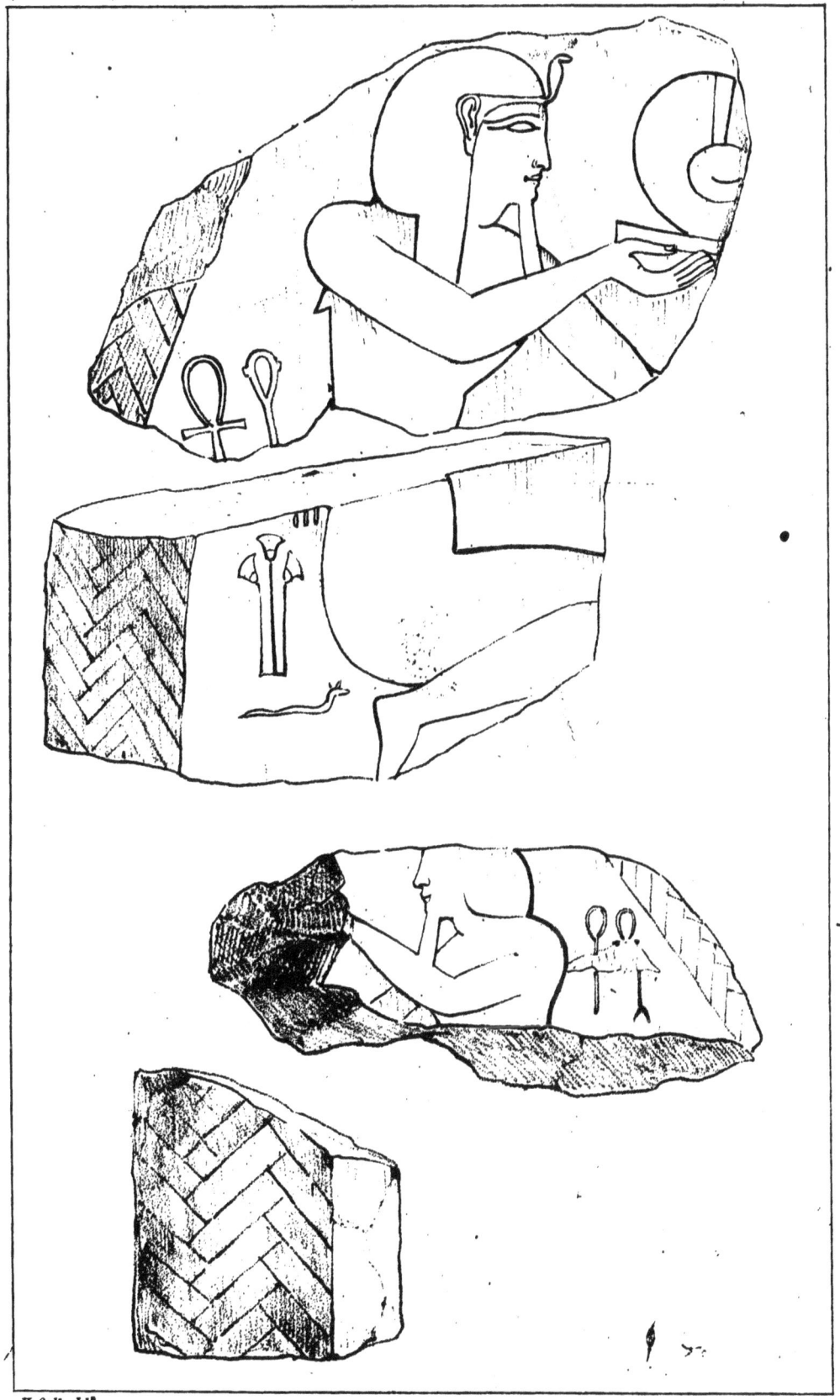

FRAGMENTS OF THE BEARD OF THE SPHINX.

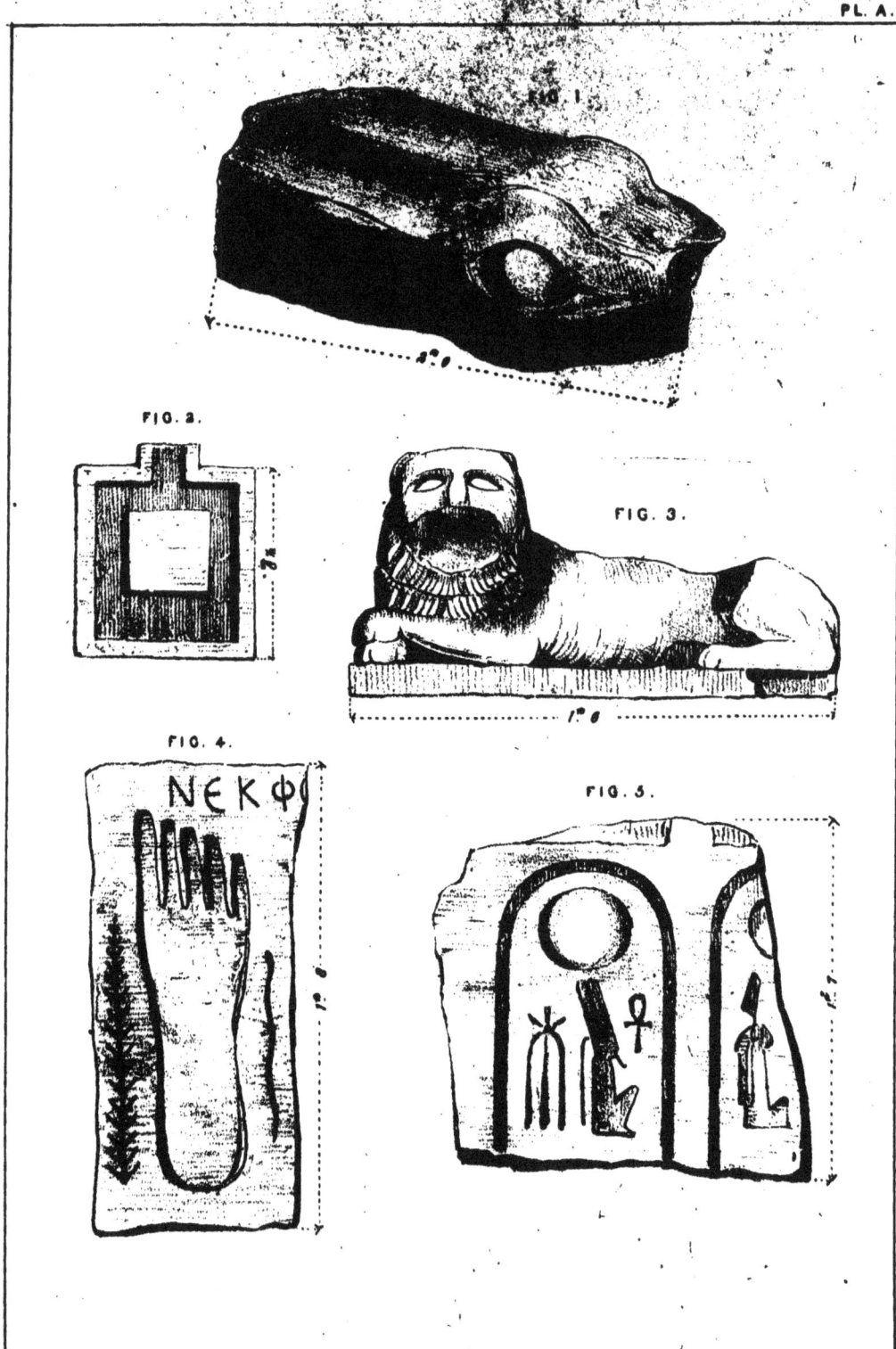

FRAGMENTS FOUND DURING THE EXCAVATION OF THE SPHINX.
(NOW IN THE BRITISH MUSEUM.)

with much care,[8] and covered with red paint. The form of the masonry was not very regular, but it consisted of three successive ledges, sufficiently broad for a man to stand upon, and intended, probably, to represent the folds of a mantle or dress. It seemed to have been added by the Romans.

"As the result of the first operation did not prove satisfactory, Capt. Caviglia determined to undertake a larger excavation towards the front, in which he employed, from the beginning of March to the end of June, from sixty to a hundred labourers. The first discovery of any interest was that of several fragments of stone, upon which was represented plaited hair, and on the sides of which were inscribed kneeling figures, and hieroglyphics. (See Plate.) Upon the first sight of these fragments I was led to imagine that they were parts of a beard, or at least of that singular appendage usually denominated a beard, and frequently attached to the chins of male personages in Egyptian sculpture;[9] this idea was confirmed by the size, and by the position of the fragments, as the largest, which must have been nearest the chin, was first found; and the opinion received, indeed, afterwards additional confirmation by the discovery of three tablets, on which sphinxes were sculptured in bas-relief, with beards plaited precisely in the same way as that on the fragments. (See Plate of the smaller tablet, and Plate B.) The rest of the beard was found in the sand, together with a stone inscribed with a double row of hieroglyphics (Fig. 5, Plate A.), that appeared to have belonged to a wall or pillar, upon which the beard was supported, and some of which yet remained. Part of the head of a serpent, about 2 feet long and 1½ broad, which had ornamented the head of the statue, was also discovered; (See Fig. 1, Plate A.) Most of these fragments were found in a small temple, 10 feet long and 5 feet broad, which was immediately below the chin of the statue, which, according to Pliny, contained the body of Amasis, the first king of the eighteenth dynasty.[1] Soon after this discovery a large block of granite (aa in ground-plan), on the eastern side of which figures and hieroglyphics were beautifully inscribed (see Plate B), was

---

[8] Mr. Salt, no doubt, meant the lower part of the statue.

[9] A female sphinx, (probably an emblem of the Nile), with this appendage, is to be seen on the statue of Memnon, and in many of the temples; but these images were usually andro-sphinxes, and were so described by Herodotus, and by Strabo.

[1] Another king of the same name reigned 570 B.C., towards the end of the twenty-sixth dynasty. Sir J. G. Wilkinson's "Thebes and General View of Egypt," p. 516.

found in the small temple (see *d* in ground-plan), together with two other tablets, composed of calcareous stone (see *bb* in ground-plan). One of these was in its original position; the other had fallen down, and was afterwards sent to the British Museum.² (See Plate, view of temple.) Between the front walls of this temple a small lion of good workmanship was found, with the head towards the image (see view of Temple); and, as small statues of the bull Mahdes are similarly placed in Indian temples, I conceive that this statue was in its original position. Fragments of other lions, rudely carved, and the head and shoulders of a sphinx, were likewise discovered. All these remains, together with the tablets, walls, and platform of the temple, had been ornamented with red paint; which colour, according to Pausanias, was appropriated in Egypt, as in India, to sacred purposes.³

"A large part of the left paw was uncovered, and the platform of masonry was found to extend beyond it; and, in the course of a fortnight, Capt. Caviglia had removed the sand from the paw, and from the outer walls of the temple (see *hh* in ground-plan), in front of which was an altar formed of granite (see *k* in ground-plan). It is now in the British Museum, and has had at the angles projecting stones, which may be supposed to have been called the horns of the altar. (See Fig. 1, Plate D.) The altar yet retains the marks of fire—the effects, probably, of burnt-offerings.

"The opening (*j*) between the two walls (*hh* in ground-plan) was raised 2 feet above the pavement, and formed a sort of window, by which, it may be supposed, that the priests only were admitted into the temple; and near it another lion (Fig. 3, Plate A), rudely carved, and apparently intended to have been placed upon one of the walls (*hh* in ground-plan), was dug up. It is now in the British Museum. The figure of an owl and three small stones, which had belonged to an altar, were also discovered. (See Fig. 2 in Plate A, and Figs. 4 and 5 in Plate D.) Fig. 4, Plate A, seems to have been a votive offering. The interior walls (*cc* in ground-plan) had probably been surmounted with small sphinxes, like that already described. *e e* mark the pavement.

² Mr. Birch, Assistant to the Antiquarian Department at the British Museum, and Assistant-Secretary to the Archæological Institute of Rome, has kindly enabled me to give an explanation of these inscriptions.

³ Diodorus says that the kite was esteemed sacred, because it brought to the priests of Memphis a book inscribed with red characters; and he also observes that those, who wrote the sacred characters, wore, when so employed, a red head-dress.

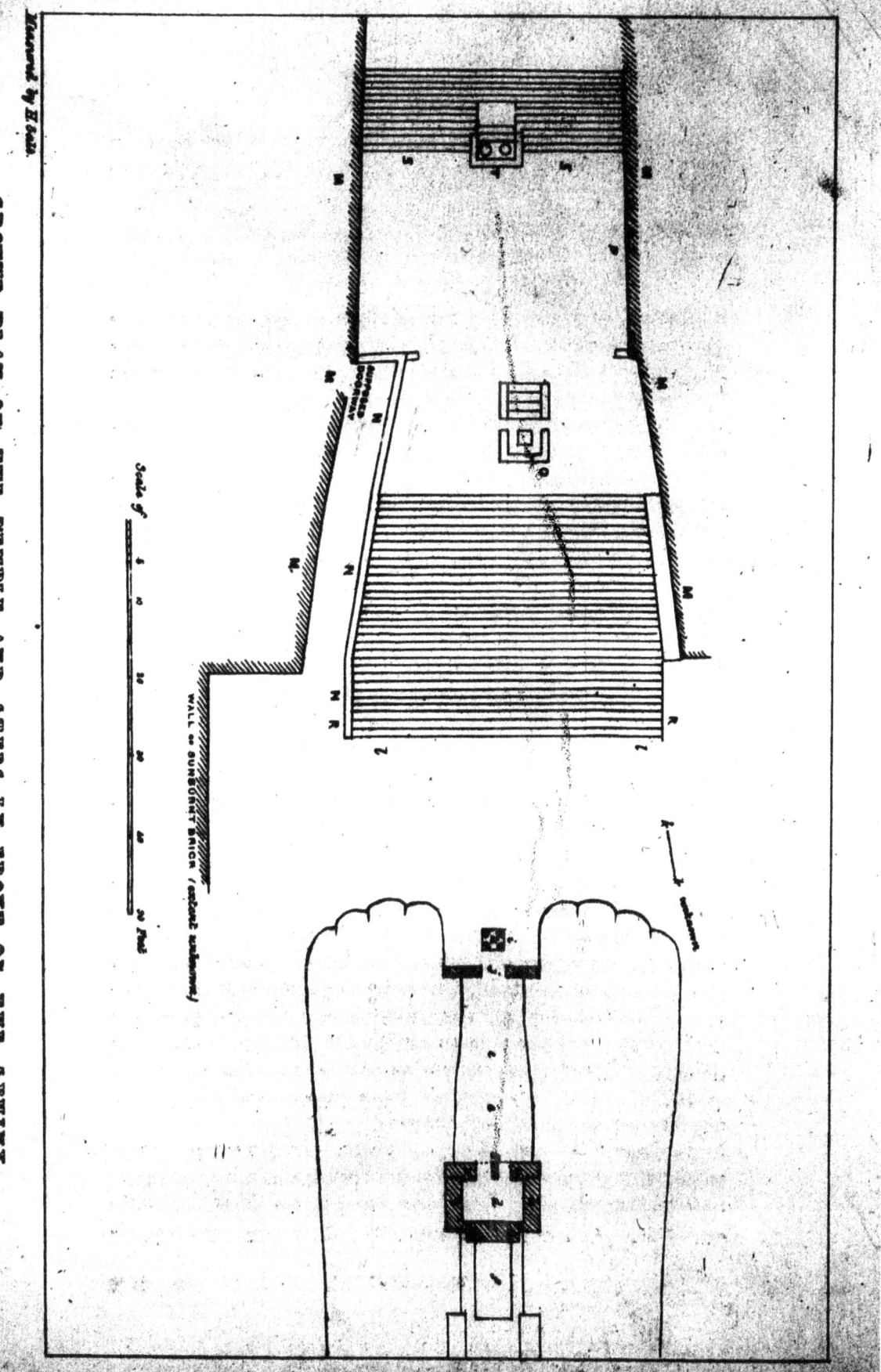

GROUND PLAN OF THE TEMPLE AND STEPS IN FRONT OF THE SPHINX.

VIEW OF THE TEMPLE BETWEEN THE FORE LEGS OF THE SPHINX.

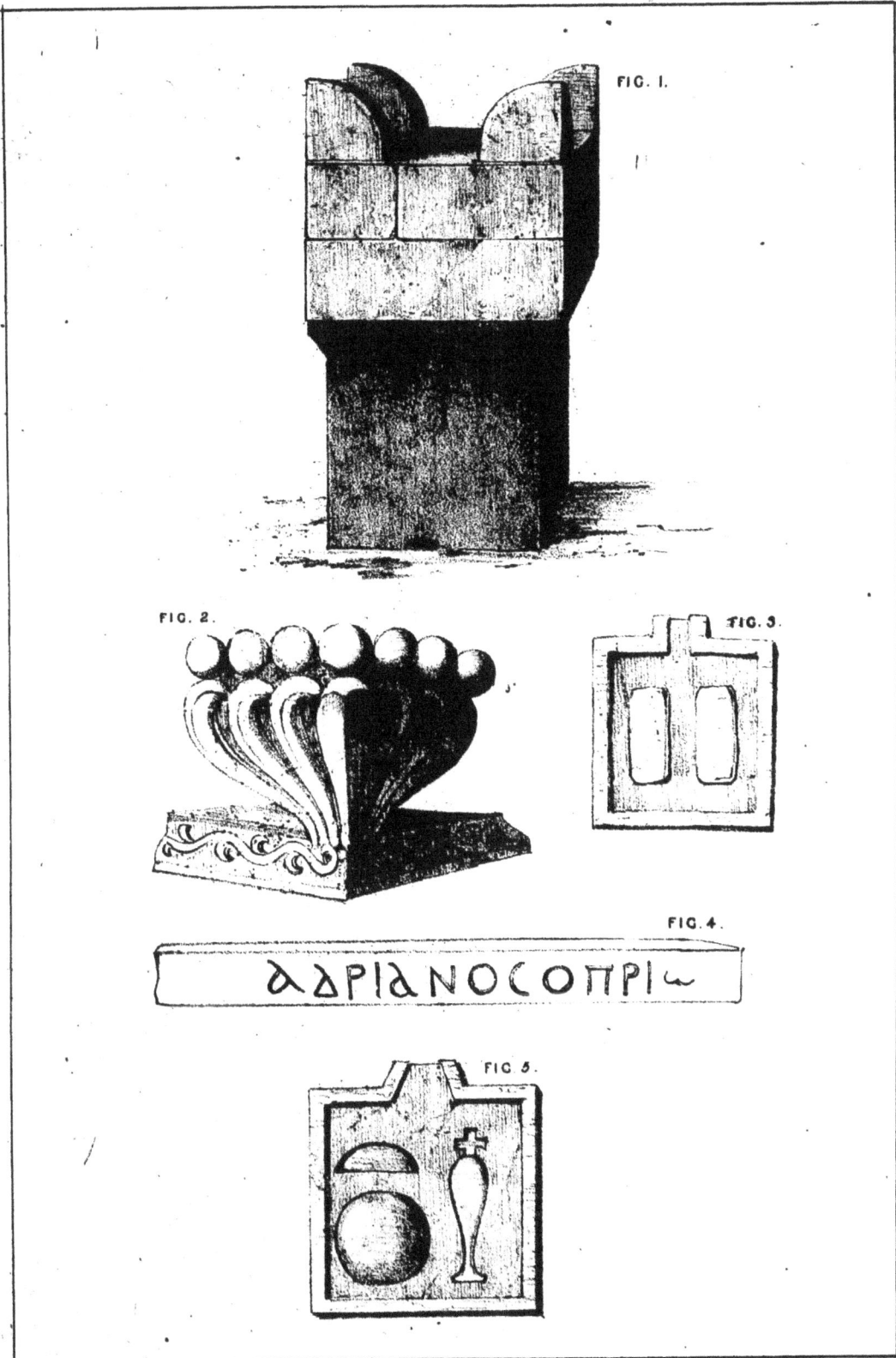

AN ALTAR, AND FRAGMENTS FOUND NEAR THE SPHINX.

"Short Greek inscriptions were indistinctly cut on the paws of the statue (see Plate E; Figs. 2, 4, 5, 6, 7, 8, in Plate F, and Figs. 3, 4, 5, 6, 7, 8, in Plate H). They prove that the image was held in high veneration; confirm the expression of Pliny, 'quasi silvestre nemus accolentium;' and contain various phrases, which elucidate many doubtful points in the sculptures in the adjacent tombs.[4]

"Capt. Caviglia succeeded in laying open the base of the Sphinx, and in clearing away the sand in front of it, to the extent of more than a hundred feet.

"It is scarcely possible," continues Mr. Salt, "for any person, unused to operations of this kind, to form an idea of the difficulties, which Capt. Caviglia had to surmount, when working at the depth of the base; for, in spite of all his precautions, the slightest breath of wind, or concussion set the surrounding particles of the sand in motion, so that the sloping sides crumbled away, and mass after mass tumbled in, till the whole moving surface bore no unapt resemblance to a cascade of water. Even when the sides appeared most firm, if the labourers suspended their work only for an hour, they found that the greater part of their labour had to be renewed.[5] This was particularly the case on the southern side of the right paw, where the people were employed for seven days without making any sensible advance, because the sand rolled down in one continued and regular torrent as fast as it was removed. He therefore only examined the end of the paw, where an imperfect inscription (see Fig. 2, Plate F) was discovered on the second digit, and a few dedicatory phrases, addressed to Harpocrates, to Mars, and to Hermes (see Figs. 4, 5, 7, 8, Plate H).[6] At the distance of about two feet to the southward of the right paw, the platform (kk in ground-plan) abruptly terminated,

[4] These Greek characters will be afterwards adverted to. Mr. Salt observes, in reference to one of these inscriptions (Plate E), that Dr. Young, probably misled by a bad copy, erroneously supposed that the eighth line alluded to one of the Roman emperors. The words are — *ωιλος Οσιρη*, and they, in some degree, confirm the account that the Sphinx was considered to be the guardian of the tomb of Osiris. Mr. Salt, therefore, conjectures that the tomb may be either in the body of the Sphinx, or in the Second Pyramid. It is to be observed, that Fig. 2, Plate H, is on a pier above Esne, and has been inserted by mistake.

[5] M. Caviglia should have begun his operations on a larger scale, and have removed the sand from the monument, instead of excavating near it. He made the same mistake in searching for the entrance of the Second Pyramid. (See p. 161, Vol. II.)

[6] Mr. Salt appears to have mistaken these names.

it was therefore supposed that the Sphinx was placed upon a pedestal; but, by extending the operations in front of the statue, the platform was found to be continued, and the steps (*ll*) were discovered. They were bounded on each side by walls formed of unburnt brick (MM in ground-plan), like those, which enclosed the antient cities, and temples of Egypt. The inner sides of the walls, nearest the steps, were lined with stone, and were coated with plaster; the stonework, however, appeared comparatively modern, for upon several of the blocks were the remains of Greek inscriptions, which alluded to other buildings. (See Fig. 3, Plate F;) and another of the inscriptions, recorded repairs, which were performed by the orders of Antoninus, and of Verus. The walls appeared to branch off towards the north, and also towards the south, and to form a large enclosure around the Sphinx; but their direction was not ascertained.[7] The steps, about a foot in breadth, and eight inches in height, were thirty in number. They ended abruptly on the northern side, so as to leave a passage between them and the wall. (See NN in ground-plan.) This passage was not examined.

"On a stone platform, at the top of the steps, was a small building (O in ground-plan), which, from its construction, and from various inscriptions found near it, seemed to have been a station (see Fig. 1, Plate C),[8] whence the emperors, and other persons of distinction, who visited the Pyramids, could witness the religious ceremonies performed at the altar below. An inscription on the front of it was much worn. (See Fig. 1, Plate F.)

"Another inscription on a stele (see Plate G) was found at *p* in ground-plan. It was erected in the time of the Emperor Nero, and bestows on him the epithet αγαθος δαιμων, which is also found on his coins, with the figure of a crowned serpent, the true symbol of that title. Dr. Young has indeed stated that αγαθος δαιμων was often represented in Egyptian mythology by a winged globe; but wings were the emblems of Ptha, and a globe of Phre, and together with the crowned snake, they formed the symbol of the great god.

"The platform above the steps was of narrower dimensions, and the abutments (RR in ground-plan) had a theatrical appearance. In a few days another flight of thirteen steps was discovered, and another small building (at T in ground-plan, see Plate)

---

[7] Part of a wall has been found in a direction from north to south, near the Shaft No. 2, in the map in the first volume.
[8] Fig. 2, Plate C, is a restoration of this building by Mr. Salt.

PLATE C.

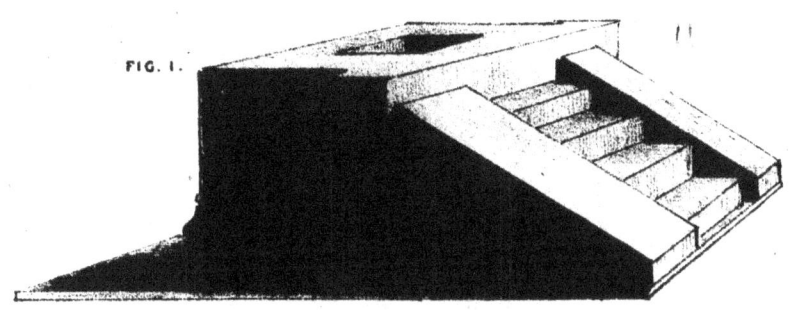

FIG. 1.

FIG 2.

FIG I. THE BUILDING ON THE STEPS IN FRONT OF THE SPHYNX, AT O IN GROUND PLAN.
FIG 2. THE BUILDING RESTORED, FROM FRAGMENTS FOUND DURING THE EXCAVATION.

```
ΥΠΕΡ ΑΙΩΝΙΟΥ ΝΕΙΚΗΣ ΚΑΙ ΔΙΑΜΟΝ        ΙΣ
ΤΩΝ ΚΥΡΙΩΝ ΑΥΤΟΚΡΑΤΟΡΩΝ

..ΣΕΠΤΙΜΙΟΥ ΣΕΟΥΗΡΟΥ ΕΥΣΕΒΟΥΣ
ΠΕΡΤΙΝΑΚΟΣ ΑΡΑΒΙΚΟΥ ΑΔΙΑΒΗΝΙΚΟΥ ΠΑΡΘΙΚΟΥ
ΜΕΓΙΣΤΟΥ ΚΑΙ Μ ΑΥΡΗΛΙΟΥ ΑΝΤΩΝΕΙΝΟΥ ΣΕΒΑΣΤΩΝ
‾‾‾‾‾‾‾‾‾‾‾‾‾‾‾‾‾‾‾‾‾‾‾‾‾‾‾‾‾‾‾‾‾‾‾‾‾‾‾‾‾‾‾‾‾‾‾‾‾‾‾‾‾ΚΑΙ ΙΟΥΛΙΑΣ.
ΔΟΜΝΗΣ ΣΕΒΑΣΤΗΣ ΜΗΤΡ ΣΤΡΑΤ ΠΕΔΩΝ ΤΟ ΣΤΡΩΜΑ
‾‾‾‾‾‾‾‾‾‾‾‾‾‾‾‾‾‾‾‾‾‾‾‾‾‾‾‾Ν ΔΙΑΨΘΑΡΕΝ ΑΠΟΚΑΤΕΣΤΑΘΗ.
‾‾‾‾‾‾‾‾‾‾‾‾‾‾‾‾ΝΟΥ ΕΠΑΡΧΟΥ ΑΙΓΥΠΤΟΥ ΕΠΙΣΤΡΑΤΗΓΟΥΝΤΟΣ
ΙΣ ΑΡΡΙΟΥ ΟΥΙΚΤΟΡΟΣ ΣΤΡΑΤΗΓΟΥΝΤΟΣ‾‾‾‾‾‾‾‾‾‾
ΤΟΥ ΣΗ‾‾‾‾
```

INSCRIPTION ON A BUILDING ON THE STEPS LEADING TO THE SPHINX.

VIEW OF THE STEPS LEADING TO THE SPHINX.

which resembled that at *o*; it appeared, by the inscription, to have been erected under the Emperor Septimius Severus; and the name of Geta is erased from the inscription, in the same manner, as it has been taken from the inscription upon the triumphal arch at Rome. At this place another inscription on a stele, erected in the reigns of Marcus Antoninus, and of Lucius Verus, was found; it was sent to the British Museum, and it recorded that the walls were restored on the 15th of Pachon (the 10th of May), in the sixth year of the reign of the Emperors Antoninus, and Verus. At the top of the second flight of steps a platform is carried on with a gradual ascent to the length of 135 feet, bounded by a wall on the southern side till it arrives nearly at the level of the ground, when the rock rapidly descends towards the Nile, whether, or not, in the form of steps was not discovered. It is difficult to convey, even by drawings, a distinct idea of this approach to the Sphinx. It was impossible, however, to conceive any thing more imposing than the general effect; or better calculated to set off to advantage the grandeur of the enormous monument, particularly in the evening, when the sun was setting behind it. Mr. Salt observes, "That the spectator advanced on a level with the breast, and thereby witnessed the full effect of that admirable expression of countenance, which characterises the features, whilst, as he descended the successive flights of stairs, the stupendous image rose before him, whilst his view was confined, by the walls on either side, to the interesting object, for the contemplation of which, even when he had reached the bottom of the steps, a sufficient space was allowed for him to comprehend the whole at a single glance. Mr. Salt concludes in the following words: "Such was the result of Captain Caviglia's exertions in June, when, in consequence of exposing himself too much to the sun, he was unfortunately seized by an attack of ophthalmia, that compelled him to suspend his operations, and shortly afterwards to return to take charge of his ship at Alexandria. It is, perhaps, a circumstance, unexampled in Mahommedan countries, that these operations should have been carried on by a single individual, attended occasionally only by one soldier, without the slightest molestation having been offered, or unpleasant circumstance having occurred, notwithstanding that numerous parties of idle soldiers went every day to inspect the excavation, and that thousands of Arabs, during part of the time, were encamped in the neighbourhood; and this circumstance indeed, strange as it may appear in Europe, presents the most unequivocal proof of the tranquillity reigning in Egypt, and does honour to the government of Mohammed Ali Pasha, who, on this occasion, as well as on many others, I have reason to testify, has shewn a remarkable liberality in facilitating the researches carried on by Europeans in any way connected with science."

"The whole expense of these operations amounted to about 18,000 piastres (450*l.*); and I have to add, that Captain Caviglia, to whom by our engagement was left the disposal of every thing that might be discovered, very handsomely requested me to forward the whole, of what I might think interesting, to the British Museum, as a testimony of his attachment to our country, under the flag of which he had for some years sailed."

MR. BIRCH'S NOTE ON THE LARGE TABLET.
SEE PLATE.

This tablet represents a proscynema, or act of adoration, offered to the Sphinx by Thothmes IV. or V., supposed to have reigned 1446 B.C.[9]

The upper part is divided by a perpendicular line of hieroglyphics, which expresses the following declaration of the Sphinx, "*We decree, that the sun, the establisher of the world* (Re-men-tor),[1] *shall be crowned on the throne of Seb; that Thothmes, the crown of crowns, shall be adorned with the glory of Athom.*"

In each of the two upper compartments, a sphinx is seated on a

---

[9] Sir J. G. Wilkinson is of opinion, that Pliny's assertion that the Sphinx is the tomb of Amasis is owing to a mistake in the names Amosis and Tuthmosis; because Herodotus distinctly says that the tomb of Amasis was near the Temple of Minerva at Sais.—"Manners and Customs of the Antient Egyptians," Vol. I. p. 192. And in Vol. III. p. 28, he remarks that sphinxes were emblems of the Egyptian kings, and that, when composed of the head of a man, and of the body of a lion, signified the union of intellect with physical force. There were two kings of the name of Amasis, one the last of the XVIIth dynasty, and the other of the XXVIth or Saite dynasty. Hence the assertions of Pliny and Herodotus may be reconciled.

[1] It has been usual to read the beetle in the cartouches the word TO, the world, because, with particular determinatives, it is thus found. Cf. Champ. Gr. p. 96, but it is the first of a phonetic group, TP Tar. or Tor, signifying to plant, pledge, &c. Cf. Champ. Gr. Eg. p. 368, Salv. i. An. Gr. 41, 75. The expression Re-men-to is, therefore, more properly Re-men-tor. The scarabæus at the Roman period was employed phonetically for T in proper names. The repetition of this phrase seems to infer that the adoration had been made about the period of the coronation.

PLATE B.

F. Arundale delt. from a Drawing by H. Salt.

TABLET BETWEEN THE FORE LEGS OF THE SPHINX.

pedestal, which resembles a doorway; and the image on the left receives a libation offered by the monarch, and is accompanied with an inscription expressing "*the sun—in his solar mountain, or the lord of the two solar abodes;*"² and with the following declaration, "*We grant life and power to Thothmes, the lord of the world, the crown of crowns.*"

In the other compartment the same monarch pours a libation on an altar, and offers burning incense to the Sphinx, which is here styled, "*Ra or Hor in the solar mountain;*" and is said "*to grant power and victory to the lord of the world; to Thothmes, the crown of crowns.*"

The remaining thirteen lines can scarcely be made out, but they begin as follows, "*In the first year, on the 19th day of Athyr, under the purity of Horus, the mighty bull; the establisher of diadems; the lord of the upper, and lower hemispheres; established with dominion, like Athom; the golden hawk; the director of the years; the conqueror of the (Libyans); the King; the Sun; the preserver of worlds; the son of the sun; Thothmes; the diadem of diadems; the giver of life, of stability, and of power; like the sun for ever,*" &c. Any attempt to explain the rest of the inscription would require a restoration of the text, which would be attended with great uncertainty; but it appears to record an act of adoration performed by the monarch to the Sphinx; to enumerate the benefits supposed to have been conferred by the idol; and also the following address of the Sphinx to the king; "*I am thy father; the god in the solar mountain; Tor, and Athom.*"³ The inscription also declares, "*That the king shall wear the two crowns, which compose the royal pschent; and that he shall sit on the throne of Seb, the youngest of the gods.*"

In the thirteenth line part of a cartouche occurs, which is apparently the prenomen of the king *Ra-shaa-f*, or *Shafre*, supposed to be Chefren; but the fracture in the inscription makes it impossible to determine in what manner the name is mentioned. It is, however, to be remarked, that the Sphinx is situated before the eastern front of the ruins, supposed to have been a temple connected with the second Pyramid, which is said to have been built by Chefren; and also, that it is proved by this tablet, which seems to have been executed in the first year of the reign of Thothmes IV., that the construction of the image had then been achieved, which, from its enormous size, could scarcely have been effected in one year.

---

² A sphinx, resembling in many respects the one here represented, has been published by Champollion, Panthéon Egyptien, 24 (F), holding in its fore paws a figure of Truth, and called "*the Sun, the lord of the two worlds, the great god, the lord of heaven.*" This image is also seated on a gateway. Salt's copy is incorrect and should apparently read "*the sun, the lord of the two worlds and of the solar abode.*" A sphinx, wearing on its head two plumes, appears in the boat of the sun at the sixth hour. Cf. Rosel. M. d C. xli.

³ Solar types.

The oldest representation of a sphinx, which Mr. Birch had met with, is on amulets belonging to the times of Thothmes IV., who is represented on the erect obelisk at Karnak under this form offering to Re, and of his successors.[4]

According to Pliny, the Sphinx at Gizeh was the tomb of Amasis, the founder probably of the eighteenth dynasty, and the form of the head-dress, and the remains of the features of the image, seem to indicate, that it was constructed under the eighteenth, or Diospolitan dynasty; and the inscriptions in question appear to assign to it as high an antiquity.

In this tablet the Sphinx is identified with the sun under the appellation of *Horus, or the god of the solar abode.* In royal cartouches a sphinx signifies, "*a lord*" or "*master*,"[5] and it is called in hieroglyphics "*okr*."[6] The Greeks imagined that it represented *intellect*, or *strength*, but they seem to have alluded to the sphinx of Thebes in Bœotia,[7] and not to those in Egypt, which usually personified distinguished monarchs, as has been proved by two inscriptions, connected with Amenoph III.[8] (or Memnon), which have been already published.

The figure of a lion appears to have been connected with the sun, because his name "*Moui*" signified splendour, wisdom, intellect, &c., and one of these animals, indeed, appears to have accompanied distinguished Egyptian kings in their conquests: who, from their heroic exploits, were often mentioned, as a lion among inferior animals. Amulets, and scarabæi have been often inscribed with the names of Egyptian kings, who are in the form of a sphinx, and in the act of treading under foot Asiatic, or Negro prisoners. The Sphinx, at Gizeh therefore probably represented, under the character of the sun, the monarch by whose orders the image was constructed; and it was afterwards worshipped in consequence of the superstitious observances, which gave rise to the deification of departed kings, to whose service priests of different orders were dedicated, and whose glory was compared to the noonday effulgence of the sun.

---

[4] Amulet, British Museum, case BBB., 2. On a fragment of a coffin Amenophis I. is personified as a sphinx, the Queen Mauthem occurs at Turin. Ch. Lett. à. M. le Duc de Blacas. Pl. I. Alexander is found under this type. Rosel. M. da C. 156, and one of the Ptolemies. Ibid. M. R.

[5] It is used for the syllable *Neb* in the name Nasht*neb*f or Nakht*neb*f Memphiticé. Cf. Rosel. Mon. Hor. T. 11. Tav. XIV. 156 b., 156 c. Nectanebo also offers the emblem, Rosel. M. R. cliv.

[6] Ch. Gr. Eg. 463. This perhaps meant victory, as Neith-okr, the victorious Neith.

[7] Οὐ τὴν Ὀθηρέας ἀροταριοι ἄς ἐπὶ Θήβαις.

[8] D'Athanasi, Giov. Researches and Discoveries in Upper Egypt. 8vo. London, 1836. Frontispiece. Burton, Jas. Exc. Hier. Pl. LXI.

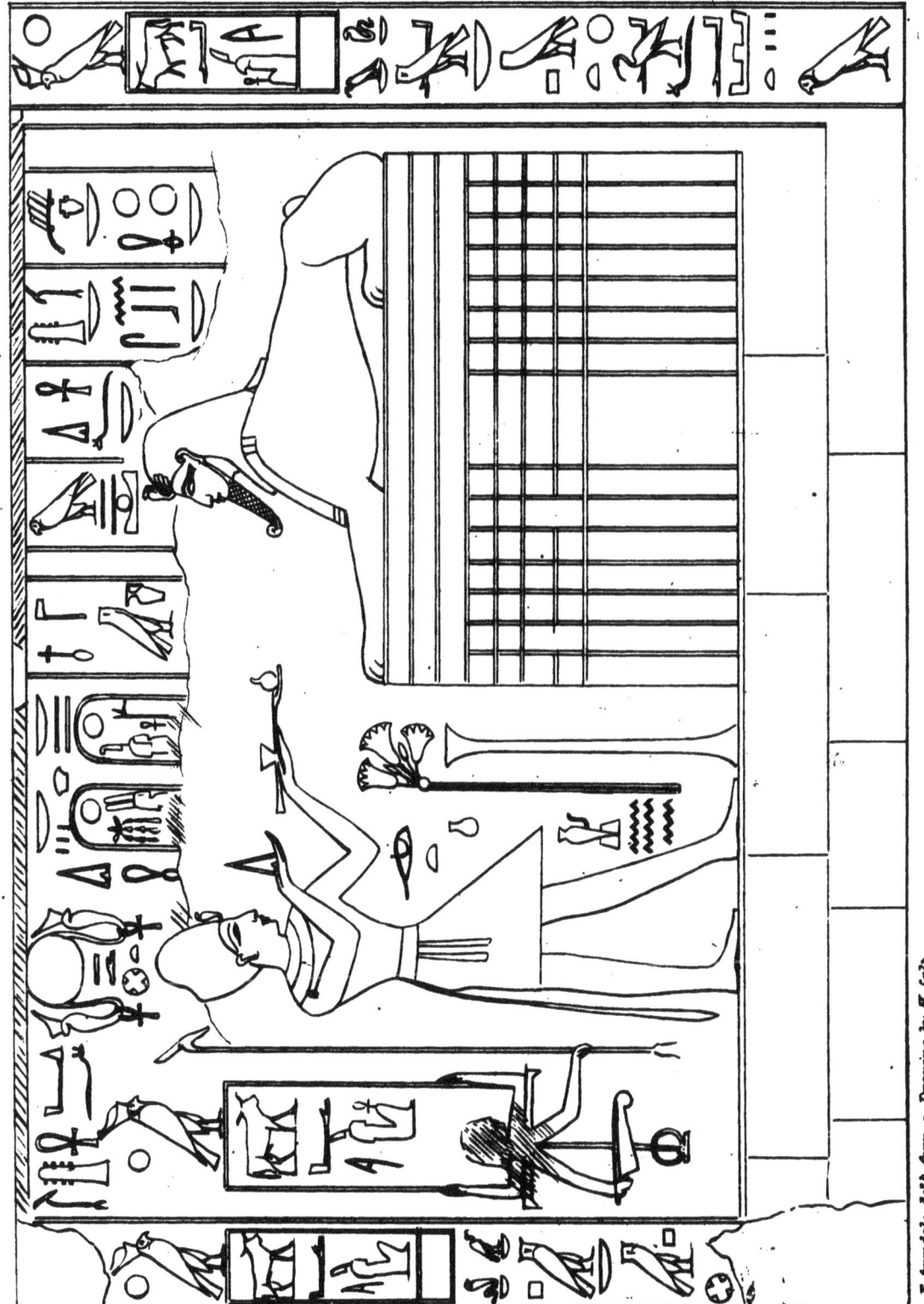

SMALLER TABLET BETWEEN THE FORE LEGS OF THE SPHINX.

APPENDIX.

NOTE BY MR. BIRCH ON THE SMALLER TABLET BETWEEN THE FORE LEGS OF THE SPHINX.

SEE PLATE.

Rameses the great, Sesostris, supposed to have reigned 1355 B.C., dressed in his robes, holds in his hand an amshoir (or censor) and a conical piece of bread, which he offers to a sphinx placed on a pedestal, which, like that in the tablet plate B, has the form of a doorway.[9] The Sphinx has the body of a lion, the head-dress of a god, or of a monarch, and the features in Mr. Salt's drawing resemble those of Rameses.

Before the Sphinx is an altar adorned with flowers; and behind the king is a royal standard, supported by a human head, and by four arms, two of which elevate the standard, and the others hold a koucoupha sceptre, and the feather of truth; below the standard are the emblem of heaven, and the staff, which ends in a signet representing the orbit of the sun. Above the head of the king is *Har of Hat*, the *Horus* of Edfou, the celestial sun encircled by uræi, which sustain the symbols of life, and the crowns of the upper, and lower hemispheres, over which the sun presided.

The inscriptions on the upper part contain the names and the titles of the monarch in question, and also those of the Sphinx. The monarch is styled "*The gracious god directed*[1] ...... *the lord of the upper, and of the lower world; the sun; the director of truth; approved of the sun; the lord of diadems; Rameses, beloved of Amoun; the giver of life; like the sun for ever; Har-Hat, the giver of life, of stability, and of power. A gift of incense and of libations. Har—of the two solar abodes*" (which refer to the Sphinx in the character of Har. ph re, or of Horus the sun), "*of life, of stability, and of power,*" with the following epithets, "*the giver of victory, and of magnanimity; like the sun continually.*"

The inscriptions on the sides of the tablet are nearly alike, but that on the right is most perfect. They express "*Har, the sun, the ruler of the upper, and of the lower world; (Aroeris) the victorious bull; the beloved of truth; the lord of the upper, and of the lower worlds; the regulator of Egypt; the chastiser of nations; the hawk (of gold),*" &c. &c. The tablet is imperfect and the inscriptions were doubtless much longer.

---

[9] The form of these pedestals has been supposed to allude to a communication through the Sphinx to the Second Pyramid, or to a temple within the body of the image. Excavations may possibly exist in the rock beneath the Sphinx; but for many reasons a communication with the pyramid is not probable.

[1] Champollion reads this group ΠΩΩ "*to direct,*" but I suppose it to mean ΠΟΤΩΩ or ΠΟΤΩΩ "*water*" and "*to suffuse*" taken in an active sense.

NOTES ON THE GREEK INSCRIPTIONS.

The characters do not appear to have been accurately copied; it is, therefore, extremely difficult to explain them; and in many instances they are merely fragments.

PLATE E.

This is an inscription on one of the paws of the Sphinx, a translation of it was given in the "Quarterly Review," Vol. XIX. p. 412.

The ever-living gods built thy . . . . . form,
Sparing the ground producing corn.
Having raised thee in the midst of the level arable land,
Having driven back the sand from the rocky island;
A neighbour of the Pyramids they placed thee;
(A line seems wanting) . . . . such to behold,
Not the slayer of Œdipus, as at Thebes,
But the goddess Latona, a most pure attendant,
. . . . . protecting the regretted good Osiris
. . . . the revered governor of Egypt,
. . . . heavenly, great,
. . . like to Vulcan,
. . the earth.
The Salutation of Arrian.

PLATE F.

Fig. 1 is an inscription on the front of the building at O in ground-plan (see plan), and it appears to have been a description of the Sphinx, but it is very obscure.

Figs. 2, 4, 5, 7, 8, were found on one of the paws of the Sphinx; and figs. 3 and 6 were on the wall, but they are too imperfect to admit of explanation.

PLATE G.

Plate G. was on a stele, and is also to be found in the "Quarterly Review," p. 414.

To Good Fortune.[a]

Whereas the Emperor (Nero) Claudius Cæsar Augustus Germanicus, the good genius of the world, in addition to all the benefits, he has conferred on Egypt, has shewn the most especial care of its interests, by sending to us Tiberius Claudius Balbillus as governor, through whose favours and acts of kindness, abounding in all good things, Egypt, beholding the gifts of the Nile yearly increasing, is now more (than ever)

---

[a] These inscriptions have been translated by M. Letronne, and are also inserted in the "Library of Entertaining Knowledge."

INSCRIPTION ON ONE OF THE PAWS OF THE SPHINX.

ΗΔΕΚΥΡΕΙΠΑΝΤΟϹΝϹΦΙΞΙϹΚΑΙΘΕΙΟΝΟΡΑΜΑ
ΧΩΜΑΙΑΡΚΗΝΟΕΕΙϹΩΦΟϹϹΥΠΕΡϹΠΛΕΤΟΤΗΔΕ
ΗΦΑΛΑϹΑΤΟϹϹΙΕΡΩΙΟΝΔΗϹΕΙϹΚΟϹΜΟΝΑΠΑΝΤΑ
ΙΕΡΟΝΙΩΥΕΦΥΠΕΡΚΙΕΠΡΟϹΩΠΟΝΕΧΕΙΤΟΘϹΟΤΠΩΥΝ
ΓΥΡΑΔΕΚΑΙΔΕΜΑϹΟΙΑΛΕΩΝΒΑϹΙΛΕΥϹΟΓΕΘΗΡΨΝ
ΕΙΝΟΝΚΨΕΝΤΟΘΕΛΜΑΝΡΕΚΕϹϹΕΙΤΙϹΓϹΝΟΤΙϹΕΙ
ΤΝϹΧΕΙΤΕΗΟΤΕΤΙΩΝΑΜΟΝΗϹΑϹΙΟΝΔΕ
ΚΕΙΚΕΤΙΑΝΤΟΛΕΙΑΙΟΜΕΔϹϹΙΓϹΕΚΤΗϹΘΕΙΟΤΗΤΟϹ
ΕϹΘΛΗϹΑΥΤΑΡϹΤΩΙΕΕΑϹΑΠΙΩΝΕΧΑΡΑΞΑ

Inscription on the front of the lower Building on the platform facing the Sphinx.

ΜΜΜϹΘΙϹΜΜΜ ΑΙϹϹΙϹΑΡΜ
ΜΑΙϹΑΥΡ ΑΠΟΔΩΜΜΜ
ΜΑΥΡ ΙϹΧΥΡΙΩΝ
ϹΨΤΗϹ ΛΑΜΜΡΟΤΑΓΜΜΜ
ΛΕΞΑΝΔΡΕΙΑϹϹ
ϹΥΝΜΜΩ ΚΑΙΤΕΚΝΟΙϹϹΤΕ
ΛΩΙϹΧ
ΕΠΑΡΙ-ΘΩ

Inscription on the paw of the Sphinx.

ΗΡΑΚΛΑΤΟΙ

ΤΕΛΕΙΛΟΥ
ΕΛΟΥϹΙΝΕΙΝΑ
ϹΥΜΒΟΛΟΝΤΕ

ΚΟΛΛΟΥΘΙΩΝΟϹ
ΤΟΠΡΟϹΚΥΝΗΜΑ

ΚΥΝΙΙΟ
ΦΑΝΟΥ

ΛΟΥΚΑϹ

ΤΟΠΡΟϹΚΥΝΗΜΑ

INSCRIPTIONS FOUND NEAR THE SPHINX.

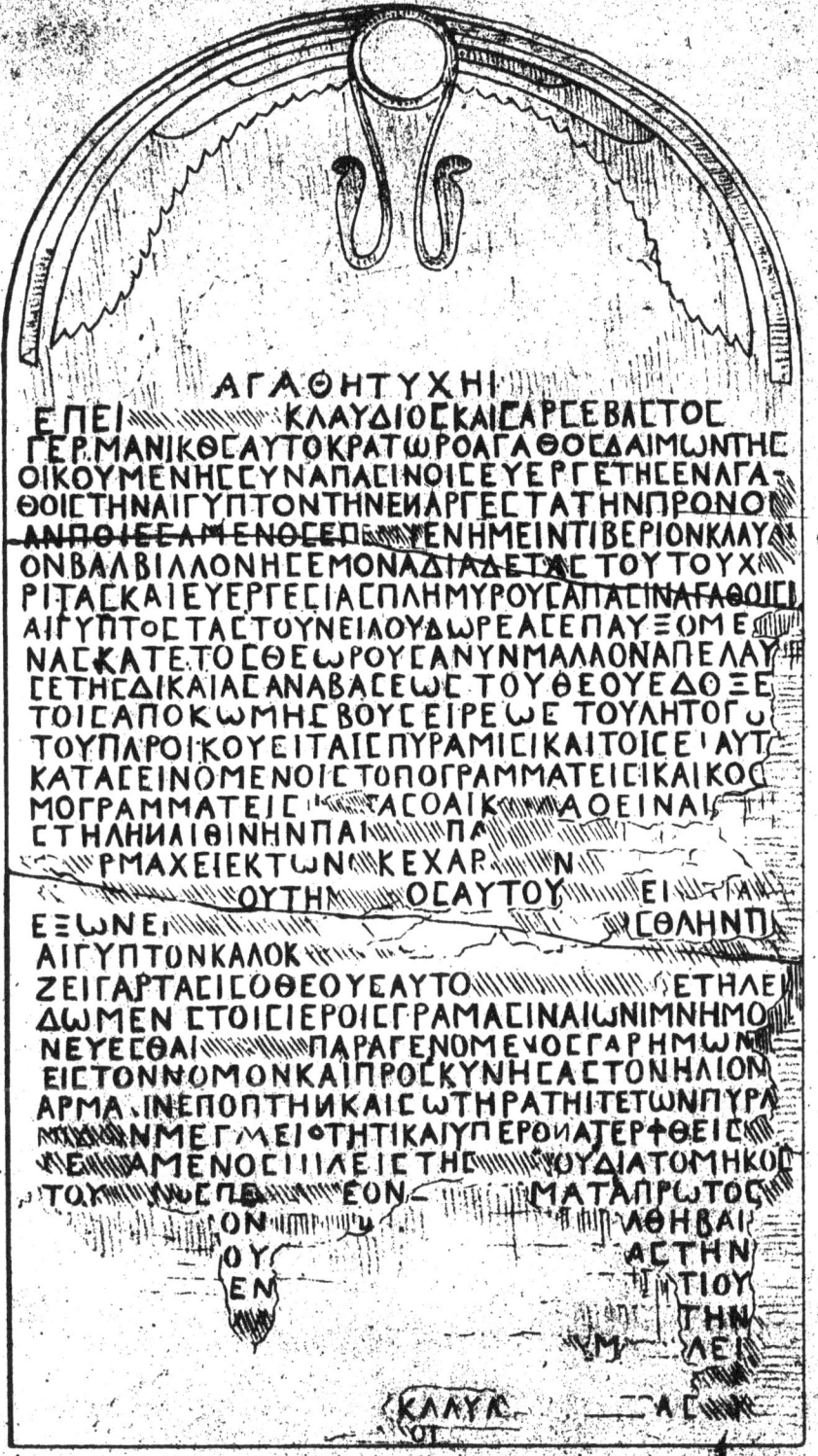

TABLET FOUND DURING THE EXCAVATIONS AT THE SPHINX, AND NOW IN THE BRITISH MUSEUM.

FIG. 1.

ΑΓΑΘΗΤΥΧΗ
L̄ ΑΝΤΩΝΕΙΝΟΥ
ΚΑΙΟΥΗΡΟΥΤΩΝ—
ΚΥΡ''ΙΑΥΤΟΚΡΑΤΟΡΩΝ
ΗΓΕ ΙΝΙΥΟΝΤΟΣ ΦΑ-
ΤΙΤΙΑΝΟΥ(ΠΙ(ΤΡΑΤΗΟΩΝ
ΤΟ(ΛΟΥΚΗΙΟΥΦΕΧΙΛΙΑΝΥ
ΣΤΡΑΤΗΓΟΥΝΤΟΣΤΟΥΝΟ
ΜΟΥΘΕΩΝΟΣ ΑΠΟ
ΚΑΤΕΣΤΗΣ ΕΝΤΑΤΙ
ΧΗ ΕΠΑΓΑΘΩΙ
ΠΑΧΩΝΙΣ

FIG. 2.

ΑΓΑΘΗΤΥΧΗ ΠΕΠΛΗΡω
L ᾱ ΑΝΤωΝΙΝΟΥ ΚΑΙΟΥΗΡΟΥΤωΝ ΚΥΡΙωΝ
ΑΥΤΟΚΡΑΤΟΡωΝΜΕΣΟΡΙ   ΕΠΙ ΤΙ ΤΟΥ
ΦΛΑΟΥΙΟΥ ΤΙΤΙΑΝΟΥ ΕΠΑΡΧΟΥ ΑΙΓΥΠΤΟΥ
ΕΠΙΣΤΡΑΤΗΓΟΥΝΤΟΣ ΤΕΡΕΝΤΙΟΥ ΑΛΕΞΑΝΔΡ⁼
ΣΤΡΑΤΑ////////////ΤΟ⸗ ΚΛΑΥΔΙΟΥ ΑΠΟΛΙΝΑΡΕ

FIG. 3.

ΚΕΚΑΡΙΚΟΥΚΕΕΥΤΥΧΗ.
ΚΕ ΤΕΡΟΝΤΙΟΥ
ΚΕ ΜΑΝΔΡΚΕΧΡΥΩΨΙΟΥΚΕΠΛΛΙΧΟΙ

FIG. 4.

ΤΟ ΠΡΟΣ.ΚΥΝΗΜΑ
ΑΡΤΟΚΡΑΤΙΟΣ
ΚΑΙ ΠΥΝΑΝΙ

FIG. 5.

ΤΟ ΠΡΟΣΚΥΝΗΜΑ
ΑΡΙΟΥ

FIG. 6.

ΤΟ ΠΡΟΣΚΥΝΗΜΑ ΕΡΜΙΟΥ ΑΛΕ
ΞΑΝΔΡΟΥ ΠΣΚΕΙΜΣΙΜ⸦

FIG. 7.

ΤΟ ΠΡΟΣΚΥΝΗΜΑ ΕΡΜΙΟΥ

FIG. 8.

ΤΟ ΠΡΟΣΚΥΝΗΜΑ
ΑΡΙΟΥ

INSCRIPTIONS FOUND NEAR THE SPHINX.

enjoying the proper rising of the deity, it has seemed good to the inhabitants of the village Busiris, in the Latopolitan Nome, who live near the Pyramids, and to the local and village clerks therein to vote and dedicate a stone column . . . . It preserves his godlike . . . . column . . . . in sacred characters to be remembered for ever . . . . for having come to our nome, and for having worshipped the sun, Armachis, the overseer, and Saviour, and for having been delighted with the magnificence and . . . . . of the Pyramids.

PLATE H.

Fig. 1 was inscribed on a stele near the building at N. in ground-plan, and is noticed in p. 414 of the " Quarterly Review."

To Good Fortune.

In the sixth year of Antoninus and of Verus, the sovereign Emperors, in the prefecture of Flavius Titianus, Lucianus Ophellianus being Commander in chief, and Theon being the general of the Nome, he rebuilt the walls under happy auspices.

Pachon XV.

Fig. 2 was found on a pier above Esne, and is inserted by mistake, on account of its having been written in the same page of the MS. with the other inscriptions.

Figs. 3, 4, 5, 6, 7, 8, were on the paws of the Sphinx. Fig. 3 is obscure. Fig. 4 is the Adorations of Harpocratius and of Punan. Fig 5. The Adoration of Arius. Fig. 6. The Adoration of Hermius Alexander . . . . . . Fig. 7. The Adoration of Hermius. Fig. 8. The Adoration of Arius.

INSCRIPTION ON A BUILDING AT T IN GROUND-PLAN.

For the eternal victory, and . . . . . . of the sovereign lords.
Septimius Severus, Pius, Pertinax, Arabicus, Adiabenicus, Parthicus, Maximus, and Marcus Aurelius Antoninus being emperors.[3]
and Julia
Domna Empress mother, of the camps, the pavement
. . . . . having been destroyed, was restored
. . . . nus; prefect of Egypt, being commander-in-chief,
Arrius Victor commanding . . . .

[3] Caracalla had the titles of M. Au. Antoninus, and is here alluded to. This inscription is also mentioned in the " Quarterly Review."

REMARKS ON THE EGYPTIAN ARMY.

The following remarks on the Egyptian army were written in the summer of 1840, and were published in the "United Service Journal" of November in that year; the account of the horses was also published in the "Sporting Review" of Nov. and Dec. 1840. These papers are now reprinted, because they are referred to in the two former volumes of this work.

It is a most satisfactory reflection that, since the remarks were written, the direction of the public affairs of this country has been intrusted to an administration strictly Conservative, and intimately acquainted with the circumstances of the times, and with the resources of the country. It is therefore to be expected, that those great principles, by which the nation has so long, and so signally prospered, will, as far as circumstances permit, be again adopted; and that the interests of the country will be better attended to than they were under the late government.

The observations more immediately relating to Syria are not inserted, because the operations, to which they alluded, are concluded, and although the result greatly exceeded my expectations, yet I consider that my opinions were well founded; for, notwithstanding the established and well-merited reputation of the British navy, it was difficult to imagine that the trifling detachment landed from the fleet (which, I believe, did not at any time exceed 2000 Europeans) would be able to defeat an organised army, in complete possession of the country, and supposed to amount to 70 or 80,000 men, at all events of sufficient strength to threaten Constantinople. The event, no doubt, is chiefly to be attributed to the mismanagement of Ibrahim Pasha, and of Suleiman Bey, who ought at once to have removed their artillery and stores from the coast, when they could no longer command it; and, instead of advancing on certain destruction by attacking our people in communication with the fleet, should have retired upon Damascus, and upon the interior; whence nothing but an European army, sufficiently strong to keep up a communication with the fleet, could have dislodged them. The noble services of the British navy, and the efficiency of the equipment, made up, however, for the want of numbers, and amply sustained the matchless glory of their former achievements.

At the same time it must be confessed, that, if the reduction of the Pasha's power was the object in view, his army should not have been allowed to have returned to Egypt, particularly that large part of it, which was composed of Syrian conscripts; and, it may be added, that the hostile disposition, which, according to Mr. Perring's account, was manifested by the Arabs on the confines of Egypt, and more especially the dreadful state of Syria even at the present time, may well call in question the policy, as well as the humanity, of destroying a government (which, however oppressive, effectually provided for the tranquillity of the country) without establishing an adequate authority in its room; and also of arming a population, irreconcilably divided into hostile sects by religious opinions, and by local circumstances; and of then turning them loose on each other, with no other control, or resource from anarchy and confusion, than the ferocious atrocities of Albanian banditti, and of a half-disciplined Turkish soldiery. The mischief, however, is done, and, unless the jealousies and discordant interests of the allies can sufficiently subside to allow of the occupation of the country by a European force,—a circumstance, which would be highly satisfactory to the unfortunate inhabitants, it will probably be found necessary to call in the assistance of Mahomet Ali, whose military arrangements, and vigorous determination, are well calculated to disarm the people, and to enforce obedience; and whose authority, however destructive and severe, is at all events preferable to license, and to insecurity.

Having briefly stated the opinions, which my visit to the East induces me to entertain, I proceed to mention, that the formation of a regular Egyptian army was first attempted in 1822, when a corps, consisting of 5000 Mamelucs, under Mohammed Bey, and of 20,000 Negroes, was assembled at Es Souan, in order that it might be disciplined by Colonel Sevres, who was said to have been an aide-de-camp to Marshal Ney, and who afterwards assumed the title of Suleiman Bey.

It is stated that the instruction of the Mamelucs was attended with considerable difficulty and danger; but that the negroes were more tractable; and were also strong and efficient, until, from some cause or other, which has not been explained, they suddenly became sickly, and were reduced to 3000 men.

As this scheme had failed, the Pasha was advised, it would appear, by the French consul, through whom he obtained French and Italian instructors, to establish a conscription, similar to that in France. 30,000 men were in consequence indiscriminately seized, and sent into Upper Egypt; and, from these people, the 3000 Negroes, and some Nubians, with the Mamelucs as officers, an army was formed, which in 1824 consisted of six regiments, each of five battalions nominally 800 strong; but the whole force did not actually exceed 23,000 men. Another conscription of 15,000 men soon afterwards took place, with the intention of eventually increasing the force to 40,000.

A corps of artillery was formed; and the army attained some proficiency under French and Italian officers, amongst whom, a Neapolitan engineer, named Chiandi, is said to have had considerable merit; but Colonel Sevres appears to have been infinitely superior in all respects to the other Franks. With an idea, probably, of increasing his authority, he turned Turk, and is said to have received his pelisse, and investiture as a Bey on Christmas-day.

The medical department was at that time extremely defective, and a college was established under French superintendence.

Ibrahim Pasha is reported to have acquired great popularity with the new levees, notwithstanding that they were drilled under his direction for four hours in the morning, and as many in the evening, till the hospitals were crowded with sick. Mahomet Ali resided also for some time in the camp near Cairo. It is said that he enforced with great strictness the observance of the hours of prayer, but that he sanctioned at the same time the open sale of wine in the bazaar.[4]

In 1836, there were fourteen regiments of cavalry, and twenty-three of infantry, besides Albanians, irregular troops, and a considerable corps of artillery. Of these, four regiments of cavalry, four of infantry, and a troop of light artillery, formed the guard. The greatest part of the men had been raised by conscription in Egypt, but several regiments of cavalry, and a few battalions, came from Syria. With the exception of some muskets made after the English pattern, they were armed, ap-

---

[4] When the Pasha was employed in the organisation of his army, a circumstance occurred, which shews his despotic authority, and the absurd mistakes, which an inconsiderate exercise of it often occasioned. His Highness happened to observe at Alexandria a pair of European shoes, which appeared well adapted for the use of his army. Having obtained them for a pattern, he directed that twelve pairs should be made, and sent to Cairo, with an order for the instant manufacture of 40,000. The order was obeyed, and the troops were furnished with 40,000 pairs of shoes exactly of one size!

pointed, and exercised, like the French army. The French language is taught in the schools, and the Frank instructors are chiefly of that nation, which has consequently great influence. The whole of the native officers were formerly, and many now are taken from the ranks, and are therefore entirely uneducated; a few have been recently furnished by the different schools, which the Pasha has established.

The monthly pay is as follows:—

		Piastres.		
		Cavalry.	Infantry.	Artillery.
	General of Division	18,000	18,000	18,000
	General of Brigade	10,500	10,500	10,500
Mirely Bey	Colonel	8,000	8,000	8,000
Caimacan	Lieutenant-Colonel	3,000	3,000	3,000
Bimbaschi	Commandant	2,500	2,500	2,500
Sarcologassi	Major	1,250	1,250	1,250
Umbaschi	1st Captain	550		600
	2d Captain	450	500	500
Metagim Awal	1st Lieutenant	300	300	360
Metagim Saim	2d Lieutenant	250	250	300
Sawuss	Sergeants	25	25	25
Mobassi	Corporals	20	20	20
	Privates	15	15	15

In 1824, the pay of a Mirely (colonel) amounted to 8383—6 paras, and a fraction.[5] The guards have double pay, 3 per cent is deducted for military stock. The troops are supposed to be paid annually, but were said, in 1836, to be a year and a half in arrear.

A Christian can attain to the rank of General of Division. Surgeons, and veterinary surgeons take rank as officers. Cavalry officers are furnished by Government with swords.

A colonel is allowed forage for 3 horses.
A lieutenant-colonel .. 3 ..
A commandant .. 2 ..
An adjutant .. 2 ..

Rank is distinguished by the following decorations worn on the breast:—

Colonel - Crescent, and star in diamonds.
Lieutenant-colonel Crescent in gold, star in diamonds.
Commandant - Star, and crescent in gold.

---

[5] In 1836, 40 paras made 1 piastre, 5 piastres 1 shilling.

Major - -	Crescent in gold, star in silver.
1st Captain -	Star in silver, with small diamond in centre.
2d Captain -	Star in silver.
Lieutenants -	Small star in silver, with one quarter of crescent.
Sergeant Major	3 Marks.
Sergeants - -	2 Marks.
Corporals -	1 Mark.

Bars on the arm were to be introduced into the artillery service.

The men are retained as long as they are serviceable, and, if disabled, or wounded, they are entitled to half pay. They receive every year a white linen, and also a woollen uniform, either red, blue, or brown, according to the colour of their regiments. The price of the linen dress is fifteen; of the cloth sixty piastres. Their necessaries are soap, one or two shirts, and a knapsack supplied by government. A company is divided into ten messes, each of which have a separate bowl. Their food consists of lentels, and bread; and meat is supposed to be served out every fourth day; married men may take their rations to their families.

Tents are provided by government; baggage is carried by camels, boats, &c. &c. belonging to the country; as there are not any baggage animals attached to the regiments. Courts-martial are composed of one of each rank.

A regiment of cavalry consists of six squadrons, each squadron of four pelotons, each peloton of two companies, each company of two escouardes, each escouarde of six men. The officers are a colonel, a lieutenant-colonel, two chefs d'escadrons, one adjutant, one standard-bearer (or cornet), six 1st captains, six 2d captains, six 1st lieutenants, six 2d lieutenants, six quarter-masters, seventy-two non-commissioned officers, with the usual number of surgeons, veterinary surgeons, and farriers. The regiments are numbered, and in 1836 three of them were to be equipped as cuirassiers with appointments after the French fashion.

A regiment of infantry is composed of four battalions, each consisting of 1000 men, divided into eight companies, of which one is composed of grenadiers, and another of light infantry. The officers are nearly on the same footing with those of the cavalry. The drums, fifes, and music, are like those in the French establishments. Four guns are attached to each regiment. As some of the muskets are made after the English, and some after the French pattern, two sorts of ammunition are necessary. Each man carries twenty-four rounds; and the remainder is conveyed in tumbrels.

The best troops were probably with Ibrahim Pasha in Syria; therefore, a fair opinion of the army could not be formed from those in Egypt; neither should the great difficulties, which the Pasha had to encounter in its formation be forgotten, arising from the idle and depressed habits of the population, their extreme dislike to regularity, and to exertion, and particularly to the military service, a dislike, that the manner, in which the conscription was carried on (however necessary), could not but have greatly increased; and, if to these considerations be added the prejudices and peculiar tenets of the Mahometan religion, the energy and perseverance which have brought the army to its actual state, will be clearly manifest; and, whatever imperfections may exist, they will not be attributed to any want of vigour on the part of the Pasha, or of his son Ibrahim. But, on the contrary, it will be a matter of surprise, how such a population could be rendered at all effective, and yet the Arab troops, particularly the infantry, are considered the best.

I cannot give a decided opinion respecting the troops in Syria, as I never saw any considerable number under arms, but I have occasionally met regiments of cavalry on their march in that country; and they were well mounted, and armed; their horses were in good condition; their baggage small; and they had few, if any, stragglers. The men were stout and serviceable, and apparently healthy and in good spirits, and had not that sullen and dejected look, so universally to be seen amongst the troops in Egypt. One regiment in particular, which I met near Jaffa, had the finest collection of high-bred horses I almost ever saw, which might well be the case, as they had taken possession of the best horses, they could find in the country.

I attended several drills near Cairo, they were entirely on the French plan, and chiefly under French instructors; from whom, as well as from the other officers, I received every civility. The stables, considering the habits of the people, were clean, and in good order; and their appointments were in a serviceable state, which was all that could be expected. They were, however, bad horsemen, their bridle hands were stiff, and ill placed, and their horses ill bitted; the whole was, in fact, a bad imitation of European equitations. They had lost the firmness and dexterity, so often to be remarked in Eastern horsemanship, and moved loosely and ill when in squadron.

I saw twenty-four squadrons of Arabs, and Syrians inspected at Tourah. They were armed with swords, and carbines, and the flank squadrons of each regiment had lances, with red and white flags. They were tolerably well mounted, and their horses, although rough, were in fair condition. They were drawn up in good allignment, but their files were open. Their officers were badly mounted, and no sort of uniformity was observed in their horse appointments. They performed several manœuvres, chiefly by pelotons, and often in regimental columns. They advanced in line, and charged very slowly; and finished by trotting past with no great exactness, or regularity. The old Turkish saddle is extremely heavy, and the large stirrups cannot be used in squadron; but the saddles in use among the common Arabs, although of the same form, are much lighter, and with smaller stirrups would be preferable to the Hussar saddles, which these people have adopted. The Mameluke bit would also be better than the one, which they have at present. Instead of blankets, the saddles are placed upon loose pannels, so awkwardly stuffed, that with a little use they would probably become perfectly unserviceable.

In an excursion to Palmyra, I had an opportunity of observing a small detachment of irregular cavalry, sent as an escort by Sheriff Pasha. The officer was scarcely in any respect superior to the common men, who were mounted on their own horses, without any uniformity of dress, or of appointments; were armed with long guns, swords, pistols, &c., and rode on Turkish saddles. How they would have behaved, if an enemy had appeared, I know not; but they were exceedingly active and alert, and appeared to be well aware of their duty. They galloped forward, and occupied the rising grounds on the front, and flanks, till the party had passed by; and pursued every horseman, or camel they saw in the distance; in marching at night they kept as close together as possible; but, when they halted in the evening, they did not appear to have any idea of precaution (possibly because no danger was apprehended), for they took off their bridles, and turned their horses loose to graze on the scanty herbage of the desert, without any vidette, or sentry; and then lighted large fires, so that their numbers, and position could be distinctly seen, whilst the advance of an enemy was completely concealed. They were probably a fair sample of this species of force, as they belonged to the guard of Sheriff Pasha, the Governor-General of Syria, stationed at Damascus.

I saw considerable numbers of the same sort of people encamped in the Forest of Basan, and near Djerash, and also in the Haouran, and I should imagine that as irregular troops they would be extremely serviceable.

The infantry stationed in Egypt had certainly a better appearance, than those, which came under my observation at Constantinople; and were better appointed, particularly with respect to their red caps, or tarbouches, which fitted the head, instead of coming down over the face according to the Turkish fashion, apparently with an intention of protecting the eyes from the sun. The Arab peasantry are in general straight, and well made, but most of them have short necks, and extremely high shoulders, which may be occasioned by the constant habit of sitting upon their heels. Besides, however, this defect, when drawn up in line, many of them seem to be deformed about the chest, and shoulders; probably from the looseness of their clothing, which, on account of the heat of the climate, is not made to fit the shape.[6] Their line appears also to considerable disadvantage from a want of attention in sizing the men, so essential, not only for appearance, but for exactness in that most important operation, advancing in line.

The officers wore a red tarbouch with a blue tassel, a white nizam dress, consisting of a waistcoat, and jacket, of loose breeches hanging over the knee, and of white leggins, and red slippers. Their swords, or rather sabres, were hung by waist-belts in the European fashion. Besides this common white uniform, they had another, made in the same manner, but of blue, grey, or brown cloth, according to the colours of their regiments.

For full dress the officers wore loose crimson jackets covered with golden embroidery, and striped silken shawls instead of sashes round their waists. As most of them were common people, although lately, in some few instances, improved by instruction, they could not be expected to carry much authority, to be distinguished by a martial appearance, or by any refinement of manners. The greater number, in fact, particularly in the inferior ranks, were little, if at all, better than the common Fellahs; and I have seen one of them, when on guard, in full uniform, and with his sword by his side, gutting and scaling fish in the public streets of Cairo.

[6] Owing to the same cause, the handsome golden embroidery on the officers' jackets had a tinsel and tawdry appearance.

I have already observed, that the dress and appointments of the men consisted of a red tarbouch, a white, dingy red, brown, or blue loose jacket, buttoned up to the chin, loose breeches, and leggins to match, red slippers, white leather belts, which were never cleaned, a pouch of bad black leather, a waist-belt, a sword, and a socket for a bayonet without a scabbard; their arms were clean, and in good order, and their bayonets were generally fixed. They had a sullen and dejected look, a most unmilitary appearance, and irregular habits. I have repeatedly seen sentries squatted on the ground, engaged in talking to other people, or in spinning, with their firelocks resting against a wall. Their arms were regularly lodged, in arm racks, at the several guards, but they turned out in a very slovenly manner; and, by the altercations, and quarrelling, that took place between the non-commissioned officers and the men in relieving the sentries, it appeared that the reliefs were not regularly told off.

The Syrian battalions were very young, and of low stature; and, as their officers, and sergeants were full-grown Arabs, they did not appear to advantage. It was said that many of them died from the effects of the climate, when stationed in Egypt.

I never examined an infantry barrack, but several battalions were encamped without the walls of Cairo in a very regular manner, and the whole had a better appearance than could have been expected; the tents were white, and clean, and the guards, and sentries were regularly posted. Their wives and families were hutted at some distance in the rear, where there was a sort of bazaar.

I saw eight battalions, each consisting of eight companies, in all about 4500 men, inspected by the minister of war, on an extensive desert plain near the encampment; they were drawn up in close order, their line was good, but their files were very loose. The drums were in their rear; and the music on the right flank; the pioneers were well equipped.

One field-officer in each battalion was mounted. Some of the officers were in full dress, but the whole of the men were in white. The Egyptian battalions were composed of stout Arabs, and were said to have served, when Acre was taken from the Turks,[7]

[7] Acre is remarkable on many accounts, and will be for ever connected with the name of a most distinguished character, whose glory is identified with that of his country, which he served with such heroic enterprise, and with such pre-eminent success. The exploits of Sir Sidney Smith are still remembered with admiration, and with respect in Syria; they appear, indeed, from the little re-

and to have made several extraordinary marches to Kerek, and to the eastward of the Dead Sea; the Syrian battalions consisted of young undersized boys, extremely wan and pale. They changed position by an echellon movement upon a central company; changed front by wheeling into column, and by countermarching; formed square; and performed several other manœuvres with tolerable exactness, but very slowly. They did not advance in line. They fired several volleys with much precision, but their file firing was extremely faint. In conclusion they wheeled to the right by companies, and marched home in quick time, the whole going over the same ground, instead of breaking off by regiments: they marched well, and with good intervals. Their music was weak and out of time.

I afterwards saw two divisions, each composed of four battalions of eight companies: one division consisted almost entirely of Syrian boys, several in the front rank were not above five feet high, and could scarcely load, or return their ramrods. They presented into the air without taking the slightest aim, and many of them put quantities of gunpowder into the pockets of their loose breeches, in order, probably, to sell it at Cairo; for which they were well thrashed by their officers with the flat of their swords. When a battalion commenced firing, the colour and two files on each side of it fell out to the rear. They performed several evolutions in the manner, which I have before described; and one of the divisions advanced a considerable distance in echellon from the right, which was the only advance directly to the front, which I had ever seen them attempt, and it did not by any means succeed.

On the 18th of November I was present when some artillery were inspected at Tourah; forty-eight pieces of cannon, (four guns and two howitzers to a battalion,) were drawn up in line; the gun-carriages were short, and were fixed by a vertical pin to the limbers, which were painted of a dark olive green, picked out with black. An ammunition wagon was in line behind each gun; six horses or mules were harnessed to each gun, and four to each tumbril; these animals were serviceable, and in good condition. The saddles and harness were made after European patterns, with winkers for the horses in hand, with rope traces,

---

gard that has been paid, till lately, to his memory, to be less esteemed by his own countrymen, for whom in perilous times he fought and conquered, than by strangers and enemies. Neglect and ingratitude cannot however obscure his well-earned and glorious reputation.

K

and with swing bars for the centre pairs: long ropes were also provided to assist in working the guns when in battery. Ten or twelve dismounted Arabs in brown uniforms, and with yellow belts, and armed with swords, bayonets, and with muskets, (which latter were slung), were attached to each gun; they were in marching order, but their knapsacks appeared almost empty. The men were clean, well appointed, and soldierlike. The officers wore dark blue uniforms, with red collars and cuffs, and golden embroidery.*

They took up various positions, and fired several rounds, at intervals of about forty-three seconds, and afterwards marched past (the tumbrils being abreast, on the outward flank of their respective guns). Some practice afterwards took place at a long wooden target, with a distance of 150 toises, during which time the guns were placed in some works, that had been thrown up on the plain for that purpose.

I afterwards observed at the barracks that many of the limbers were fitted with seats, but those, which were inspected, carried only small ammunition boxes.

The barracks and their whole establishment appeared in good order, and the men were stouter, better fed, and cleaner than those in the other services. Much of this efficiency was owing to the talents and exertions of Colonel Seguerra, a Spanish officer of great respectability and merit, who, from some cabal or intrigue, was soon afterwards compelled to leave the Pacha's service.

HORSES IN EGYPT AND SYRIA.

During my first visit to Cairo, in the spring of 1836, I had frequent opportunities of seeing the Pacha's stud at Shoubrah; it consisted of three or four hundred mares, and of about forty stallions, and was in very bad order. But the best of the horses and mares were afterwards sent to a new building, about two miles off, and were much improved in condition under the care of M. Amand, a Frenchman. The stallions, before their removal, were picketed with heel-ropes under open sheds, had

---

* Those in the light artillery belonging to the guard had light blue uniforms.

very little grooming or exercise, and, as the weather was chilly, were extremely rough; added to which, their feet, from the Turkish way of shoeing, were in a very bad state.

The shoes in Egypt, like those in Syria, are usually circular plates, with a small hole in the middle; but, in the latter country, they have sometimes the usual form, and the ends of the shoe are turned up across the heels, as a protection against the sharp edges of the rock; for the roads in the mountainous parts of that country are for many miles a series of broken steps, and of steep declivities, and a horse could scarcely travel without some such defence. It is true that the form of the hinder shoes, to a great degree, prevents overreaching; but this mode of shoeing can, in general, only be applicable to travelling at a slow pace and in a dry country; for a horse shod in this manner cannot move with security on moist or on slippery ground; nor be ridden at any pace for a considerable distance on a hard road, without injury. Upon removing the shoe, the foot is found so much compressed that the several parts of it cannot be distinguished, and, it appears, are never considered; for, preparatory to being shod, the leg is held up by one man, whilst another cuts away from him with a buttress, and reduces the whole foot, by removing large slices of the frog, bars, sole, and crust, altogether, and the plate of iron is then nailed down as it would be to the bottom of a post. The shoes are not fullered, and are fastened in each quarter by three large nails, which resemble those used in France, and have good hold; for, except by being broken against the rocks, or worn out, the shoes are seldom lost. The clenches are twisted round in circles, and hammered into the hoof. My horses were scarcely ever lamed by these shoes, and went in them over the most difficult roads with confidence and security. Of course, it is impossible to clean the foot.

To return to the stud. Amongst the stallions were several of a peculiar white breed:[9] they were said to have been sent as

[9] By a white breed I mean to infer that the horses had been foaled perfectly white, and that their colour was not the effect of age. A breed of this kind was once famous at Girgenti, in Sicily, and I believe still exists in Hungary; and it is to be remarked, that many of these Arab stallions had grey eyes like the Hanoverian horses. As far as I could discover, it was equally necessary in the East, as it is in England, that either the horse or the mare should be grey, in order to breed a grey colt, and that in those countries, as in Europe, colts of all other colours may be indiscriminately produced; but the rule does not seem to hold good in the white breeds; indeed, I have seen in England an instance to the contrary.

a present from Mecca, or to have been taken during the war, and seemed to be thoroughbred: they had in general more power than the other horses, were from 14·3 to 15·2 in height, extremely handsome, of great substance, and had capital legs and feet. The greys and bays were, in general, smaller. Many of the latter were colts three and four years old, had been purchased at great prices, and were supposed to be high-bred, but they were, of course, much out of condition from being exposed to heat and to cold, and from being constantly tied up. The manes and tails of the colts were closely shorn, which did not add to their appearance.

The finest horses were the following:—Mufti, a grey horse, six years old, brought by an officer in the Pacha's service from Mecca. He was very lengthy, had great substance, and remarkably large bone, and was about 15·2½ in height, and able to carry fourteen or fifteen stone. He had the finest action, the highest possible show of blood, and was said to be of the purest breed. When I afterwards saw this fine horse at the new stables, he was still rough from neglect, and from want of exercise, and his eyes appeared weak and dull; excepting on that account he would have been worth bringing to England. A dark chestnut horse, with two white legs, and a white face, was of equal power, but was rather heavier in his forehand; he was also considered to be of a valuable breed. Two or three of the white horses were particularly fine, but were not quite so lengthy, and had rather coarser points. The highest bred, however, was a bay, about 15·1½, and fourteen or fifteen years old. Nothing could exceed the strength of his limbs, or the perfection of his make, excepting that he was rather upright in his shoulders; his head and neck were extremely handsome, and his display of high breed, and of action was equally striking. He was very muscular, and able to carry twelve or thirteen stone. There were several stories of his having been taken in battle, and of the reluctance, with which the Arabs parted with him, on account of his blood, superior excellence, and great value.

There was, likewise, a bay English horse, of good size and shape: he appeared to great advantage, as he was in a box, and, consequently, in better condition than those in the sheds. He was very like Gulliver (by Orville, out of Canidia), and his stock were better than those got by the other horses.

Considering the value of these fine stallions, I was a good deal surprised at seeing a sick horse loose amongst them, which, according to M. Amand's account, was infected with *la morve* (the glanders): the disease appeared to me to be only the strangles; but, even in that case, it was highly improper that he should be loose in the same yard,[1] and have access to the water and the forage, from which the rest were fed.

The mares were fastened by heel-ropes in large barns, and it may be easily imagined that their foals were in the worst condition. Some of the mares shewed blood, particularly a grey from Thebes; but many were of the common breed of Egypt, crossed with Arab, or with Dongalese blood. A few had been imported from the latter country, and had the distinctive marks of their race, namely, long heads, extremely round in the nose, a good deal of white on their faces, and legs,[2] large limbs, and lengthy narrow frames. They shewed blood, and had a great resemblance to our horses got by Blacklock. The slope of their shoulders was most extraordinary; their action, as it might be expected, was loose and disunited; but they had great liberty, easy paces, and probably excellent wind. They were not, however, in high repute, nor had the Mamelukes formerly much opinion of them, notwithstanding the statement of M. Burckhardt.

A considerable number of mules, and of asses were also bred at Shoubrah.

When I revisited the stud on the 12th of November, 1836, the finest mares and stallions had been removed to the new establishment, which was situated in a fertile plain, abounding in

---

[1] One of the white stallions had a disorder, which I had never seen, but which I was informed was not uncommon in the East, and was generally fatal. I only saw two instances of it. The dock was swollen to a large size, and became knotty, and callous, and the hair stuck out and was rough. It did not seem to be attended with pain, or with inflammation, and, therefore, did not appear to have any resemblance, to the Plica Polonica. I was told that it had a connexion with the blood-vessels in the interior of the horse's body.

[2] White marks are not, at present, more esteemed in the East than they are in Europe; nor have the stallions, lately imported into England, been usually distinguished by them, excepting the Cole Arabian, who was said to have been very speedy. There is, however, an account in Evelyn's "Memoirs" of three horses which were taken at the relief of Vienna, and brought over for Charles II., in December 1684; the best is described as a bay with two white feet, and a blaize. The Derby Arabian (the sire of Childers) had four white feet and a blaize; Childers had the same; it may be added, that Eclipse, Selim, Velocipede, and many of our fastest horses, have been marked with white.

luxuriant crops of corn, cotton, &c. Two large enclosures in front of the stables, fenced in with reeds about seven feet high, contained one hundred and ten yearlings,[2] many of them were promising—the best were two colts, got by the English horse. The produce of Mufti were strong, but coarse, which is often the case with young Arab stock: those from the fine bay horse were small. These horses were in tolerable condition, and had the great advantage of being at liberty. Seventeen later yearlings were turned loose in a large barn; one or two of these, particularly a small bay colt, were very handsome; but they were in bad condition.

The buildings were very extensive, and, being new, were perfectly clean: they surrounded large courts, into which the brood mares ought to have been turned, in lots of twenty or thirty, with sheds to shelter them from the sun. There were forty-eight barren mares tied up in a large stable, some of which were handsome and apparently well-bred. In another stable were sixty-one mares in foal; they shewed much blood, and five of them (two white Nedgid, and three greys from Syria, Nubia, and Thebes,) were remarkably fine. I did not observe at these stables any mares that had foaled, they were probably in separate buildings. Twenty-two stallions were in another stable; the grey horse Mufti, the fine bay, the chestnut already alluded to, and five other bay horses—one of which was a capital horse from the Hedjas, and two of inferior value, which had been selected from the army. Eight extremely handsome grey Nedgid, and six white horses,—of which five were Nedgid, and one an Egyptian stallion.

These horses and mares were in large boarded stalls, and were not fastened by heel-ropes, but by halters attached to posts let into the bottom of the stone mangers. The stalls were not paved; the mangers were high; and, by a singular arrangement, the horses stood in two rows facing each other. A narrow path had been made along the walls behind, and a broad high walk extended in front of the stalls down the middle of the building. The horses had nothing therefore before them but the manger; and were consequently kept in a continual state of alarm and uneasiness, by people coming unexpectedly before them: many of them, indeed, which were easily excited, hung back, with the imminent

---

[2] The mares generally foal about October and November, and in the ensuing months, on account of the green crops, that come in at that time.

risk of pulling up the post, to which they were fastened, and the whole place to pieces, and it did not appear to be very substantially built. It is difficult to imagine why this absurd plan was adopted; which, beside other inconveniences, precluded the possibility of examining the horses, without passing close behind them by the dirty path near the walls. The stalls, however, will not last long; and, it is to be hoped, that these fine horses will eventually be kept in loose boxes, and the mares in sheds, which will not only save much expense, but contribute vastly to their health, and enable them, by moving about, in some degree, to make up for the neglect, and the want of exercise, to which they are exposed. The stud, however, is, upon the whole, much improved since it has been removed to this place; and the French superintendent has been of service. Even the two-year-old colts sent to the stables at Cairo are in better condition; but nothing can compensate for want of air, liberty, proper exercise, and good keep, particularly to young horses; and the colts at Shoubrah, it is to be observed, are principally fed with chopped straw, and have little or no exercise.

In Syria, horses are generally fed with green forage during the day, are watered at sunset, and their allowance of grain is afterwards given to them in a nose-bag. It is to be observed, that these horses are generally ridden at a slow pace, and are seldom overheated.

In Egypt, the cattle, and in many instances the sheep and goats, when turned out to graze, are necessarily tethered in rows, as the plains contain a variety of valuable crops, and are entirely unenclosed, on account of the annual inundation. Under such circumstances, heel-ropes are not only the sole expedient, but the most secure manner of picketing a horse, either with regard to his own safety, or to that of other horses with him. About February, most of the horses in Cairo are turned into the bersin (a fine sort of clover), and are fastened in a line; the sizes, (or grooms,) being encamped behind them. And in the immediate neighbourhood of the city, they are often picketed under trees on the banks of the Nile, and are regularly attended to, and clothed.

But, notwithstanding the fine climate, they are generally, both in the stable, and in the field, in the condition of grass-horses. They are rough from want of exercise, and are never sufficiently cleaned, although a sort of currycomb, a brush made of twisted rope, and a coarse hair-cloth, are used for that purpose. It is scarcely necessary to add, that their manes and tails are seldom touched; and it appears odd to an European eye, to see a horse, dirty and rough, as if from a strawyard, brought out with a velvet saddle, and with a bridle covered with golden embroidery and fringes, and with tassels of the same material.[4]

Instead of the large Turkish saddle with Eastern stirrups, a stuffed pad with a low round cantle, covered with black or with red cloth, is generally used. It is furnished with smaller stirrups shaped like those belonging to a hussar saddle, and with short spurs on the inward sides. The bridles are of different patterns, and are generally made of webbing. Over them headstalls are put on, composed of a number of silver chains, and adorned with small flat ornaments, particularly on the nosebands.

The Mamelukes were formerly no doubt well mounted, and armed, and could ride well; but I never saw a fine horseman in these countries. Abou Gosh, (an Arab chief near Jerusalem), and an old Mameluke at Cairo were the best. Some of them, indeed, were well placed on the old Turkish saddle, (which is still used by the Arabs, and is by no means an inconvenient equipment), yet they had bad hands, turned entirely on the outside rein, and the hand and the heel seldom, if ever, accorded. Skirmishing, and the exercise of the jereed, were not usually performed with much address, although with considerable violence: and few of their horses were really fast, although many of them were quick in getting into their speed. When the colts belonging to the Pacha's stable were occasionally exercised, they were suddenly galloped for a short distance, and then stopped in the most violent, and awkward manner, without any regard to the action of the horse, or to the momentary position of his legs, and therefore, with great danger to his joints. By application through the consuls strangers can procure horses from these stables, and the Pacha himself, and many of his officers were mounted from them.

There were a number of remarkably fine mules at the same place, which were employed in conveying provisions for the troops.

The stud at Shoubrah was intended in some degree to supply

[4] The Arabs are very particular in walking the horses about till they are quite cool; they water generally once a-day, and feed in the mornings and evenings, and indeed, from the intense heat of Eastern climates, the morning and evening are the proper times for eating, for both man and beast.

the cavalry; but in this, as in other instances, the best supply would be procured from the people, by securing to them the peaceable enjoyment of their possessions, and by paying a fair remunerating price.

Opposite to the stables at Cairo was the establishment for the Pacha's carriages. I heard that he had procured through Mr. Galloway a tolerable coach and harness; but the carriages, which I saw, were worse than common hackney-coaches; and the horses, harness, and particularly the coachmanship, were bad beyond all description: the whole, indeed, was conducted in such an awkward manner, and was attended with so much difficulty and embarrassment, that it was no longer a matter of surprise that carriages appeared to the Turks most extraordinary inventions. Those, although belonging to the Pacha, were never cleaned, excepting that the linings were occasionally brushed out. I forget the colours of all of them, but the one most constantly used was a dark blue chariot, with a red hammer-cloth; the varnish had long since disappeared, and the paint scarcely remained. The harness was of a common sort, like that used for breaks, it had breast-collars, and did not appear to have been either cleaned or repaired; there were no bearing reins, and the cruppers were seldom put on; the reins of the leaders were only passed through the head-terrets of the wheel-horses; and their traces were fastened to a large swing-bar at the end of the pole; the horses were driven with bridoons, or with bits without curbs. There were several sets of horses, white, bay, and chestnut, apparently very old, underbred, and out of condition. Their thick manes and tails were never combed, and, when they were fastened to the carriage (for " put together" they never were), the pole-pieces were put on first, and then the traces.

The coachman, (and the best performer was a black), was dressed in a white Nizam suit, with a red tarbouse and slippers, and drove with a pig-whip. He leant forward on his box, with his legs stretched out on each side of the foot-board, and, having taken the off-side reins in his right, and the other reins in his left hand, he ascertained their purchase by two or three violent pulls, that brought the horses' heads alternately round in opposite directions; and then setting to work with his whip, started his straggling team through foot-passengers, camels, asses, &c. in a most surprising manner. On his return, however, the horses had got quite steady, and by taking a long circuit (if nothing accidentally interfered), the equipage was safely deposited through a large gateway, into the *remise*.

The women of the harem seemed, however, to enjoy this mode of conveyance, and often took long drives, and returned in the evening by torch-light. I once saw, in an exceedingly hot day, four fat women veiled up in a coach, with a black slave sitting, as a guard, on the floor between them. Abbas Pacha had also a close carriag, eand a phaeton; and one or two of the Franks had gigs, and four-wheeled chairs; there were also one or two carriages at Alexandria.

The stud of Ibrahim Pacha was in much worse condition than that at Shoubrah; but several of the mares, of which there were between two and three hundred, appeared to be superior, shewed a great deal of blood, and, although rather slight, had fine racing shape. They were tied up by heel-ropes in large stables. Some of the foals and yearlings were handsome and high-bred, but were starved and weak, for they were principally fed upon chopped straw, and had not any exercise. The stallions were also confined by heel-ropes. Most of them were coarse, particularly a German horse; but there were some good Turkish stallions, a fine white horse from Shoubrah, and a good shaped ambler, a pace which is much esteemed by the Turks.

Ibrahim Pacha generally rode mules; and he had some very good ones, and in tolerable order. There were also some remarkably fine stallion asses from Syria, and from Arabia, by which mules were bred from Arab mares.

The horses, taken at Acre, had three round spots burnt in their hind-quarters (which was not an unusual mark); although it did not appear to denote any particular breed.

I requested permission to examine the shed belonging to the Shereef of Mecca, as the best horses came from that place; and as, I concluded, that his would have been of the purest breed. I had, indeed, observed, during the time the Shereef was encamped at Gizeh, that his attendants were well mounted, when they practised with the jereed on the sandy plain below the Pyramids. Amongst those, however, which were afterwards shewn to me at Cairo, I did not recognise any that I had seen before. They must, therefore, have belonged to some of the other chieftains from Mecca, or to the stables at Shoubrah. The Shereef's stud did not appear to be numerous. The stables were, as is often the case, underground, and upon entering them, my attention was particularly directed to a grey mare in foal by a white horse, then in the possession of Abbas Pacha; both the mare and the horse were of the purest breed from Mecca, and were esteemed of great value, and the best, which the Shereef possessed. The mare shewed much blood, had a very handsome head, and good length, but was slight. The horse, which I afterwards saw at the stables of Abbas Pacha, was about fourteen hands three inches high, had good substance, and also shape, but not that of a race-horse; I could not judge of his action, as he was led out in heel-ropes, and with a heavy bit fastened into his mouth by a cord. There was also in the Shereef's stable a bay yearling, got by the white horse out of the grey mare, which I subsequently brought to England on account of his blood. I procured this colt with great difficulty, most probably because the Shereef perceived that I wished to have him. He said that he belonged to his son, and offered me any other of his horses, but I was determined to have the colt, because I had previously heard that his sire was the highest-bred horse in the stud, and because his dam had the appearance, and also the reputation, of being of the purest breed; and because a yearling was more easily conveyed by water than a larger horse. I employed on the occasion a Frenchman named M. Riga, and I was so fortunate as to obtain likewise the assistance of Mr. Bretel, who was an English engineer in the Pacha's service, and had had the superintendance of the mines of Mount Lebanon. As the horse is stated in the pedigree to have been given to me, I subjoin the following extracts, which will shew the way, in which affairs are transacted in the East, and will prove that it was expressly stipulated by the Shereef that I was to send to him, in exchange for his horse, a golden watch, and an English carriage with harness for four horses. The letters I received at Alexandria, at Malta, and on my return to England, and the watch and carriage were sent out immediately afterwards.

Extract from Mr. Bretel, dated Cairo, August 9, 1837.

" It affords me much pleasure to be able to announce to you that the Shereef of Mecca has this morning presented for your acceptance the horse, which you admired; he requests that you will send him, as an acknowledgment, a small watch, not larger than the circle below, also an English carriage, a description of which he has not, however, given. Mr. Hill has sent thirty dollars as presents to the servants of the Shereef, he has also sent to Mr. Walne for a tesheree to forward the horse to Alexandria without delay," &c.

Extract from M. Riga, dated Cairo, August 13, 1837.

"You will see from the enclosed document[5] that the Shereef's views in giving you the colt are not quite disinterested, or rather his son's, who has been the chief party in the business: this document stipulates for a carriage, with harness for four horses, and for a small gold watch. I was required to get the Consul's guarantee that these would be sent, but, without orders, that gentleman would not do it; however, you told me to make them any offer, I thought proper, and to carry my point at all hazards, and I took it upon myself to guarantee that you would do what they required, and I hope that you will approve of it."

The stipulations with Mr. Bretel, and with M. Riga, and the formal demand attempted to be made through the Consul of a carriage, and a watch, form a curious contrast with the following account of a communication received by Mr. Bretel from the Shereef.

Extract from Mr. Bretel, dated Cairo, August 17, 1837.

"I have the pleasure to acknowledge the receipt of your letter dated the 12 inst. On the following morning I waited on the Shereef of Mecca, and stated to him the contents of it. He appeared, and expressed himself, to be much pleased, when I told him that you felt highly gratified by his present. He then said that, as his son was anxious to have a small gold watch, he would

---

[5] The official translation of the document into Italian is as follows, a literal English version can scarcely be given, but it evidently contains a formal demand, through the English Consul, for a watch and a carriage.

"Non e nascosto nel nostro amore che voi serivercte una lettera dalla parte del Console alla Signoria del Nostro Signore Nobile Abdallah, in questa guisa, e di dirlo per sigillarla col suo sigillo, questo vi avvisamo."

"*La forma della lettera.*

"Discendenza dei Re Nobili, nostro Signore nobile Abdallah, iddio allunghi la sua vita.

"Non e nascosto da voi che Mohamed Effendi Bekkati Capo del Divano del consiglio aveva avvisato che voi dimandate dalla Signoria del Bey una Carozza, ed un piccolo orologio. Con ajuto di dio altissimo avvisamo quello alla sua Excellenza il Bey, e lo riceverete, e vi ringrasiamo molto, ed iddio vi doni la saluta.

(Signed) "MOHAMMED EFFENDI BEKKATI ZAADA.
"Scrivano del Consiglio Nobile di Mocha."

accept it as a present, and in remembrance of you, but the carriage he positively declined receiving. In order to have a specific answer I wrote to him, translating that part of your letter relating to him, for which purpose he gave me in writing his address, 'The noble Mohamed Ebn Aioon, the exalted Prince of Mecca.' I enclose his reply, addressed to me, and sealed with his seal (Mohamed Ebn Aioon). After the usual compliments, and recapitulations of my letter, he says, 'The name of the horse is Abeiāān, that of his mother El Bäĕah, of the Arab Nedgid breed, and the name of his father is Hadbaan, our horse[6] from him, which is called Gerboa.

"' You tell us that the English bey, Colonel Vyse, requests us to receive a gold watch, which he will send from England for our son for his acceptance, and a carriage; we told you that he must not send any thing for having received the horse, but, because he has prayed that our son will receive from him this present, it imports not; let him then send the carriage, one for four horses, and let the colour be green. When we shall have received the carriage, we will give him another of our Arab horses,[7] and we pray that he will accept of it. We beg of you to write to him our regards. Ginmad el Ewwel 15, 1253.'

"The above date corresponds with August 16th, 1837.

"I have sent you as nearly as possible a literal translation of a part of his letter, as you may, in fact, perceive by the singular style, in which it was written."

In another letter, dated November 21st, 1837, I received from Mr. Bretel the original pedigree, and the translation here given, and, in reference to the former account given by the Shereef of the breed of the colt, Mr. Bretel adds, "I could not exactly understand what the two names, 'Hadbaan,' and 'Gerboa,' had to do with the pedigree of the colt. It has been satisfactorily explained by the Shereef. When a Nedgid horse is very celebrated, his descendants take his name as a peculiar breed; Hadbaan was a celebrated Nedgid horse, and 'Gerboa,' the father of the colt, being of his blood, is called a Hadbaan. Whilst the Shereef was explaining this to me, a person of some consequence from Mecca, who was present, asked, 'Was the colt a Hadbaan?' 'E' wullah,' answered the Shereef; the stranger appeared to be rather surprised that the Shereef should have

---

[6] This, as well as other parts of the translation, are obscure.

[7] It is scarcely to add that no other horse was sent.

parted with a Hadbaan colt. So, also, with the other names, the Hendees, and the Nedgid."

The translation of the pedigree was as follows:—

(SEAL) "All which is attributed herein is correct; the Shereef Muhammed Ben Aioon, Shereef of Mecca, the honoured, has written it. The pardon of God be for him.

"This history is the truth of the bay colt, which we presented to his Excellency the Colonel Howard Vyse, the English Bey at Cairo, the protected. His name is Abeiān; his breed is pure Nedgdi; he was born at Cairo, in our habitation, on the 21st of Giumal el Aker, 1252,[a] and his father and his mother are of the best Arab horses. His mother's name is El Abeiēh, daughter of El Abeiēh, her colour is white, and the colour of her mother was bay; and her father's name was Abeiān the Hendees, his colour was white, and he pure Nedgdi. The father of the beforementioned colt is a Hadbaan, by name Gerboa; his colour is white, and his mother is Hadba, the Nedgdi, her colour is white, and her father's name is Gelwan, the son of Hadba, and the colour of his mother is white. The whole are from the Nedgdi horses, celebrated amongst the Arabs.

"THE SHEREEF ABDALLAH,
(SEAL) Son of the Shereef Muhammed Ben Aioon.

"*Shabaan*, 6t. 1253."[b]

As far as breed, soundness of constitution, and good limbs, are desirable, a cross of Arab blood may be of service; but, with some few exceptions, such as those mentioned in the Pacha's stud at Shoubrah, Arabs have not in general the form or length necessary for race-horses; in fact, the use, to which they are applied, does not require them, nor are they bred with a view only to swiftness. The colt in question is very low, barely fourteen hands, and has small bone, but is muscular, and so much furnished, that his age has been doubted, till repeated examinations of his mouth proved that his pedigree was correct. He shews blood, has fine action, is remarkably healthy, and has great courage, as he some time since proved by leaping a gate three feet nine inches high, and a boarded door seven feet from the gate, and five feet six inches in height; which he cleared with his forehand and

[a] October 1, 1836.   [b] November 5, 1837,

body, and broke through with his hinder legs, without any other injury than a scratch below his stifle. The whole leap was about eighteen feet in breadth. The horse has also good length for his size, but he has not the shape of a race-horse; what his progeny might eventually turn out is another question.

Several of the other horses shewed blood, and were of good substance and height. The Shereef himself, when at the Pyramids, rode a five-year-old bay horse, which had the appearance and action of an English hunter; and one of his attendants was mounted on an animal of unrivalled beauty and animation. Although of low stature, he was the strongest and most magnificent war-horse I ever saw; but he was old, and had been in the stud at Shoubrah. I saw also in the Shereef's stables a bay and a fine five-year-old grey mare, belonging to one of his sons, and one or two other clever horses, any of which I could have obtained with much less trouble, and with less expense, than the yearling. They were in better condition than the horses belonging to the Pacha, but in point of value could not be compared with the best of his stud, which I have already described to have been brought from Mecca; indeed, I believe that some of them were taken from the Shereef's stables.

It is to be observed, that most of the best, and highest bred horses from Mecca, and from the Hedjas, had great bone, and were of good size, (like the grey, and the chestnut Wellesley Arabians), they had also the finest muscular shape, and indications of high blood; but, with a few exceptions, particularly amongst the mares, they have not the length and character esteemed in England.

The horses in the mountainous parts of Syria are of a different breed and form from the Arab, with which, however, they are often crossed, they are taller and larger, but not so muscular.[1]

The Druses of Mount Lebanon, (although, from the extreme difficulty of the roads, mules might have been supposed preferable to horses,) were finely mounted, chiefly on mares, and have a highly picturesque costume, composed of shawls of rich and various colours.

I tried a great many horses at Beyrout, and bought two grey mares, that answered for the journey, but neither of them were of any real value. One of them, a slight white mare, shewed

---

[1] It is probable that the mountain Arabs mentioned in our old stud-books were of this race.

much blood, and had very fine action, and was remarkably serviceable till she became thin and weak, probably on account of her age, for, I had been informed, that old horses would not stand work in the East, and I was recommended to buy two or three year olds. The pay of the seis, or groom, was fifty piastres per month, his keep, or two piastres per day board wages, and a pair of shoes every three months, as he always attended his master on foot in towns. A person of consequence is generally accompanied by two of these people, who support him in difficult places, and in going up or down hill. They require to be well looked after, and endeavour to cheat in every possible way.

The stud of the Emir Bechir was supposed to be excellent; I, therefore, expected to meet with some mares at Ebtedin, that, after having carried me through the country, might have been worth sending to England. The best, which I saw at that place, was a large white mare, about fifteen hands two inches, she shewed much blood, and had the most perfect shape, excepting that, from the height of her forehand, and the fineness of her loins and quarters, she appeared rather low in her saddle-place. Her tail was dyed red with henna; and I understood that Ibrahim Pacha always rode her when at Ebtedin. Her price was 200*l.*, which, as she was eleven or twelve years old, and barren, was more than her value. She was also too tall for the mountain-roads. I offered 100*l.* for her, which was as much as she was worth, particularly as she was shy, and easily alarmed, which induced me to believe that her eyes were bad. This mare came from Akkar, between Homs and Tripoli, where a number of very fine horses are bred. They are not, however, of so high a caste as the Nedgid, but more like the Turcoman, Circassian, and Persian horses.[2] I could have purchased at Ebtedin, for about 80*l.* each, two fine Arab mares of the Koghlani breed, but they were heavy in foal; they were a grey and a bay, very handsome, and said to be high-bred. Many inferior horses, belonging to other persons, were to be sold at this place; and

---

[2] In the autumn of 1836 I saw at Kalisch in Poland a corps of cavalry from Karabah (near Teflis); their horses were low, but very strong, and appeared to be well-bred. They were remarkably fresh after a long and difficult march from their own country. The men were the most picturesque people imaginable, but, as soldiers, of much less value than the Caucasus Cossacks, who, from constant warfare as frontier troops, have succeeded to, and eclipsed the famous Don Cossacks, although the latter appeared to me to be much superior.

a gentleman, who travelled with me, bought for 17*l.*, a very active mare, said to be Annecy; but she was coarse, and evidently not thorough-bred. It should be remembered that, although the climate has great influence, there are nearly as many low-bred horses in the East as in Europe.

In my way to Sidon I saw the Emir's stud at Djoun. There were two stallions, a grey of good size, and substance, but heavy and calf-kneed, said to be Seglowee, and a chestnut with white legs, of much power, but apparently ill-bred; both these horses appeared much neglected; they had swelled legs, and were rough for want of exercise. There were four mares with foals (two Annecy, two Seglowee), picketed in clover; they were in very bad order, and their foals were weak and sickly. The mares themselves shewed much blood, but were completely ill from neglect, and from want of food, and of care. There were likewise, seven barren mares. Five of them white; one, which was a fine specimen of the mountain breed; and another from Akkar, which was remarkably large and handsome; the latter was marked across her arms, and thighs with a firing-iron; the two others were a fine bay three-year-old filly, bought of the Annecy Arabs, and a starved yearling. Djoun is sheltered by surrounding hills, and there is abundance of water and tolerable pasture, the wretched state of these horses must be therefore owing to ignorance, and to neglect. The Emir had informed me, when I was at Ebtedin, that he had very few horses, and wished to increase his stud, by which I concluded that he was afraid that the government would take away those, which he had, if they were seen.

The foals both in Egypt, and in Syria are frequently docked; and the points of their ears, and those also of the young asses, are often sewed together. Their manes and tails are shorn till they are four years old, when the tails are cut square, with a lock left in the middle from the end of the dock, after which they are allowed to grow down.

The breeds of Seglowee, Kohlani, and Annecy, are in much esteem in Syria, particularly the former. The horses from Akkar are Annecy. There is also a breed called Abeian, which is the name of the Arab colt, that I bought at Cairo. Good horses were chiefly to be found at Jaffa, Nablous, and Nazareth, and also from the eastward of the Jordan; but, when I was in Syria, the Arabs were afraid to shew their horses, for fear of their being taken away by the government; otherwise, I have no doubt that

Arab mares and horses might be always bought (although, perhaps, those of a particular breed, or excellence, would be dear), for an Arab will never refuse to sell any thing in his possession, if a sufficient price be offered.

With respect to the care, which these people are supposed to take of their horses, I have to state that, although many of the horses belonging to the escort, which attended us to Palmyra, were foundered and infirm, they were ridden about in the most violent manner; and also that one, upon which a soldier, who attended me as a guide from Hebron, was mounted, was dreadfully lame, (owing, it was said, to his having fallen into a well) his off thigh and hock being, not only bruised and swollen, but also cut through with a lacerated wound nearly two feet in length, yet he was galloped about without the least consideration. I may likewise add, that, having lost my own horse in going from Damascus to Palmyra, I rode the mare of an Arab Sheik, and that, during the journey, I was obliged to keep watch when she was feeding, to prevent the Sheik taking away the corn from his own mare, which, after all, I believed he frequently did, and he finished by stealing the nosebag. On our arrival at Palmyra, he took away the mare, under pretence of taking care of her; and, when I returned to Kariathain, I found that he had cut out, and stolen the pannel of my saddle, and that the mare's back was injured to such a degree, that she could not continue her journey to Damascus.

There are six or seven breeds of Nedgid horses. The best blood is supposed to exist between Bassora and Mecca. The horses sent to England, many years since, by Mr. Manesty, then consul at Bassora, were probably from that part of the country.

I saw several well-bred mares belonging to the Arabs in the Haouran, and many fine horses among the irregular cavalry encamped in the forests near Djerash; but those of high caste were generally old and worn out. I tried a great many horses and mares at Damascus, and also at Jerusalem: several of them belonged to the Hadji; one, a small bay mare, had a long pedigree, and came from Bagdad; but none of them were particularly worthy of notice. When I called on Abou Gosh, at Jerusalem, I tried a grey three-years old colt, which he strongly recommended, and said was a Koghlani: the colt was kept constantly saddled, and was picketed with heel ropes in an underground vault, or stable. He was about fourteen hands three inches, had a tolerably good head, but was rather coarse about the jaws; had a short, low neck, pretty good shoulders, good ribs, and carcase; high, narrow loins, short quarters, good legs and feet, but was coarse, and had the appearance of a Welsh galloway: he had broken knees, and had been fired for thorough-pins; his tail was cut square, with a lock left in the middle; he moved well and firmly, and, when six or seven years old, would be probably very close and muscular. I was told by the superior of the Latin convent that the governor had seized the horse for the Pacha's service soon after I tried him; which appeared to me extraordinary, as Abou Gosh was on good terms with the governor, and as he immediately sent into the country for another horse, which I by no means wished him to do, for fear that he would be taken by the governor also. This horse I afterwards bought, and sent to Malta; he carried one remarkably well, and was extremely active, and serviceable, particularly in rocky mountains. I gave 2520 piastres (about 25l.) for him. When animated, he was very handsome, but had not a very high show of blood. I got, however, the following attested pedigree; the original was given to the English officer, who bought the horse, and who was afterwards, I believe, drowned in the Nile. "The red (bay) horse is Koghlani, son of a red (bay) mare, which I bought from the Arabs near Gaza. I declare that he is Koghlani, and that his mother and his father are Koghlani, and that all his ancestors were Koghlani for fifty years, being known as to their sires and grandsires till now, when I sold the horse to Colonel Howard Vyse, an Englishman; and this is the horse, which is above described, and he is pure Koghlani. 25 Gilfi, 1261 A.H." Signed by Abou Gosh, and certified by the authorities in Jerusalem. This horse had good substance, was about fifteen hands and one inch high, good head and neck, very strong shoulders, short, but strong quarters, thin thighs, capital legs and feet, and good loins; he was rather flat-sided, but was deep and good in his girthing-place. He had been roughly fired above and below his off hock; his tail was cut square, with a lock in the middle, and his mane was tufted and thick; he did not appear very high-winded, and went rather round in his gallop; he improved, however, in these respects, and became an admirable fencer.

The Governor of Jerusalem had some tolerably good horses; and Mr. Farren (the consul at Damascus) had a remarkably fine bay horse, apparently of the best blood; but he was old, and out of condition. That gentleman had also a bay filly, which had been purchased from the Arabs; she shewed much blood, but was underlimbed and heavy. The horses belonging to the Persian princes, who had at that time gone to England, were also at Mr. Ferreau's. They were well clothed, and taken care of, but did not appear to be well bred. I heard of a mare at Damascus for which 500*l.* had been refused, but I did not see her. Eight or ten horses had also been bought for the Emperor of Austria; but, with the exception of two bay stallions, they did not appear to be of any value.

THE END.

LONDON:
PRINTED BY MOYES AND BARCLAY, CASTLE STREET,
LEICESTER SQUARE.

www.ingramcontent.com/pod-product-compliance
Lightning Source LLC
Chambersburg PA
CBHW080433110426
42743CB00016B/3159